VOLUME 1

Turkey Men

VOLUME 1

Turkey Men

Thomas R. Pero

Illustration by Jack Paluh

WILD RIVER PRESS

www.turkeymen.com

Library of Congress Cataloging-in-Publication Data
Pero, Thomas R.
    Turkey men volume 1./Thomas R. Pero.—1st edition
    p. cm.
    ISBN 9780989523653
    1. Wild turkey. 2. Hunting. 3. Super Slam records. I. Title.

    Library of Congress Control Number: 2016915404

Book and cover design by Gregory Smith Design
Front cover photograph of hunters by Matt Lindler of National Wild Turkey Federation
Front and rear cover photographs and throughout book of live wild turkeys by Timothy C. Flanigan of Nature Exposure

Published by Wild River Press, Post Office Box 13360, Mill Creek, Washington 98082 USA

Wild River Press website address: www.wildriverpress.com

Book series website address: www.turkeymen.com

Printed in the United States of America by Jostens

10 9 8 7 6 5 4 3 2 1

DEDICATION

This book is for all the young hunters, teenagers and younger, boys and girls,
who will pull the trigger on their first wild turkey this year.
May you always be as thrilled.

Special Thanks
To Jeff Budz and Rob Keck, who helped me shape and sharpen my questions.
This book is better for your help.

ABOUT THE AUTHOR

Thomas R. Pero is a lifelong fly fisher and bird hunter. He a full-time professional writer, editor, photographer and publisher, and has been an active member of the Outdoor Writers Association of America since 1981. He is the owner of Wild River Press, a publisher of fine fishing and hunting books. Many of these titles have won international awards for graphic and editorial excellence, including multiple gold and silver Benjamin Franklin Awards from the world's largest association of independent publishers.

Pero was just 18 when he started the Southeastern Massachusetts Chapter of Trout Unlimited, the youngest chapter president in the organization's history. In 1977, at age 23, he was named editor of *Trout* magazine. During his 16-year tenure, *Trout* was twice named Conservation Magazine of the Year by the Natural Resources Council of America. In 1992 Pero co-founded the non-profit Wild Salmon Center. In 2010 he was awarded the prestigious Starker Leopold Wild Trout Medal at the Wild Trout Symposium in Yellowstone for a lifetime of influential writing about coldwater fisheries conservation.

Pero is the author of *Till Death or Fly Fishing Do Us Part* (2009), the editor of *A Passion for Grouse* (2013) and the author of *Gettysburg 1863—Seething Hell* (2016)

CONTENTS

PREFACE

One of the great wildlife conservation success stories of our time is the restoration of the wild turkey to America's woods, fields, mountains and swamps—and expansion beyond its original range to 49 states, everywhere but Alaska.

The happy spread of all four regional subspecies of *Meleagris gallopavo* (eastern, Merriam's, Osceola, Rio Grande) has created hunting opportunities of a scope unimaginable to earlier generations of American hunters.

As wild turkeys again flourished and the 20th century was coming to a close, a handful of avid hunters set their individual sights on pursuing an ambitious feat: killing a wild turkey in each of the 49 states where they now thrived. One by one, these individuals topo-mapped their way across the country, methodically planning hunt after hunt, and tagging a prize bird in state after state, year after year. And then, one magic spring day, each pulled the trigger on the bird in his 49th state.

Two hunters accomplished the remarkable feat in 1997: Jim Hascup of Ringwood, New Jersey and Rob Keck of Edgefield, South Carolina. Bill Wilson of Hulett, Wyoming and Clyde Metz of Givhans, South Carolina each killed their 49th-state bird in 2003. Earl Mickel of Beach Lake, Pennsylvania completed his quest in 2005. Tom "Doc" Weddle of Bloomington, Indiana followed in 2006; Jon Pries of Trout Run, Pennsylvania in 2008; and Randy Stafford of Franklinton, Louisiana in 2010. In 2011 the National Wild Turkey Federation recognized Daniel Rorrer of Pulaski, Virginia for being the first hunter to register birds tagged in all 49 states, officially calling it a United States Wild Turkey Super Slam. The same year, 2011, Doc Weddle repeated with an amazing second Super Slam, only five years after his first. In 2012 Clyde Neely of Kingwood, Texas and James Wilhelm of Eagle Rock, Virginia joined the exclusive club. Two years later, in 2014, Jeff Budz of Okeechobee, Florida registered his 49th state with N.W.T.F. Then, as I was planning this book in the spring of 2016, three more hunters completed the Super Slam: David Ellis of Crestview, Florida; Tony Hudak of Noxen, Pennsylvania; and Dave Owens of Acworth, Georgia.

As I began my research, I learned that Metz and Mickel were deceased. All the others were still alive.

I was fascinated with this saga. Who were these guys? What made them tick? Who taught them to hunt? What did they do for a living that allowed them the lavish time off to hunt for weeks on end? Were they ordinary hunters or were they wealthy? What motivated them to chase wild turkeys from coast to coast, north to south? Did they drive or fly to all these far-flung places? What challenges did they face? What adventures did they experience? Were there secrets to their success?

How secretive were *they*—and would they even talk with me?

I started making telephone calls. I learned that they would indeed talk with me. I heard passion and enthusiasm in their voices. I reached several while they were in the middle of hunts, their cell phones cutting out when mountains got in the way. To a man they called me back.

How to proceed? Long talks would be required. To get their full stories, I would have to interview them. For more than four decades, a core part of how I have earned my living has been interviewing talented hunters and anglers. It's been fun. Along the way I have met some amazing people while becoming a better sportsman myself from listening to their generous storytelling. I have always respected my colorful subjects and tried to work hard at my craft to accurately portray their extraordinary lives.

To interview these turkey men, I considered my options. In short order I concluded what I suppose I really knew all along: that the only way to do this right was to go see these devout turkey hunters in person. I had to sit down with each in his trophy room or living room. I wanted to hear their stories first hand, eye to eye, across their kitchen tables or on their porches. I started booking airline tickets.

During June 2016, I visited and interviewed the six individuals featured in this book, *Turkey Men*. Later in June and in July I visited six other turkey hunters who have reached the coveted Super Slam; their equally compelling stories will be featured in the soon-to-be-published second volume of *Turkey Men*, later in 2017.

A word on style and approach. I have definite ideas about how an interview should be conducted and presented in print. I came of age reading the great, free-wheeling interviews in *Playboy* and *Rolling Stone*. Later I discovered the treasure trove of interviews in *The Paris Review*. These were long, rough, rambling talks. They were not neatly organized. Most were barely edited, or so it seemed. That's what made them so riveting. There was a rawness that spoke to me: I felt I was listening to this person unvarnished or, in today's jargon, unfiltered. When I read these interviews I had the sense I was sitting right there, eavesdropping on conversations with the likes of Jim Harrison, Hunter S. Thompson, Clint Eastwood, Pete Rose, Stephen King, Ted Turner, Johnny Cash, Tom Wolfe, Jack Nicholson, Keith Richards and many, many others.

So off to talk turkey. Tongue in cheek, I called my whirlwind trip Tom's Turkey Marathon: up and down in the sky every other day, from one airport to the next; in and out of rental cars; chasing the dozen extraordinary turkey hunters across the country with the same intensity they chased the birds. The irony was not lost on me. At each stop I turned on two Sony IC digital recorders simultaneously—one for backup. Upon my return, I uploaded the MP3 digital files to an online program called VoiceBase, which produced rough machine transcriptions of my interviews. I spent the next three months of summer and into autumn working every day, including weekends, replaying and listening to every word, every sentence. This process was tedious and neck-searing. Progress some days was glacial. It was a slog. But I was committed to getting it right.

My work demanded attention to detail on several levels.

First, for authenticity, I had to make sure my first working draft matched exactly what each person said—no easy task since machine voice transcriptions, as I quickly learned, don't do especially well with technical terms such as extra-full-choke and with regional dialects (hens became "hands").

Second, once I had listened carefully to the conversation and was satisfied I had not missed anything important, and had it down verbatim, I went back and started in again. I eliminated distracting repetitions of words and phrases (which we all are guilty of when speaking extemporaneously). I cleaned up some—but not all—run-on sentences. I removed a thicket of "you knows," which many of us routinely interject as pauses in our comfortable conversation, while leaving enough *you knows* scattered throughout so as not to drain the speaker of his natural manner of speech. Answer after answer, I did my best to listen carefully, often multiple times, to preserve the speaker's cadence and original voice. I left in as many colloquialisms as possible.

I went back through each entire interview a third time, focusing on fragmented sentences and responses that were begun but not fully completed. Sometimes I deleted them, sometimes I fleshed them out discreetly to clarify what I was pretty sure the speaker meant. The whole point of my editing was authenticity, after all, not incoherence.

Where I could not decipher the exact spelling from the pronunciation (try Atchafalaya River!) I looked it up. When I was unsure of the spelling of someone's last name, I asked the interviewee. I fact-checked dates, numbers, brands, names of towns and counties, rivers, National Forests, and so on. I tried diligently to weed out and correct all errors. But I have been in publishing too long to imagine that I got them all, for which I apologize to Jeff Budz, David J. Ellis, Tony Hudak, Rob Keck, Clyde F. Neely and Randy Stafford— and to you, dear reader.

Finally, a word about grammar and usage. English majors, please put down your red pens and blue pencils. I am well aware that while in a phrase such as "where we were hunting at," the redundant preposition "at" should be dropped. I am also aware that when "I was laying down next to a big old oak tree," the hunter was actually *lying* next to it. But that's not what they said.

Welcome to *Turkey Men*—I cannot imagine a series of richer or truer conversations with and between highly accomplished wild turkey hunters. You will hear remarkable stories. You will be entertained. You will learn a great deal. You are in for a treat.

THOMAS R. PERO

Jeff Budz

HOME:
Okeechobee, Florida

OCCUPATION:
Hunting Outfitter with Tag It Worldwide

FIRST WILD TURKEY:
1989, Illinois

COMPLETED U.S. SUPER SLAM:
2014, Arizona

David J. Ellis

HOME:

Crestview, Florida

OCCUPATION:

Aortic Clinical Specialist with Endologix, Inc.

FIRST WILD TURKEY:

1988, Georgia

COMPLETED U.S. SUPER SLAM:

2016, Hawaii

 HE BROKE HIS HEART. The family of the girl he was dating had some property where he bow-hunted. At Christmas he was going to ask her to marry him. Instead she gave him a "Dear John" letter. He was a skinny cross-country runner without an extra ounce of fat; in 30 emotional days he lost 20 pounds. One morning he woke up and looked at his Timex: 02/01/1992. He thought: *I'm done. I'm done with moping around. I'm done with beating myself up.*

Observe, observe, *observe*. Spotting birds from a distance, coming up with a game plan, and implementing it is key to Jeff Budz's success. "I don't know what I would do without my 10 x 42 Leicas," he said. Little escapes his attention in the field.

That summer Jeff Budz, age 22, moved from Springfield, Illinois to Boulder, Colorado, where his father lived. Jeff's father and mother had divorced when he was four. He was raised by a single mother. In Boulder Jeff found employment as a waiter in a restaurant, eventually working his way up to management. But that didn't leave much time for pheasant hunting in the corn stubble of eastern Colorado or for his dreamed-of long-range turkey trips. So he started painting houses. A friend loaned him a sprayer. He worked like a demon all summer, every daylight hour of every day. It suited his sense of order: cleaning up a scruffy, peeling house and leaving it gleaming. The owners appreciated his work ethic. Jeff stashed the cash and began plotting his future as a consummate hunter, a bona fide pro.

In May of 1993 Budz awakened in his truck and stepped into the Chadron National Forest in northwest Nebraska. A decade earlier, in 1980, biologists had released one gobbler, two jakes and 24 Merriam's there. The population exploded exponentially. Now there were more than 3,000 wild birds on the loose. Most hunters were buying one tag, going afield, and, if they were lucky, coming back into town for a second tag.

Why waste time? Budz thought. He bought two tags. First morning out: BAM! First bird. Two days later: BAM! Second bird. He had his first Grand Slam. Now he wanted a single-season slam. Off to Florida swampland, to hunt notoriously stingy state habitat, where only a few hunters got even a single bird. He knew he had to up his game. He would have to put distance between all those out-of-state license plates and the Osceolas that were out there somewhere in the misty pines and palmettos. Before daylight Budz jumped right in, floating his clothes and his vest and his shotgun in two Hefty trash bags across a waist-deep murky creek. He was scratched up when he got to the other side. Par for the course. He was naked and holding a little Maglite in his mouth so he could see to clamber up the bank. He switched on the light to the startling sight of dozens of eight-inch baby alligators all around him, their eyes aglow.

BAM! BAM! He got his two Florida birds.

All these years later, Jeff Budz has a record 94 Wild Turkey Grand Slams beside his name. No other hunter has come close. And he is showing no signs of slowing down, although he talks about someday doing so, once he reaches 100. Maybe.

When *Field & Stream* sent writer Bill Heavey to profile Budz ("The Slam Man: A Road Trip With the Greatest Turkey Hunter Alive," April 2016), the writer found himself instantly

sucked into the vortex of a human tornado: "Jeff's World," he called it, in which all activity spirals around the frenzied, unrelenting pursuit of bagging another wild turkey. And then another. And another. Whatever it takes, wherever it takes him—and *you*, if you are along for the ride. Hang on, buckaroo. A walk in the woods it ain't.

The magazine writer found an alcohol- and caffeine-eschewing, devout Christian pounding on his motel door at 3:45 a.m. after driving all night because wasting daylight on the road rather than in the woods is a sin.

"A germophobe who carries disinfecting wipes everywhere, he prides himself on traveling light but cannot imagine life without Chapstick, hand lotion, and Charmin," Heavey wrote. "He's an obsessive-compulsive who likes things organized his way. When friends want to mess with him on trips, they don't rearrange the whole truck. They move little things. They put the pen tray over on the console or a seventh shell in a pouch that had six."

Budz led Heavey jogging, scrambling and belly-crawling for hours, barely stopping to catch a breath or devour a meager protein bar, an exhausted Heavey clawed his way up to the top of the South Dakota ravine wall and whispered, "Look, dude, I'm in decent shape for a guy my age, but I can't keep up with you."

"Nobody can," Budz whispered back.

For nearly three decades Budz has steadfastly remained wedded to one all-consuming passion: turkey hunting. His advice to new hunters who wish to succeed? Take off your wedding ring and finish it off with a sledge hammer. Women in Jeff's World have come and gone—mostly gone. A while back he and one of his girlfriends who had kept their relationship going for several years set off in Jeff's truck on a hard-driving cross-country turkey chase. They got only part way. Arguments over when and how many kids they would have filled the cab of his pickup by day and motel room by night. Jeff drove her to the nearest rental-car agency and told her to have a nice drive back to Florida. Gone. He Photoshopped her out of his turkey pictures.

Which brings us to David J. Ellis.

Ellis flies around the world—Australia, New Zealand, Singapore, Thailand, China, Japan, Belgium, France, Germany—for a company that makes medical devices, aortic

FACING PAGE: After his "honey hole" fell through on opening weekend of the Oregon season in April 2011, Jeff Budz scrambled and started knocking on doors to acquire permission. An hour and a half after introducing himself to a farmer who was loading hay bales, he was wading this icy river on his way back to the truck with this beautiful Rio Grande.

stints. The week after we met he was heading to Amsterdam. He hoards the points he accumulates with Delta, National Car and Hilton Hotels, and cashes them in on spring-time turkey travels.

D. J. Ellis was born in 1982 in the then-rural town of Conyers, Georgia, southeast from Atlanta. It was a laid-back farming community where you knew your neighbors, and just about everyone fished and hunted. David's father hunted deer when he could squeeze a day away from his busy schedule as a physician. When Dad was in medical school he had fished for bass competitively in the Redman Tournament Trail. The Ellis family home sat beside a small lake where, as kids, David and his younger brother Daniel paddled around in canoes and staged their own little tournaments.

And then the year David turned six he caught turkey fever. His three-quarters-blood-Cherokee paternal grandfather took him into the woods, sat him down at the base of a tree with a Sears, Roebuck .410 shotgun perched on a forked stick. A strutting gobbler appeared and the boy was blinded by the light—literally, as you will soon read. He killed his first wild turkey. He was in first grade.

Years later, his obsession did not go over well with his Ecuadorian-born wife who had moved to Queens, New York when she was 12. She and David met when they were both in the U. S. Air Force and married at age 22. Four years and two children later, her mother moved in. Mom spoke barely any English. "I couldn't understand her," David said.

They ganged up on him, he said. They urged him to update to a more stylish wardrobe. Lose some weight. Spend more time at home. He started working out. They went back to church. He didn't hunt for a year. The relationship unraveled.

"Good woman—perfect mother to our kids," Ellis said, "But she didn't understand my turkey hunting."

David was then an x-ray technician at a hospital in Fort Walton Beach, Florida. Through the stress of David's marital woes and eventual divorce, at least he could talk with a woman at work who had been through a similar experience. She could empathize. They got married.

New wife—same story. She had no real hobbies, no passion of her own. David's turkey hunting became a mistress.

FACING PAGE: David Ellis said this hunt in Skyline, Alabama in March 2014 was an "absolute blast." He chased this longbeard up and down a range of mountains before finally getting on the same bench with the bird and calling him right in.

"As long as I can get out the door," he said, "I know that when I get on the plane and have a couple of drinks, I'm on my way. I know I'm lying to her but I'll deal with it when I get home.

"I've been caught so many times," he told me, mildly moaning. "You can put this in the book because she knows about it."

He has a second set of camouflage clothing and guns locked up in the truck. He flies somewhere for business and surreptitiously tacks on an extra day or two to kill turkeys. If he gets one he gets so excited that he posts a photo on Facebook. He can't help himself. And then the phone rings. It's Jessica: "What the hell are you *doing* out there?"

The tension starts building after the holidays. When January rolls around and it's time to apply for turkey tags, she starts asking, "Where are you going *now?*"

David Ellis smells spring coming: "If there are turkeys gobbling in another state, I want to be there."

In 2016, at age 33, Ellis became the youngest hunter ever to register his 49th-state bird with the National Wild Turkey Federation.

FACING PAGE: One of Ellis's most memorable hunts was in Paradise Valley, Nevada in April 2014. He shared the hunt with two great friends, (left to right) Ron Collins and Scott Culpepper. All tagged-out their first morning.

On a soft June evening I was sitting in a rocking chair on the porch of a delightful century-old hunting camp on an island in a shallow, reed-filled freshwater lake. I was sipping a scotch and smoking a Nicaraguan cigar to the tune of a loud chorus of cicadas singing in the ancient and magnificent moss-draped live oaks surrounding the weathered camp. Just before midnight, in the distance I heard Jeff Budz's airboat roar to life and speed off. He was going to meet David Ellis across the lake and escort him here.

Why do you hunt?

JEFF BUDZ: I have had knockdown dragout arguments with PETA and tree huggers—and I say it's a great excuse for me to get outdoors and stay in shape. Their answer was for me to go hiking. But it wouldn't be the same. I wouldn't have a purpose. Hunting is the core of who I am—and now it's the way I make my living. To me it's like asking why do I breathe. I have been fortunate enough to get four Grand Slams a year since 1999 and I'm getting close to 100. People say, "Well, what are you going to do when you get to 100?" But because I've done it for 20 years—and of course I live in Osceola country, which is the hardest—I don't even think about it. I plan on still doing what I have for a long, long time to come. Turkey hunting is all I know. In the spring I guarantee you that my vest is in my truck, my gun is in the rack up top, I keep a jacket and a hat in the back. If I have to jump out and turkey hunt *right then*, any time from March through May, I'd need about 30 seconds notice.

What motivates you?

BUDZ: I think what motivates me to hunt now—and getting sort of deep—but I've become so good at it and so successful at what I've done, and met so many people. Call it a badge of honor, ego, whatever. However you want to slice and dice it, it's sure nice to have done all that hard work, all those early hunts and gotten little or nothing for

years. Now I'm spoiled. David is so accomplished as well in the woods. You're talking to all these guys and I know after you get done interviewing everybody you're going to come up with a lot of the same reasons. I mean, we're definitely cut from the same mold. Now it's about taking others and keeping our ability to hunt alive for generations to come.

Same question: What motivates you—deep down what drives you to hunt?

DAVID J. ELLIS: There's this, this fire—this desire. For me, you know, once you've heard that one bird gobble on the roost and you've seen him come in, there's a passion, there's a fire that's lit. It doesn't matter where you are, it doesn't matter what's going on in your life, turkey hunting is constantly on my mind. I lost my father the year before. Turkey hunting was the thing that kept me out of trouble. It was *the* one thing that kept me going. It's something to look forward to every year. Like Jeff, to me, it's all I know. I learned how to do it and learned to do it well. And, you know, being able to get out and see different parts of the country, integrating hiking with hunting—just being able to seeing beauty across the country—was the perfect combination.

Jeff, what specifically is it about hunting wild turkeys that you most love?

BUDZ: It's the interaction—interaction and communication with the bird. Forget everybody else. Two hunters in the woods is one too many. For me it's mano a mano—me against that bird. It's also the chess match. Turkey hunting changes through the season and through the years. Traveling from state to state, boy, that's the match I live for. You have to think and you have to be a step ahead to get him.

What is it about this singular animal, David?

ELLIS: Springtime. Everything in the woods. It's a rebirth. Everything is turning green. The wind starts to clear in spring, especially here in Osceola country. Being out there first thing in the morning, hearing the woods come alive, hearing that bird gobble, knowing what your game plan is, you know, and figuring out how you're going to tackle it. I mean, anyone who says that they go out to see a longbeard strutting—if that's all turkey hunting does for you—then you're totally missing it. Like Jeff said, it's the interaction, and I tell everybody the same thing: it's a chess match and you need to know the next move. If there's a bird hung up at 70 yards, what do I need to do to make it happen? Some guys freeze up. They don't want to make a move because they're afraid they're going to get busted. But there's a point when you cross that turkey-hunter threshold. When you call to a bird and he's working back and forth on a strut zone and he's wanting you—in nature the hen comes to the longbeard—if you can't figure out how to decipher that and make a move successfully to get in position, you'll never do well. You have to be able to think ahead of the game. It's like going to war with a bird. In the end, who's got the upper hand? And, I mean, I get goosebumps thinking about that experience I lust for every spring, that one spot and one moment I share with a longbeard.

When did you kill your first turkey?

BUDZ: April first, 1989. I was 22 and a buddy of mine had taken me turkey hunting for the first time. He said, "Buy a tag." We were going to college

Home away from home while hunting Kansas public game land in 2003. For decades Budz has logged tens of thousands of miles by himself, chasing turkeys in every corner of the United States, hunting every day the law allowed.

at Southern Illinois University. We went out on some public property. We heard a shock-gobble and two birds came running in, two jakes, and I knew—I have the picture of me holding that bird—and I knew right then that turkey hunting would always be a part of my life. And no one in my family had ever hunted. I wasn't around anybody who hunted. I was a city boy. Yeah, I had a BB gun and was a better shot than any of my friends. But when that happened—*whooo*—it was like hook, line and sinker.

What about you, Dave—what do you remember about your first bird?

ELLIS: My grandfather was a great woodsman; he 75 percent Cherokee Indian. I went out with him when I was five. I never woke up that well but he said, "Come on, let's go." In our family if you commit to something you'd better follow through with it. When I heard that first bird gobble that's when it first struck me, like, I didn't really know what it was. But once I saw him come in and my grandfather harvesting it I knew then there was something special going on within me. I didn't understand why I was shaking. I told my grandfather I'd like to go next year. My grandfather had a .410, a bolt-action Sears model because my grandma worked

Jeff Budz (right) with his first wild turkey, bagged April 1, 1989, with his friend Jim Lynch, who introduced Budz to hunting during their junior year at Southern Illinois University. "Two hours into my first turkey hunt I was a little let down," Budz recalled. "Didn't see or hear a bird." His luck and destiny were changed when two scrawny jakes shock-gobbled.

at Sears. And I remember sitting at the base of this tree. He had scouted everything out. I was sitting in his lap. He had cut a little makeshift fork in a stick to prop my gun on and had it pointed down this little lane where he had seen them strutting. This bird starts gobbling and I was *done*. He comes strutting down the lane and I'm to the point where I could not *see*. To this day I have the same problem: everything around that turkey goes white. It gets real blurry. I have to look off to the side of the gobbler so I can see him to shoot— seriously. I don't know if it has to do with the blood pressure in my eyes or what, but whenever that gobbler was coming, I had issues with keeping one eye partially open partly and focused on that shotgun bead. That's why I now use a red dot; I

used to have a scope. So anyway he's coming down towards us and he's about 25 yards away and I'm just completely losing it. I shot and killed that turkey and I jumped up to get him. I was ecstatic! It was about the best thing that had ever happened to me my life. I felt like everything I had built myself up for the whole year was right in front of me. And each bird I kill, you know, whether it's this last bird I took in New Hampshire this year or number 49, it's just so sentimental. It's perfect. Those feelings, those emotions have not changed since that special day when I was six years old.

Let's talk about getting into turkey hunting. What vital piece of advice would you give a beginner?
BUDZ: Spend as much time in the woods as you

can. Get the best gear that you can afford and cover as much ground as you're physically able to. Be aware of everything around you in the woods because all the answers are out there. You should do your homework to learn the basics but you have to be out there. You can chalkboard it. You can read. You can watch videos and listen to CDs all you want, but there's no substitution for being in the woods. There was almost none of that when I started. In 1989 I called Primos because I had bought my first call—a pushpin call—and I tried it and thought, *This thing doesn't sound right*. They said, "Hold on I'll send you to the back." "Hello, this is Will—what can I do for you?" It's funny to this day, you know, looking at what he's done with

David, have you kept track of how many turkeys you've killed over the years?
ELLIS: To me it wasn't about a number. The only time I wanted to kind of keep a tally was when I was going for the U.S. Slam. But the last time that I kept track I had 200 birds and that was my junior year of college—2008. I know a lot of guys like to keep a journal and I did. But I live such a busy life it's hard to dedicate the time. I used to keep a blog, too. And having a family, when you come home, the last thing you want to do is to make it even more, you know, stressful within the household by spending time on some forum and blogging about your hunting experience. Everything's here [points to head]. I can recall just about every memory,

> This bird starts gobbling and I was *done*.
> He comes strutting down the lane and I'm to the point
> where I could not *see*. To this day I have the same problem:
> everything around that turkey goes white. It gets real blurry.

the company and his career. But today it's totally different. There's so much out there for a guy if he really wants to beat the bushes and put in some work.

That's behind my question because the sheer amount of information floating around can be overwhelming.
BUDZ: In follow up, once you get out there, don't be afraid to call. I'm not in David's league—he calls in competitions. My competition is in the woods and honestly I don't really think I'm that great of a caller. I've heard stuff come out of people's mouths that is just sweet as sweet. But they couldn't call in a bird to save their life because they are not good woodsmen. And then again I've come around the corner thinking there was another hunter ahead making horrible calls and, whoa, a hen flies away with the tom right behind her. So don't ever be afraid to call.

every successful hunt—even not successful. Every time you go out there it's a learning experience.

Any idea how many birds you've tagged?
BUDZ: Somewhere north of 400. I'd have to look. I keep an Excel spreadsheet. My girlfriend doesn't buy it but I *really* don't have a good memory and the older you get you realize it. That's because I could literally go to public property and get there in the dark at 3:30 or 4 o'clock in the morning—after being 15 years gone—and find the tree that a bird was roosted in. But at a cocktail party I shake a guy's hand and before I've let go I've forgot his name. So the net is I started a spreadsheet to keep track of date, weight and other basics.

And nearly all of those 400 were part of Grand Slams.
BUDZ: Ninety-two of them.

Do you remember when you started thinking about the U. S. Super Slam?

ELLIS: I do. I remember like it was yesterday, actually. I was in the U. S. Air Force and I got orders to Andrews Air Force Base in Maryland. I was devastated. I was like, *Oh, God, I'm going to a place where I'm going to have to carry a concealed weapon 24/seven.* I was worried. There was a girl in my class who was from Connecticut. She was assigned to Wright Patterson Air Force Base in Dayton, Ohio. We swapped so she could be closer to her family. So once I finally got down to Dayton and I'm like, *There ain't crap around here.* There's cornfields all over. I started doing a little research with the National Wild Turkey Federation and found out that in southeast Ohio there's a local chapter called the Jackson County Longbeards

road—I'm going down this road." So we go and hunt and we both kill turkeys. We come back do the whole turkey-calling seminar showing all these kids how to call and blah-blah-blah. And the kids were stoked—it was just the best feeling ever. Well, I had gotten a concrete slab in one of the state forests to put my tent on for the season opener, and Ron's like: "No, no, no. You're going to come stay with me. We'll hunt together." We hunted maybe two or three days and he brought up the whole chasing a U. S. Slam thing. He knew Earl Mickel. He knew everybody. And I'm like, "The U. S. Slam—what in the heck is a U. S. Slam?" "You know, getting a bird in all 49 states." And I'm thinking to myself, I was like: *Wow! Now I've got something to think about.* I mean, nothing against the Grand Slam. But I had gotten a few Grand

> I hunt primarily public land. I don't pay guides. I did not pay anyone—period—the whole time I was chasing the U. S. Slam. To do it all on your own kind of hits the pinnacle of awesomeness.

that has a youth turkey hunt every year in the foothills of the Appalachian Mountains. They have many acres of public land and game wardens would open the gates for the youth hunt, you know, to make it easy on the kids. You want to get them involved and make it fun. That's what I try to do. The last thing you want to do is beat the crap out of them. Jeff and I could walk 15, 20 miles but these kids would be like, *Forget this— I'm playing video games for the rest of my life.* [laughing] I get down there and it was like a God-send. It was like the absolute meant-to-be situation. And I teamed up with a guy named Ron Collins, who is one of the best turkey hunters I've ever met. After my grandfather, he was my mentor. And when my father passed away he became like my second father. So Ron coordinated everything. He's like, "Take these kids and go down that

Slams before. You can get your subspecies here and there and change it up to successfully do it, you know, and do it the right way, for me. I hunt primarily public land. I don't pay guides. I did not pay anyone— period—the whole time I was chasing the U. S. Slam. To do it all on your own kind of hits the pinnacle of awesomeness. And Ron Collins led me to it. And after he told me about it I hunted and took birds in every state surrounding Ohio that year. Then it was like a fire: *Oh, my God, this is so cool. I'll get to see cool places and go hunting and do it all on public land.* It was perfect.

And when did you start thinking about aiming for all 49 states?

BUDZ: You know, I don't have a specific time that I said, "Oh, I think I'll go for it." I had traveled and hunted, not knowing anything about the Super

In March 2103 David was successful with his buddy Rand Rose on Rose's Alabama hunting lease.

Slam, until I think I was probably around 17 or 18 states

ELLIS: You had a bunch already—you were halfway there almost.

BUDZ: And somebody said something about it and I thought, *That's cool.* And I think I dabbled with it for a few years and then I finished two years ago, in 2014. So I probably spent eight years actively pursuing it, saying, "Okay, this is it." For those of us that have done it—or me I know for sure—I don't want to say it became work but I think I heard you [David] say: "Gosh, I don't have a schedule. I don't know what I'm going to do now." There's no regimen. There's no *have* to do this and *have* to do that.

ELLIS: For me, once I began chasing the Super Slam, that's all I looked forward to every year. For me, turkey season is ongoing. Meaning that as

soon as one season is over I'm already thinking about what I'm doing next year. I'm already looking at and compiling maps. I'm talking to people—foresters, biologists. It's like putting it all together, studying it all and then trying to execute. This year I was discombobulated because after Hawaii I was done. I mean I love to hunt here and there and everywhere. And it was fun. But the U. S. Slam has been my drive.

How long did it take you?

ELLIS: I started in 2006. So 10 years, although I missed a year from my divorce when I didn't hunt.

BUDZ: I cringe when I hear you say that. *Didn't hunt for a whole year?*

ELLIS: It was terrible. Trying to change for a woman to try and salvage a marriage, when you're not that person, it never works. I gave up a whole year and

I'm telling you I wish I could have that back.

BUDZ: Not the wife—the year. [laughing]

ELLIS: She's a great mother to our kids but I lost something—if that's not you then you shouldn't do it.

BUDZ: Well, the truth's going to come out. You can fake it for a long time but the truth is going to come out and it's going to rear its head sooner or later. If it's later it's going to be uglier when it does.

ELLIS: And it's not just that my buddies were sending me pictures of a dead bird. It's a feeling. If you have that instinct to be out in the woods, once that spring air hits, the smell of it, the way that the leaves start to bud. It's almost like I *am* a turkey to some degree. I feel it's my time. Just like in the fall. If you're a big deer hunter, once you feel that cool fall air move and you can smell it, you know that it's not far from rut. You know that's when you want to be in the woods. Things will never change. It's who I am.

What was your last state?

BUDZ: My last state was Arizona. May 14 of 2014.

ELLIS: I remember the picture. You got it with a bow. You had it on a rock.

BUDZ: A fire went through this whole area. Where I was hunting there were all pines. I don't know how everybody else does it but before I even get to a state I envision what I want a picture to say. When I started pictures were everything for me. I can look at a picture and say, "Oh, that was Tennessee; that was Ohio; that was Maine." Something stands out—whether it's the morels or whatever.

ELLIS: That was a good picture. I'm very big on that, too. I think out of respect for that bird it deserves the best picture. That's why I dislike shooting a wet turkey. I'll go buy a blow dryer and blow that thing dry before we take a picture of it. We did it. We did it in Hawaii. So out of respect for that elusive bird, the bird that I respect so much,

you know, it deserves that last victory that we both had together.

David, we talked earlier about not only your last bird, but your next-to-the-last. Take us back to Maine.

ELLIS: Maine would make the 48th continental state. This was last year, 2015. One of my good buddies, Randy Rose, me and him have been hunting since we were little. He's a lawyer, a public defender in Tuscaloosa. And he's also chasing the U. S. Slam. We kind of always talk back and forth about where we've been hunting and how it's going. I knew Randy had reached out to a biologist up in Maine. The U. S. Slam is a network—we take it seriously. We don't openly throw out information. Every single year after the season there are people who are, like, "Hey, man, you have G.P.S. coordinates for this place or that?" "No—you're taking the fun out of the whole journey. Taking the fun out of it." I talked to the same biologist and he told me about a wildlife management area and said things were looking good, the woods were greening up early, they're feeding well, blah-blah, blah. So I flew to Portland. My wife thought I was going to Portland, Oregon—*don't put that in there!* [laughing] I drove up to check out this place and I'm putting on my camo I go to go pee over this ledge and I see a dead turkey lying there. I mean it had like an 11-inch beard. Spurs were still on it. And I'm like holy hell! I was pissed. I'm like, *what the hell?* Had a rope, like a lasso around its neck. I don't know if somebody hit it with a car or whatever and they put it around its neck and drug all the way over there. I don't know. The biologist told me he had seen only one bird. I don't know if this is him but I'm still going to go and check things out and I walked the property thoroughly. I didn't see crap. I called and heard nothing. I didn't have a good feeling. I wasn't 100 percent but my instinct told me to move on. I never have all

FACING PAGE: Two weeks before his May 2014 hunt and aiming to complete his U. S. Super Slam, the Budz realized he had bought a turkey license from the right Indian reservation Arizona—but for the wrong year. "After talking with my local contact I realized that my only option was to buy an over-the-counter archery-only tag," he said. "I hunted hard for four days to harvest not only my most beautiful Merriam's to date but, most exciting, finally accomplish No. 49!"

my eggs in one basket. So I drove north to check out some other place. I'm sitting there talking to the biologist on the phone and I said, "Man, there's a turkey!" I'm seeing a turkey strutting right through this field.

Was it private land?
ELLIS: You know, in Maine, if it's not posted you can hunt it. A lot of the New England states are that way. If it's sprayed with red paint on the trees you can't hunt it; if it's posted you can't hunt it. But even if it's not posted, still, out of respect, let the landowner know that you're going to be out there. Ask him first—don't just tell him. So I drove by and I saw this guy on a tractor, an older man with his grandson. I stopped and started talking

He told me where they are and what they do and everything. I went back the next morning and killed two.

Your 48th state.
ELLIS: Absolutely. It was a great time. I went back and told the guys I was successful and I thanked them so much for their generosity. You know, being nice and upfront goes a long way. Whether the Northeast or the Pacific Northwest, you tell people that you're chasing a turkey, and they're going to look at you like you're crazy. A turkey is nothing. If you call asking to go kill a whitetail or muley or something else, you'll probably get the finger or a quick kick in the butt. But in a lot of these places during the winter months, the birds,

> Then I started telling about who I am:
> I'm a country boy chasing wild turkey all over the United States,
> trying to get a bird in all 49 states and they're like,
> "You're from *where*—you're from *Georgia?*"

to him and I asked him if this was his place. He was like, "Yeah it's our place." He kind of like beat around the bush. Then I started telling about who I am: I'm a country boy chasing wild turkey all over the United States, trying to get a bird in all 49 states and they're like, "You're from *where*— you're from *Georgia?*" "Yeah, I'm from Georgia, living in Florida now. I'm here in Maine trying to get a bird." He told me he doesn't usually let people hunt because they have bison. So then his son comes out of the house and the old man introduces me and tells him what I'm doing and that he wanted him to drive me around the back side of the farm. It took me by surprise. After him basically saying that he does not allow people to hunt, I just wasn't expecting that. And of course the son shows me around and I go back to the hotel to get all ready. I just can't believe it. I was excited. Because I knew there were turkeys there.

they get into the hay, they get into the oats. So killing one or two of their turkeys is not a big deal.

And then you were off to the South Pacific to tag number 49. Jeff, please jump into this conversation because you both experienced the same hunting in Hawaii, although many years apart.
ELLIS: Me, Dave Owens and this guy named Kenny Mount went together. Dave won the Georgia State Turkey Calling Championship and Kenny won the Alabama Championship. Dave got his 49th bird this year; I think Kenny is about eight, nine birds away. Those guys are really good callers.

So they know what they're doing.
ELLIS: They know what they're doing. Those boys have killed quite a few birds. So we flew into Kona on the big island and I rented a car and we drove to Waimea and got a room at the Waimea Inn, a

Rebel yellers on the Big Island of Hawaii: (Left to right) Ellis, Dave Owens and Kenny Mount take the high ground at Mauna Kea Game Management Area in March 2016. D. J. said he couldn't have asked for a better crew of hunters.

really nice place. From there to where we hunted on Mauna Kea is about 30 minutes. So when you land in Kona it's about 30 feet above sea level. You get to Waimea it's about 2,500 feet above sea level. It's about 55° in the morning. When you get up to the check station on Mauna Kea you're at about 8,000 feet above sea level. When you go to Hawaii you can spend the money and hunt the Parker Ranch and use their shotguns or you can do it on your own. Only thing is if you bring your own shotgun you have 48 hours from the time the plane lands to make a reservation with a local

police station. They do the paperwork. You give them a $14 money order. They make sure that the gun you have is what you say it is and record the serial number. It took us maybe 45 minutes. Once you get your gun cleared it's good for the rest your life—you can bring that gun back to Hawaii if you have the paperwork. By the time we got up there to the check station it was like 30°—30! It was *chilly*. Then it's a good seven-mile ride in. We went deep down into Mauna Kea and hunted there and it was a turkey man's candy land. I've never heard that many birds—in every direction. [Makes rigorous

OVERLEAF: Ready for his closeup, David posing with the pair of birds he killed on his single-morning hunt in the Aloha State. Nothing tops the beauty of Hawaii with wild turkeys in abundance. It's D. J.'s No 1 place to hunt. Dress for cold.

gobbling sounds.] And you know we were early. We were there on opening day, which is March first.

How did you approach the birds?
ELLIS: Our tactic was we just got in front of the birds. They were not responsive. You couldn't call 'em or nothing because they had so many hens. There was a group of bachelor longbeards, three or four sitting there, and it didn't matter how you called to them—how soft, how sweet, how low, how whiny. Nothing. It didn't phase them. So we had to get down. I call it the Mohican Sneak. Like my grandfather said, it's the Indian crawl. You gotta get down and move on them. Use your terrain, use your greenery, your shrubbery to get as close as you can to kill them. Because they weren't coming to any calls. They would gobble back at you but they wouldn't come. Why would you leave a group of fine honeys, fine honey hens all around you? It wasn't happening.

Jeff, you hunted Hawaii many years earlier.
BUDZ: I went in 1999 and did the same thing. I stayed with a friend right on the ocean. We got there the day before the season, February 28, to scout it out. We got a rental car—it was too expensive to get a four-by-four, so we got a two-wheel-drive and we said, "Well, we're going to drive as far as we can until we get stuck."

How far did you get?
BUDZ: Seventeen springs ago? Holy cow, I have no idea, but I remember my friend and I split up from the car that afternoon before the opener. We rendezvoused just before dark having locating several toms. The next morning we left from 20 feet above sea level and drove an hour and a half up Mauna Kea to where we had scouted the night before. We jumped out and froze! To this day it's the coldest I've ever been. I had nothing but thin camo to wear. I mean, why would I need warm clothing in *Hawaii?* I didn't have to learn that lesson a second time.
ELLIS: Mauna Kea is a dormant volcano. It's not active but there's ragged rocks and very unstable

Jeff taking a final look before descending into a farm valley in eastern Washington in hopes of maneuvering closer to a prize gobbler. He is thorough in his constant scanning.

ground. If you have bad ankles I suggest you put ankle wraps on because you will break your ankle. I'm saying this because there's been a lot of older people out there that have broke their ankles. Just very unstable ground. The roads aren't really maintained. The east side is the wettest side; the west side is drier. They do a lot of goat hunting there so that road is constantly being driven. They don't maintain it even though they had a skidder out there. The furthest you might get with a car is about seven miles. Once you get up to the eucalyptus trees, that's when the road starts getting bad.

No problem finding birds?
ELLIS: It's bird paradise! Number one, Hawaii has no natural predators. Two, they have about every kind of bird you can imagine—Franklin grouse, quail, pheasants, turkey, peacocks. They've got

plenty of nesting. But the trees are very small. It's weird seeing this. I mean, I've been to Texas and seen birds roost on top of fenceposts. But when you have like eight or nine birds in a little bush, they look like a bunch of buzzards. It was hilarious to me. Different. It was different.

BUDZ: Roosting on rocks. Flying down in the pitch black because they don't have any predators.

ELLIS: Actually running down a trail in the dark. We all were on the plane to Hawaii laughing and wondering what what are we going to encounter on this trip. You know, you hear stories and talk to other people who have hunted there. The Parker Ranch has some nice big trees. But where we were at the trees are very small because of the elevation. In Hawaii you'll find turkeys in different environments like rain forests or open country like Texas. You might get an environment like down here in Florida. Hawaii was different. It was certainly different.

What is the maximum number of wild turkey states you've hunted in a single year year.

BUDZ: Sixteen. I think it's 16 states—probably 30-some birds.

When you were pursuing the Super Slam, how many of your birds were taken during the spring and how many in the fall?

BUDZ: All 49 of mine were in the spring. I have shot plenty of birds in the fall because I just want to hunt turkeys as much as I can. But I set off right from the very beginning and I said, "I'm going to kill a spring tom—no exceptions." If you're going to start the quest, there's no sense in shooting a jake somewhere and then a couple years later go, "Oh, man, I wish I had not counted that jake." And there's nothing wrong with a jake, but ask yourself that question and decide right off the bat.

How about you, D.J.?

ELLIS: I've never killed a fall turkey.

BUDZ: Of the 49 or any turkey?

ELLIS: Every turkey I've ever killed has been in the spring.

BUDZ: Really?

ELLIS: I'm not one to judge anybody because I believe everybody has a right to do things their own way. But for me, the idea of killing a turkey anytime except in the spring doesn't give me that fire, that desire. I actually went one time in the fall with a buddy in Virginia and they had these turkey dogs and they did all that but we never had any luck. I'd rather be sitting in a tree looking for a big buck.

Jeff, you are a professional hunter—managing hunting properties is how you make your living these days. Have you ever hired a guide?

BUDZ: The closest I came to using a guide was in North Dakota because a nonresident can't hunt turkeys on public land there. On the Standing Rock Sioux Reservation you have to have guide. And I said, "Hey, I'm on my way to Minnesota." That was my 16-state year and I hunted 10 states in 10 consecutive days and took 10 toms—it was just surreal. I told my guide: "All I need you to do is just point me in the right direction. Show me a turkey." We're driving separate trucks and we came around this corner and he slowed down and said: "Look there's a couple over there. What do you want me to do?" I said, "Take a nap." [laughing] Forty-five minutes later we were taking pictures of two beautiful toms.

Of the 49, how many were bearded hens and how many were toms?

BUDZ: All toms. I've shot plenty of bearded hens. That's the exception. I said I would not shoot a jake but if I would have seen a bearded hen I would have shot her in lieu of taking a tom. I've shot a Grand Slam of bearded hens. I mean, I've shot a pile of them. I'm just crazy about bearded hens.

During your quest for 49 what firearms did you shoot?

ELLIS: I used a Browning Gold 12-gauge, shooting Nitro shells loaded by a guy in Missouri. It's a blended load of Nos. 5, 6, 7. Then I went to a 20-gauge.

Bingo! on a late-season hunt in May 2015 on a local dairy farm near the town of Preston, Connecticut, which had been pressured pretty hard. It took D. J. all morning before he finally got the cagey bird into shooting range.

For the past four years I've been hunting with a Benelli M2. And I hand-load that ammo. It's Tungsten Super Shot. I want the best when I'm out there. Just like if you're playing tennis, baseball or bass fishing, you want to do it the right way. You might as well invest in equipment that's really good. I feel the same way when it comes to turkey hunting. Some people might think I'm crazy for spending the amount of money that I do but— you know what?—it's my hobby. That's what I love. That's what I'm passionate about. I like that Benelli M2. It's light—it's roughly 5.4 pounds. As much as I walk, I mean, it's ridiculous. I shoot this 20-gauge load of Tungsten Super Shot No. 9. and it actually has the same amount of kinetic energy as a No. 5 lead. At 55 yards—and I don't shoot that far—it can put those little BBs through a metal barn roof.

BUDZ: My bread and butter was a 12-gauge Benelli. I've shot them with 10 different weapons, including bows. That's my new goal—a slam with all the weapons. But my go-to gun is still the 12-gauge three-and-a-half-inch Benelli Super Black Eagle with a Carlson's Choke Tube. I shoot Hevi-Shot,

blended. In today's day and age the technology makes 40 the new 20. You wouldn't even bat an eye. I mean, when I started, if you shot a bird over 25 yards people would say, "What are you *doing?*" ELLIS: My grandfather would slap me. He'd say, "Dude, you're not respecting the bird." Because the last thing you want to do is wound him. But, yeah, like Jeff said, so much has evolved.
BUDZ: The technology is so much improved.

Did you ever feel you were competing—either against other hunters who had completed the quest or others who were well on their way to doing so?
ELLIS: It was personal because, to be honest, I didn't know a lot of people. Most of the guys that I knew I respected so much and I felt like, who am I to try to beat somebody to the punch? If, you know, No. 1 they've either been helping me or No. 2 they've been doing it longer than me. So it's never been competitive. My thing was being the youngest guy to ever do it, to register 49 states. I just love to get out. It was that thirst that I had for each spring to see if I could do as much as I could. So for me it was purely personal. Because when it gets competitive you start making poor decisions.
BUDZ: And that's in life. But if you don't have a deep-seated—and I don't know if *passion* is even the *word* because it's way beyond passion—need or drive to accomplish this, you're going to fall by the wayside. I don't care if you're a billionaire and you say to your 10 assistants, "Hey, line this up," and then go on a bunch of guided hunts. David and I are so similar in the away we approached this. I'm not taking anything away from anybody. If someone killed all 49 birds with a guide and they flew in and shot 49 yardbirds it's still going to take a long time to do it. You have to have something deep down, some deep desire to fulfill. And you can't take any selfish shortcuts. It's not like saying, "Oh, I want to go buy a Ferrari," or something for an ego boost. To kill a wild turkey in every state you can't just write a check or swipe a black Amex.
ELLIS: I think there's a core. The core is we have a

passion. We have the desire, the drive to get out there because we love chasing the wild turkeys. Being able to succeed in a new place it's almost like you're conquering. In your mind it's like: *All right. I've killed a bird here. I can get it done. Now can I take what I've learned and get it done somewhere else?* I've heard stories about Rios or Merriam's being easy. Turkeys are turkeys. I don't care—you can go kill a bird on some farm. They're going to do their thing. I mean that's just what they are and is what they do. But being able to decipher that one turkey, because I've been hung up on one turkey. There might be one gobbling over here but this one right here is given me heck—and I can't get my mind off it when I probably can go over and kill that other bird. But there's a core, there's

Okay, well that's a perfect segue into the next question. Did your Super Slam quest ever put a strain on your personal or family relationships? Don't both speak at once. . . .

ELLIS: I'll let Jeff take a swing at that one. [laughing]

BUDZ: I guarantee there have been a few girlfriends that have gone by the wayside because my passion for turkey hunting got in the way. I've never been married. No kids. I'll be 50 in November—proudly 50. Now I have the best girl of my life. Jenny is the best that I could dream of. And she's gone with me and gotten her single-season Grand Slam. Even at that she does it, I think, more for me. She definitely wants to see what it's all about. I said, "I want you to do this once." She went last year, shot four times and got four

> And you can't take any selfish shortcuts.
> It's not like saying, "Oh, I want to go buy a Ferrari,"
> or something for an ego boost. To kill a wild turkey in every state
> you can't just write a check or swipe a black Amex.

a drive that puts us in a place where everything else around you just goes silent. It's all about that bird. And then being able to take off and do that across the United States. You just thrive on it. It's hard to understand unless you live for it.

Did you ever feel like quitting?

BUDZ: No. I *always* woke up early, never was afraid to drive all night, and always found the money to go do it. I never had a problem finding the money to be able to go do this. When I first started, I lived in the back of my truck. It just wasn't even a question. I'd have sooner stopped breathing. Not a question. Not an option. *Hoooo. . . .*

ELLIS: I'll stop turkey hunting when I end up in a casket 'cause it ain't happening.

BUDZ: There's no way that I won't be in the spring woods. Maybe if I'm incarcerated or dead—that's the only way. [laughing]

toms—her first Grand Slam. I mean, that's like too good to be true, unheard of. And I said, "You better tip your guide!" [laughing] So this spring I said, "Hey, you in?" And she said, "Absolutely." It's like several things in life—I don't know if either of you has ever parachuted. The first time you don't remember a thing. You're so overwhelmed. You do it again and *everything* just slows down and you're like, *Wow!* It's just insane. So anyway we had a great time this spring. She did it again and, you know, I've got hope and faith that she stays with it.

ELLIS: I have definitely lost many relationships because of my passion for turkeys. I have had baseball coaches pissed at me because I didn't show up Saturday and Sunday because I'm "sick." I've been through a divorce. I actually tried to change into what she wanted me to be and I was miserable, absolutely miserable. And if I'm miserable

everybody around me is going to be miserable.

BUDZ: She was not a hunter?

ELLIS: No, she was from Ecuador. When she was 12 she moved to Queens, New York. We are polar opposites—just polar opposites. Then her mom moved in with us and it was just a cluster. . . . I lost a year trying to please her in these stupid-ass clothes—pardon my French.

Having been through the Cuisinart of life, what would you advise young hunters about surviving turkey season with their relationships intact?

BUDZ: Don't have one. [laughing]

ELLIS: You have to find someone that has a desire or a passion for something outside of everyday life—and I'm not talking necessarily about hunting, but in general something that they've done from a young age, their own thing. Because otherwise they'll never understand. They have to be able to fathom your passion to some degree, knowing that turkey season is short, even though it does carry on a little bit longer for guys like me and Jeff because we take it to the extreme. Some will never understand it. And I tried to tell that to my ex-wife and now my current wife, but they've never really been devoted to anything other than their family. So being around the family 24/seven is all they know. But if they do not have something that they love to do or something they're passionate about they'll never understand. And if you don't set some sort of expectations up front—*Hey, come spring I'm going to be turkey hunting all the time*—I can promise you it's not going to last. And if it does she's probably got a boyfriend on the side. [laughing] They need to understand. But they don't understand. It's like, "I don't understand how you can be gone for six days, seven days and not think about me or anybody else." When I'm in the woods, when I'm out West, by the time you get done—whether you're two miles, three miles from the truck—it's 10:30, 11 o'clock by the time you get situated. It's already 1 o'clock, 2 o'clock

in the morning back home. Then in the morning you're taking time out of your hunting making phone calls. It just doesn't work.

Is finding a woman who understands your obsession enough, wise bachelor turkey man?

BUDZ: I think it's important to find somebody with her own passion. But when you fall, you fall. I will say that if you want to have a relationship after turkey season, you had better check every single "honey do." Before the season you better check every project. You better have a smile on your face every waking moment. If you think you're going to come home and gripe about being tired. Ha! Forget about it. Because they'll never forget. I know for me and anybody at this altitude of our sport and passion, I would rather be gone for three or four days and come back with my batteries fully charged. I might be physically spent because I haven't slept two hours a night. Mentally and to the core I went to my thin place. [Ancient Celtic name for a mesmerizing place where the distance between heaven and earth dissolves.] Other people—I know you fish—have different ways to get to that thin place to get back grounded, centered, recharged. If someone who claims to love you is preventing you from doing that you're going to be miserable. And as D. J. said, everyone around him was miserable. Don't stop just to make somebody else happy. For me, I start scouting the last week of February and beginning in March I hunt for three months—so I'm going for four months straight. Luckily, elk don't rut and bugle for months like turkeys gobble in the spring. If they did I literally would not ever have a relationship or job. Elk have a far shorter window. But when I'm not in the woods I'm nonstop making *everybody else* happy. So we can, as hunters, we can get our little crumb of happiness and that is just being in the woods. And it's not about pulling the trigger and just the kill. Yeah, that sure makes it nice. But it's about being out there and it's about the challenge.

FACING PAGE: Time to celebrate! Jeff's girlfriend Jenny Slayton shot her first Merriam's on May 15, 2015 in South Dakota. This tom completed her first single-season Grand Slam. Jeff calls this countryside his "thin place."

You better be ready to buy some really nice purses and shoes and jewelry and go out for dinners and do all that extra stuff that's so important to women. I could have a peanut butter-honey sandwich and bottle of water and say: "That was a great meal. I'm going to bed." But what they want is just *so* much different, you know, and that's Venus-Mars kind of stuff—we don't need to go there. But you better be ready for a challenge if you're going to really pursue the Super Slam. Now, you could do two states a year. And there are guys that do it and it takes them 20 years. And they maybe started off with 10 states before they decided. You could take a couple trips like that and nobody would even notice you're gone. But if you're going to really

states touch and within a four-hour range, let's say, you can hunt different states. If you get a bird in one state you can cut across that state and hunt another. Start reaching out. If it's a National Forest call the district office. Call state biologists and see what kind of hatchings they've had in the past couple years. Has there been any winter deaths? Is there a good population of birds in the area? I start downloading maps. I get on Google Earth. I start plotting points. Each state file has all the wildlife management areas I'm planning on hunting: how large they are, the closest hotel to that place, how long of a drive is it from that hotel to where I'm going to be hunting. I have G.P.S. coordinates I'll name like A, B, C or D—the areas I'm going to

> And more guys want to listen to a bird or see a bird from their vehicles before they go after him. Heck, my vehicle could *blow up* and I wouldn't hear it—that's how far away I am when I either hear a bird in the morning or when I hear a bird going up to roost at night. I want to be a mile plus.

hunt like we do, hunt hard, and take off back and forth across the country—*whew*—it's going to take a toll. So be prepared for it. And if you're not willing to make that commitment, go shoot sporting clays down the road.
ELLIS: Is it okay if I take a time out for a pee break, real quick?

Call your wife. [laughing]

Let's shift focus from women back to turkeys.
BUDZ: Thank goodness.

Let's talk about strategy. All this is, of course, second nature to you guys. But if one aims to bag a turkey hundreds—even thousands—of miles away from home, where do you begin?
ELLIS: I basically looked at a map of the United States and I tried to find places where two or three

park at and then, you know, point 1, point 2, point 3. One might be a high knoll that's close to water, so when I get there I can listen at dusk or daylight to see if I hear any birds. Then I can take my G.P.S. and plot where I hear birds. That was always my starting point—knowing where I'm going to go before even getting there, even though I've never been there. But reach out. The foresters are out in the woods the most. They're out there marking and cutting trees. They know where the birds are. I don't ask specifically for spots but maybe one will be, like, "Hey, this road right here, 12-A off 32-something, I seen a turkey crossing the road." Well, that was probably a couple weeks ago, but at least I know that there are birds there. Now all I have to do is find a good vantage point and listen.

Jeff, you're the master at this. You've been exploring new turkey country for decades starting with

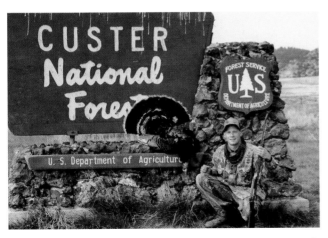

May 5, 1998 was the only day Jeff hunted Montana: "I stopped at a Forest Service office and got some directions," he said. "Thirty minutes later, I was following a flock to their roost." This bird slipped by him that evening—but not the following morning.

rolled-up topo maps.

BUDZ: Good old-school, yeah! Of course, you know the Walla Walla story because you picked me up in Seattle and we drove out there together. Walla Walla is a beautiful little town in southeastern Washington with vineyards and farms all around it. Before our trip I got on the phone and I started calling and talking to anyone I could. But no matter what information you collect, you still have to deal with the conditions you find on the ground. We got there with great intel, you remember, for opening day and there was inches of new snow up in the high country in the National Forest! Which meant there were *no* birds up in that high country. So we started knocking on doors and we fell into some incredible luck: three states—Washington, Oregon, Idaho—three toms, four days. It was great. On opening weekend we ran into a farmer loading hay along the Columbia River and he said: "No, I don't have any birds here in Washington but my farm over in Oregon has some. If you want to follow me over I'll show you

where." So we drove across the river to Oregon and you sat watching me from a little apple orchard climb up this hill and it was incredible. The birds were everywhere. His son was the only one that hunted that property. So we got lucky. But it's best to have something lined up well in advance. On bigger tracks of public property, the first thing I look for is the largest area the farthest away from any road. Because every species—Man's at the top of the list—is lazy. And more guys want to listen to a bird or see a bird from their vehicles before they go after him. Heck, my vehicle could *blow up* and I wouldn't hear it—that's how far away I am when I either hear a bird in the morning or when I hear a bird going up to roost at night. I want to be a mile plus. And guess what? A mile in the woods is a long ways when you're in the dark and never been there.

ELLIS: You're in higher elevation. That mile up hill beats the shit out of you. You get out there in the West, people are going to drive down the road, calling. They don't walk far. The West has always been easy to me because I could walk about a mile and I hear something and end up killing a bird. That B.L.M. and Forest Service land has a lot of gates which they keep closed until pretty much towards the end of May. You can get in there and get after them if you want. I've hardly ever run into another hunter.

BUDZ: Florida is the only opener I hunt because, of course, I'm here through our season. Everywhere else, I want to hunt the last week of the season because there's no hunters. Usually the bad weather is over. The hens are going to nest and the toms are getting pretty receptive. But, you know, it's doing a lot of homework before. One thing you can be sure of and that's anybody doing this is not going to say, "Oh, I just showed up and a bird fell in my lap." As D. J. said, we try to maximize every hour. When you're out West, you drive from

OVERLEAF: The road-warrior hunter from Florida walking through one of the many vineyards around Walla Walla, Washington, where expansion of high-end wineries has created a bonanza food crop for wild turkeys. "I was thinking about what a roller coaster ride the week's hunt had been after showing up for the opener to hunt some promising Forest Service land," Budz said—"only to find the only thing plentiful was six inches of snow on the ground."

southern California to northern California, or in Florida go from top to bottom. Then there are states like Texas—heck, you're in that state the entire day!

Once you get there, how do you find the birds?
BUDZ: I cover as much ground as I can to acquire as much intel as possible. I have no problem driving because I can cover a whole bunch of ground. I just need to see a bird. Once I see a bird at a certain time in a certain place—especially strutting—if I see that bird twice in the same area, around the same time of day, I'm already thinking, *Where am I going to take a picture of this joker?* Because if you stay out of their way they're going to do the same thing. Anybody that's been out there and is worth their weight in salt has stopped U.P.S. drivers, Postal Service drivers, FedEx drivers, forestry guys, people that are out there that live it. For the most part everybody is happy to talk about what they know. Repeatedly I hear, "You're from Florida doing *what?*" Now it's more commonplace. But they love that strange oddity kind of quirky thing. I mean, it's cool to help out somebody in need; we all like to help out other hunters. I help more people than I book or guide each year. I help them go places and give them information. I'm not giving you G.P.S. coordinates—you go figure that out yourself. There's absolutely no possible way I'll give up a pin-point location. I'll give him Chadron, Nebraska, Pine Ridge National Forest. That's it. That's all you're getting from me, buddy. I'm happy to share all kinds of helpful information, but never a roost tree or a strut zone.
ELLIS: There's turkeys in there. [laughing] What I value so much is being able to go from the beginning to the end. If you skip the beginning you're missing figuring it out. It's like all they're trying to do is kill a turkey and that's it. It makes no sense for me to tell you exactly where you need to go and kill a turkey and then you're like, "Oh, I got one!" Well, you really *didn't*. You did shoot him. But you didn't hunt him. You're not doing all the fun stuff. I went down into the north rim of the Grand Canyon last year and didn't really have

anything. We flew into Las Vegas, me and Scott Culpepper, and we drove all night. Everybody calls me "Dale." And the reason why they call me Dale is because I drive like Dale Earnhardt Jr. when it comes to turkey hunting. 'Cause I'm telling you, whenever I got turkeys on my mind it's, you know, a rush. It's probably my crank. I go and I go *fast*. We gave ourselves two days to scout. That first morning while Scott was sleeping I walked for miles on trails trying to find any mud hole, looking for turkey tracks. That was my No. 1 thing, trying to find tracks in the dirt, trying to find fresh droppings. Come to find out, I walked different benches. I walked probably 25 miles that day. I changed elevation three different times. I started low because it was really cold and I moved my way up and I ended up on that middle bench which was about 7,000 feet above sea level. That's where I found turkey tracks, old ones, and I just scoured the mountain. I went all the way up and then walked around and I started finding spots and heard a gobble.

So it starts with finding tracks.
ELLIS: If you can drive in there, at least part way, like Jeff said, it will help you save some time. And then if you can find a good mud hole or where the water has been you can possibly see fresh tracks that's a great place to find sign. But you've got to get off the beaten path and just walk and try to find tracks and listen for birds gobbling. Find a good spot where you know there's water and where you have a good vantage point and then get out there at dusk when they want to roost. Out there you can blow a coyote howler. Ninety percent of the time it's going to work. You'll hear them answer with a real loud shock-gobble. [makes noise]

And this is perhaps an impossible question because you've had many, many, but which were one or two of your most challenging birds?
BUDZ: Well, two birds in two states—New Jersey and Arizona. New Jersey took me three trips—the only state I had to go back to that many times. I

"Wow—the North Rim of the Grand Canyon!" Ellis said. "Absolutely makes my top five places I've hunted the wild turkey. Some of the most gorgeous scenery you can imagine." This hunt in Arizona was on the 12-A Unit. D. J. killed this magnificent bird in May 2015 with his buddy Scott Culpepper. The day before he hiked 25 miles looking for sign.

only had one morning my first trip and two mornings the second, all without success. When I got there the third trip I said, "I am not going to leave this state without a turkey." I roosted a bird and got him the next morning. It was sort of anticlimactic because I just wanted that bird so badly. He was my last Northeast bird. That specific bird wasn't hard. But it made finishing the Northeast memorable.

What do you mean, the terrain or access?
BUDZ: No, no. When I went there I actually had some really good access, but the birds were just silent. You can plan all you want and have everything lined up perfectly. When you get there you don't just sit around. But easterns especially can

get tight-lipped during the season. You can be on the best property in the world and if they decide they are not going to be vocal it will be brutal.

What happened in Arizona?
BUDZ: Arizona was my 49th bird. I called ahead of time in January. I didn't realize that the draw deadline for hunting public ground is way early, in September. I thought, *Oh, no problem because I can hunt the reservation.* So I called the reservation: "I'm coming coming out West this spring and I want to hunt turkeys there. She said: "Sure. Fill out this application and pay your money." I paid the money and got my tag and I was driving out, straight from Florida to California. My plan was to hunt California, Nevada, New Mexico and

then Arizona. On my way and I called my guide on the reservation to touch base and he said, "What's the date?" I said, "The 19th," or whatever. And he said: "That's a Friday—the season opens on Saturday. What year?" *Huh?* I looked at the tag. And it was for the *next* year! She sold me a tag for 2015.

Oh, no!

BUDZ: And I about fell out of the truck going 80 miles an hour. So I called my contact in Arizona. He said my other option now is archery only. Me being the pro traveler and the planner—how I let that slip through the cracks? How didn't I ask her that one question? How didn't I see the date on that license when I got it? SAN CARLOS APACHE

after my father passed away. On a lot of those trips I would always talk to my dad afterwards. He wasn't a big turkey hunter but he loved to hear my stories. And you know if I had an issue with a bird that was giving me shit, you know, I would call him up. and talk it through. He would bring a little bit of reasoning to the whole situation: "Be grateful for what you've got. Don't worry about it. It's a turkey!" In the Southeast, hunting on public land is way different than any other place you'll ever hunt. It's the quality of hunters.

What do you mean by quality?

ELLIS: Quality that's lacking. It's the number of hunters. It's the lack of respect. If I come to a gate and it is, say, a 200-acre place, if I see a truck there,

> It's the lack of respect.
> If I come to a gate and it is, say, a 200-acre place,
> if I see a truck there, I'm not going to stop. I keep going
> because I don't want to mess up somebody.

RESERVATION TURKEY TAG 2015. I was so miffed. I called the reservation back for a refund and she would not give it to me.

But you got your Arizona bird.

BUDZ: I got my bird. Four days into the hunt. I got that bird with a bow, which was great, too, because your last bird gets a lot of air time. I look at that picture on my wall all the time. If I had to point to one bird it honestly would not be because it was 49 but because I messed up. Because I am supposed to be the specialist. And I know better. I was just so excited that I got that over-the-counter archery tag and my 49th bird.

How about you, D. J., do you have one bird that you most remember?

ELLIS: I would say the most difficult bird I killed was my bird in Mississippi. It was 2011, the year

I'm not going to stop. I keep going because I don't want to mess up somebody. I would not go in there and try to do anything because No. 1 it's disrespectful and No. 2 there's plenty of other places to hunt. In Alabama, Louisiana, Mississippi, Arkansas, Tennessee Georgia, and Florida too you don't get that at all. Every once in a while you might meet a guy who says, "Hey, man, which way you going?" In Louisiana after I parked at the gate and am walking down the trail and this dude is running down the side in the woods past me trying to beat me. What in the *hell?* It's aggravating. I hunted Mississippi for two years. The first year I drove all the way down and had issues seeing—I missed more turkeys because when the turkey comes in I'm still seeing white. I just can't see the target in plain view. So I put a scope on—one of those Pentax, you know, it has like the diamond reticle in it. When you're shooting a 12-gauge and

a three-and-a-half-inch magnum your receiver takes a beating from the force when that scope's on there. I had a turkey actually fly across a creek and landed 25 yards in front of me. And when I was looking through that scope, I saw the turkey but it blurred out the little tree that was right in front of me. I freakin' whacked it—blew it all over. The turkey flew off. I'm beating myself up. I looked at my shotgun. The damn scope's going back and forth. It's not even attached to the receiver anymore! Maybe by one screw. And I'm thinking to myself, *Well, my hunting trip is all screwed now.* I had only one gun. The next year I drew a permit for Bienville National Forest and Caney Creek. I walked through a boat load of water moccasins and the next morning I got on this bird. He was like an Osceola. Came strutting right through water and everything. I mean, I had water up to my ankles. I shot him two times. I've never shot a turkey twice [chuckling] but when he came up I hit him in his wing. Once again it was just people pressure. It was nonstop. I could never make anything happen right. I'd be on a bird and then somebody would come from the other side and start calling. He'd bugger that bird, calling too much, blowing that hen squealer or whatever the hell kind of call it was. And it just never worked. Well, that one morning it worked. It was probably the most emotional hunt I've ever had. Hard on two different levels because, No. 1, the people that I was basically forced to hunt around would not give me the space that I needed to make the hunt successful and, No. 2, when I was done I didn't have that opportunity to call my dad about the experience: The one state that had been giving me heck I finally got it done.

BUDZ: How many birds do you get to hunt in the spring and keep chasing after that bird until you get him?

ELLIS: Not often really.

BUDZ: Me neither. That's the one drawback I hear guys talk about.

ELLIS: They start naming them: "There's Leroy over here and I've been hunting him for five weeks."

BUDZ: Yeah, yeah.

ELLIS: And I'm like: "You ain't killed him yet? You ain't figured him out?" "Old Leroy he's been giving me hell. [mimicking] He's got hooks that you would *not believe.* He's got a beard that drags the ground." I'm like, "Obviously, then, something ain't going on right here."

Do you have a keen memory of a particular bird that challenged you but that you never did end up tagging?

ELLIS: I had one in Iowa. I was hunting with my cousin. [chuckling] First off I knew it was going to be a cluster of a hunt from the get-go. This was really the beginning of the U. S. Slam for me. I trusted him. I trusted his word, [sighs] trusted he knew the seasons and all that. So anyways we get out there the first morning and I have tags for the unit that I failed to look at because it was all internet—I bought it over the phone. There are birds gobbling all over the place. It's kind of a Jeff story. We're in a spot easily accessible by anybody and everybody else. I'm sitting there and I say: "Okay, Jordan, you're shooting first. I'll stay behind you." And I'm thinking to myself, *This just doesn't seem right.* It is opening day. And there ain't nobody around us and there's turkeys gobbling their damn heads off and there's tracks going in and out of there. Thank God we didn't shoot a turkey—it was the *day before* opening day. It could have been a disaster. That was the last thing I wanted. It was my lack of attention, you know, not being gung-ho about getting the exact dates right and everything. It taught me that you've got to be on top of it wherever you go.

Did you go back?

ELLIS: Oh, yeah. We get in there the next morning and we find this turkey that had paired up with a peacock. [laughing] I'm not kidding—I swear—

OVERLEAF: Tennessee's Laurel Hill Wildlife Management Area, April 2014. For Ellis, these lush woodlands makes his top 10 list of spots where he has hunted turkeys. Each year some 30,000 birds are harvested in the Volunteer State.

paired up with a peacock! And this was a wild eastern turkey. I sat there and watched this turkey. He was like, "We need to go, we need to move." I was so amazed that I just sat back against a tree and fell asleep. There comes a point in the season when you're turkey hunting all the time and your nights get shorter and shorter. As soon as you put your back to that tree you're done—you're out of it. I call it "barkolepsy."

Ha! "Barkolepsy?"
ELLIS: You go to sleep. Some of the best sleep I have ever had was up against a dang tree. I tried to pull every trick out of the book to kill this turkey but that damn peacock would scream and

Jeff, what's the most challenging individual bird that you never killed?
BUDZ: You know, I don't recall any one specific bird. It's just such a blur. I think probably the ones that are burned in are the misses. I've missed some layups, just because I was so excited, I guess. You can say all you want but it was just buck fever and I'm glad that I still get it. There are some birds that I should've gotten. There's been a slug of those that got away. But it all works out and I always shake it off and figure there's a reason for everything. Here's one: I shot my first bird in 1989 and in '90 I said, "Okay, now I'm going to call in my own bird." I went out and I peeled off from the same National Forest property with the same

> Oh, yeah. We get in there the next morning and we find this turkey that had paired up with a peacock. [laughing] I'm not kidding—I swear—paired up with a peacock! And this was a wild eastern turkey.

the turkey would gobble and they would go back and forth and strut for each other. And there was a couple hens around but it was weird. And I *know* it was not a pet turkey. That was probably the hardest turkey of my life because I really had never seen anything like it before. I ended up coming back. The season there was like four or five days so I left there and I went up to northern Iowa and hunted on another unit. But, yeah, we ended up killing him.

Did you bag the peacock?
ELLIS: No, we didn't kill the peacock. [chuckling] I think it was somebody's pet. It was still there but it wasn't with the longbeard. I could hear him screaming real loud [makes high-pitched sound like cat screeching]. Boy, every time he did that you heard the turkey [gobbling sound]. That's all you heard.

friend in the same area as the year before. I had that pushpin call that I had called Will Primos about and he gave me directions on: "Yep, that's how it sounds." I went back and forth on a bird the first morning—maybe because I worked him all morning, he went the other way and I never saw him again. I didn't know what spittin' and drumming was until many years later. Then I knew how close he really was! So, for me, it's the failures that fire me up more than the successes. But I went two years—1990 and 1991—when I got skunked. Had those birds just come in like a layup, I honestly don't know how hungry I would have been to this day. How engrained it would be in me that I want to get every bird I can. It's funny, I remember that I crawled under this bush because there wasn't a tree to sit behind. They all said, "Oh, get by a tree that's bigger than your shoulders and dah-dah-dah." There was a deadfall and I crawled underneath and I sat there on that pushpin because I didn't know what a diaphragm was. That bird in 1990—oh, boy, that bird lit a fire under me.

Where's the strangest place you ever killed a gobbler?
BUDZ: Strangest place? I really don't know. Walking on lava rock in Hawaii—that was a surreal hunt. It's a blur because for me it was one bird out of each state. I did have one fly across a mountain to come to me. Last year in South Dakota there was a foot and a half of snow. I *stalked* a turkey. He wasn't calling. I stalked him and I shot him with a 28-gauge from 15 yards. I mean, how many guys have shot one in a foot and a half of snow?
ELLIS: Not many.
BUDZ: It was pretty cool. But no garbage dump stories. I sat in an old car once in South Dakota. That's what they do out there on the reservation. They break down, they run out of gas and they just leave the car wherever it is.

Any strange places for you?
ELLIS: I actually got two good ones. One was Delaware. As soon as I got there I had people asking me for money. Every time I pulled into a parking lot of a state forest: "Hey, man, you got 20 bucks? I'm outta money and I gotta get some gas"—and yada yada yada. I'm like, *Man, this is not going to be good.* Delaware is different. You have to take the turkey hunter safety course in person and you have to put in for a lottery draw. It's a pain in the butt. So I get there and I'm thinking *Delaware,* you know, *the first state.* And it was just dirty. There's cans and trash all over. So I go out to scout and I'm not there five minutes and someone's asking me for money; I go to the next place and I'm taking a leak and someone's asking me for money. I don't know what the hell's going on. I go back to the hotel and get out of my car—someone else asking me for money. So the next morning I go to this one spot where I found these birds and it's getting light and I'm sitting up against this tree. [chuckling] A bird comes in. I shoot him. He takes off running. I start cussing myself—I cannot believe it—blah, blah, blah. I look down. I have never

From his first hunt for the Osceola subspecies in the Sunshine State years ago, Jeff Budz's instincts told him that success on hard-pressed public reserves would demand that he get as far away from the competition as he could—gators and water moccasins be damned.

seen so many damned used rubbers in my life. They had a blow-up mattress in there just going to town, I mean, just humping like you wouldn't believe. They were everywhere. There were reds, greens and purples all over the place. Obviously they got the assorted pack. [laughing]

So did you get your First State wild turkey?
ELLIS: Sure enough, the bird ran five or 10 yards and died.

You said you had two stories.
ELLIS: I was in Rhode Island right across the Connecticut line with my friend Ron Collins. It was the last day of the hunt. I had already killed my bird. I told Ron, "Look, you go down this trail I'll go down that trail and let's just listen for one when it goes up to roost. So I'm sitting there and after five or six days of nonstop hunting, I was exhausted. It's basically in line with the Providence airport. So this airplane goes over. It does something, it drops the afterburner to burn some fuel off or whatnot. And as soon as it does that [makes gobbling sound]. Out of instinct I jumped up and ran as fast as I could to the top of that hill. I could tell it was a good ways off but I wanted to be up

high so I pinpoint it.

Seriously? The bird was actually responding to the jet?

ELLIS: It gobbled. I swear to God. It shock-gobbled to the afterburner—first time I've heard that happen. So get up on the hill and I hear him gobble. I take my G.P.S. and it looks like it's in somebody's backyard. [chuckling] The next morning it rains. We're flying out at like 12 o'clock. I was like, "Let's go get that bird." So we go back and we walk down this trail along these rock walls. We don't hear him gobble at all. I tell Ron- "Look, I'm going to get on the road. I'm going to drop down I'll pick you up on the bottom and call on the way down. If we don't do anything we'll go back to the hotel, change and whatnot and get ready for our flight." I'm walking out and I hear this bird gobble. I run back in there and I'm all excited and I tell Ron, "We can get him, we can get him!" And Ron's like, "He's right there—I think he's in that person's backyard." [chuckling] So we come back off this rock wall about 100 to 150 yards. I get behind him in this ditch and I start calling. I'm running a slate call and a mouth call to make it sound like two birds. So the turkey jumps this wall and comes running right into Ron's lap [chuckling] and he kills him. Pretty much that bird was roosting in some guy's backyard. I know that in the Northeast there's lots of turkeys getting into people's yards and roosting all over the place but the experience was definitely unique for me.

Jeff, have you ever purposefully passed up a turkey you could easily have killed?

BUDZ: When I'm hunting by myself my thin place is when it's bad weather. I don't have a camera. I have no pack. All I have is my gun and my mouth call. I'm never going to pass up a bird. But when I've been with other people, or a significant other, waiting for them to shoot first, and maybe it doesn't happen, I think that's the only time. I'm out there. Unlike D. J.'s story, I don't travel with people. I'll say it: I'm selfish. My goal is to get a turkey and to go to the next state. That bird is on ice in the cooler and *still warm* by the time I cross the border.

ELLIS: It's hard. I have the same drive. I want to go to the next state and you have to set some sort of expectation like, "Look, if by this date even if only one of us has killed a bird we have got to move on."

BUDZ: And how many times have you had to do that?

ELLIS: We have not had to do it at all to this day. Well, actually, I take that back. We did it one time, that trip that I went on to Rhode Island. I killed a bird in New Hampshire; Ron also killed one in New Hampshire. I killed a bird in Vermont; he did not kill a bird in Vermont. He wanted to go somewhere else. We went down on the Massachusetts line and I ended up killing a bird in Massachusetts, right on the Vermont line. He did not kill a bird there. But at that point I was like: "Look, we've been successful. We've killed birds. Let's give it one more day." Then we went on to Rhode Island and we both got birds there. Had we not gone to Rhode Island we both wouldn't have gotten those birds. So it all worked out. But if you're going to travel with someone else you've got to have that discussion—we cannot stay in one place for more than three days when we have tags and permits everywhere else. And that sucks because, like you said, Jeff, you're chomping at the bit ready to go to the next place to get it done. I'm the same way. You got to be the bearer of bad news: we've been here for two days—we gotta go.

Has either of you dared add up what those 49 birds cost you?

ELLIS: I've gotten that question plenty of times. I haven't ever gone down that road, honestly.

FACING PAGE: Small geography and a limited number of nonresident tags make Delaware a difficult state. "This hunt was not easy by any means," Ellis said about his April 2014 experience. "I had only one day to scout and all the turkeys I could find were on private property. I finally found this lone bird on a small section of the Redden State Forest Management Area."

BUDZ: For a long time I used to keep a journal of everything for each year. I was *neurotic:* miles driven, hours slept, miles hiked, dollar spent, etc., etc. I was averaging $750 a bird. I think that was probably a fairly accurate number. That scares me because I just did the math—I had never done that before—and 49 at $750 is just north of $36,000 and $750 times 400 is $340,000. *Wow.* I don't know—maybe this passion was a bad idea. [laughing]

Your top turkey states?
BUDZ: South Dakota—if I had to hunt one place it would be South Dakota.
ELLIS: That's a tough one because I have so many. No one place really strikes me as my best because

there's nothing like seeing a longbeard coming through some palmetto patch, strutting all the way.
BUDZ: It was always Florida for me until I moved down here 11 years ago. Now it's work. For me, when I hunt an Osceola, spring or fall, it's not a hunt. It's, *I'm going to go kill a bird today.* Because I have *so* much property and *so* many birds and that's all I do is watch them all year long. I usually have my work shirt on. I pull on a camo jacket over. I'm just *so busy* trying to get everything else done around home. When I wasn't living here, Florida was my No. 1 thin place. I couldn't wait to be in Florida. I'd come out until I got my two birds; it usually happened fairly quickly. But now it's South Dakota because there I have so much

> For a long time I used to keep a journal of everything
> for each year. I was *neurotic:* miles driven, hours slept, miles hiked,
> dollars spent, etc., etc. I was averaging $750 a bird.
> I think that was probably a fairly accurate number.

each place has its own little title to best. I wouldn't be doing all the other states justice.
BUDZ: Before you started on the Super Slam quest I know you lived in a couple places and hunted around there. How many states did you hunt each spring?
ELLIS: Georgia, Tennessee, Alabama, Texas and then, of course, South Dakota. I like the Black Hills. It is different.
BUDZ: Where in the Black Hills—the reservation?
ELLIS: No, on state ground. To see turkeys in the evergreens was just totally different to me than what I'm used to. And then also—I'm not gonna lie—south Florida is different. It's totally different and if you can find good ground, you know,

land to hunt and because there's such a physical aspect to it and there's so many birds and I push myself. As you know you're going to bed at midnight. You're waking up at 3:30 and you're *go, go, go* all the time.
ELLIS: I guess it depends on how you define favorite. If you're talking about a place that's, like, "Oh my God!"—you've got this kid's big smile where you just walk into a toy store and you have everything you can ever imagine in front of you, Hawaii was one of those states. You heard birds gobble everywhere. That's what puts a grin on my face. Just hearing them do their thing, regardless if I'm in the action or not. You could just sit there in the morning and listen all down through there

FACING PAGE: Budz harvested this fine Idaho tom the day after attending a National Wild Turkey Federation fundraising event in Orofino in April 2011, and getting permission to hunt a small, private ranch on a bench area high above the Clearwater River. Jeff invests a great deal of off-season effort cultivating distant connections.

[makes multiple gobbling sounds] and realize, *Holy—there's at least 100 birds right here.*

How about your least favorite state?
ELLIS: California—another good story. We were in Troy, Oregon and I'm working this bird. I take my hunting vest off because I like to get light if I'm trying to make moves to get up on a bird, if I know he's hung up. I get within 30 yards and I can see his tail fan over this little knob but he would not pop his head up. I did everything. He moved on. (Dave Owens ended up killing that bird later. He wasn't having any luck in Oregon and I sent him in there. He didn't even call. That bird flew right down in front of him.) But I couldn't find my turkey vest; I had walked maybe 150 yards from it. So I started doing this little military sweep, like looking for an unexploded bomb or something and I'm sweeping and here's this 175-inch whitetail rack that someone had shot during deer season. It had been so cold and icy up there that it was preserved. And I'm like: *Wow! I want to take these antlers home with me.* I found my vest but ripped my pants on dead cedars laying down—I mean, they are *jagged*. So I get back in the truck and I've got this huge rack and half my pants are hanging off and Ron is like, "What happened to you?" Ron's like, "You can't put that thing in here." It stunk so bad. So we put it on the back of our Jeep. So we headed south through Oregon on Interstate 5. We are going to hunt the Klamath National Forest. As soon as you enter California there's a toll booth and all the signs say is NO VEGETABLES AND FRUIT. We're legal all the way. So we go through and keep going and you can see this beautiful view of Mount Shasta on the horizon. This game warden passes by us and I'm driving and I'm thinking, *He's going to stop us and ask about the rack.* Sure enough, he turns off and comes right in behind us and puts on his lights. We pull over. And he's like, "So where did you get the buck?" So I told him we were turkey hunting and I found it in Oregon and I've got a tag—blah, blah, blah. "Well, did you report it when you came through the check station?" I'm like: "No, sir. I

promise you, I've read the regulations and they says nothing whatsoever about checking wild turkeys. You can see I'm wearing camo. The lady waved us on through." He goes, "Do you have any other game?" I told him we do, we have some turkeys in the cooler. He's like, "Did you check those?" I'm thinking to myself, *What do you think, Captain Obvious?* He made us pull everything out of the cooler, took pictures of all the beards—okay, this beard is with this tag from Washington and this one is from Oregon. He gives us a $500 ticket. We decided to fight it. We got an attorney. We paid $1,000. We got expunged. I was so pissed off. And he took my horns, too!

These days, Jeff, is it most satisfying to you to hunt a familiar piece of land or learn a new place?
BUDZ: Familiar. Because for so long it's been show up in the dark, never get to see the area and then leave in the dark. For so long it's been so *unfamiliar*. This year I hunted Texas. I only had one morning. But I was in the area—two states away [laughing]—and I told a buddy I'd stop by to see him. And I hadn't seen him in 15 years. I'm not out to get any more states. I guarantee you 40 of those states I'll never hunt again and I'll never set foot in 30 of them again.

How many days each year do you devote to turkeys?
ELLIS: Forty-five, maybe 50 days. It's a lot. When I'm home and the season's on I'm hunting. Outside of that if I can travel I'm gone. It's all about turkeys.
BUDZ: That's tough because I spend three-quarters of my time in the woods not carrying a gun because I'm guiding. I start off scouting. I've got 90 days in the field doing something. I went out West—Kansas South Dakota, Nebraska—and I was there for 10 days. Yeah, I shot seven birds in a little over four hours of actual hunting because they were places I hunt and have hunted for years. Most of my time is spent guiding others. But my own personal days? When you're used to the same old haunts and you've done it for so long, your time in the field goes down exponentially. So I've

never thought about how many days I spend hunting myself now.

How do you go about pre-season scouting?
BUDZ: Well, for me it's all in Florida. I've got oodles of properties. But it's really easy. The "yellow yelper" is the best call known to man. And I have corn feeders on most of my properties. As I said earlier, if given the opportunity, all species are lazy. And if people stay out of the way those birds will do the same thing day in and day out. Yeah, they might have a coyote spook 'em right before they roost but they'll roost somewhere else. All my blinds and feeders are in the exact same spot for years. That being said, I'm still a turkey whore and I want to be in the woods every opportunity. So when my alarm goes off, I jump up. It was funny. One morning this year I jumped up as I scratched

guessing: "I wish I would have. . . ." Before hand do every single thing possible to succeed. And that doesn't go just for turkey hunting. That's how I live my life. I want to do every single thing possible to succeed. And if I fail—and I will, everybody will, that's part of what makes success that much more sweet—I want to fail saying, "Doggone it, man, that was *pretty cool* because I did everything I knew." I can live with that. You know, sometimes success is just not in the cards. *Intel, intel, intel.* Cover the ground. Don't plan on sleeping. Get the best gear you can. Flat out scout. Get off the beaten path. Look at the obvious stuff. Heck, when I go to an area, I want to know, "Ma'am, excuse me, when was the last time it rained here?" I mean, *right here*—not five miles over there. Because I want to know about every track I see, how fresh is that? And it goes from there.

> I can live with that. You know, sometimes success is just not in the cards. *Intel, intel, intel.* Cover the ground. Don't plan on sleeping. Get the best gear you can. Flat out scout. Get off the beaten path. Look at the obvious stuff.

my head and cleared the cob webs and I said, "What am I doing today?" Jenny said, "Aren't you taking Carl's daughter?" "Oh, yes, right—I got to go!" This was a month into the season and I literally couldn't have told you—I mean I knew I was turkey hunting—but it's just a blur. Every day somewhere different, someone different, someone new. But every day out there.

What advice do you give beginners or journeymen hunters?
BUDZ: Cover as much ground as you can. On your feet or in the vehicle. Talk to as many people as you can. Do not be bashful. You are there for a purpose. When your trip is over and the season is done, your plane is off the ground or you're driving back home, that's not the time to be second

ELLIS: To add to that I think if you can find someone that's willing to help you out, take you under their wing—a good woodsman. Go out and shadow them. See how they do it. I think a lot of it has to do with knowing the lay of the land. Maybe there's a little patch. Is there some water over here? Maybe there's a good field over there where they're feeding on bugs. So it's being able to get into the woods and feeling it out and understanding the lay of the land.
BUDZ: How many times have you had a bird just *shredding* it but not coming and you're wondering, *What's going on?* You turn your phone on, you look at the map and you're like—duh! Yeah, there's the barrier in his way. I know I'd better react to this quickly because he's going to shut up soon.
ELLIS: That's when a lot of guys just sit down and

wait. They think he's going to come over but he's not. That bird is saying, "Look, if you're a hen you can come to me—I'm gobblin' my head off over here." You have to decide whether you circle in front of him or make a big loop and come back from the other side when he shuts up and stop gobbling. You make a big loop to get in front of him and then call. Now he's coming to you: POW! You don't have to be the best caller. Whenever you're playing the sitting hen [makes continuous yelping sounds of a hen] and you have a bird that is gobbling his head off [vigorous gobbling sounds] there comes a point where he does lose interest. Because you're calling him way too much. It's not going to do anything. Instead, try walking around him in a big circle, talking to him in the same cadence. That's my idea of being a good woodsman, you know, making those right decisions that mean the most at that right time. I've killed a lot of birds from that last movement, that last point where I'm sitting down. He's acting a certain way. I know it's not right. I know he's not committed. And I need to get another 15, 25, even 50 yards away. Sometimes it's just getting to another spot and calling from there and then maybe calling away from him going back the opposite direction. He thinks she's moving around. I might go back to that same tree and call again. He ends up running over to look and I shoot him. So there's tactics or ways of doing things.

BUDZ: And how many times does a guy realize that the opener is next weekend and goes, *Wow, I have to go through my turkey stuff.* Friday night before opening is not the time to do it [chuckling] and the time to scout is not the Saturday before your state opens. Yeah, you better be out there that day, but you should be out there several times before that.

FACING PAGE: Budz spied this prime gobbler strutting with a group of hens on a hillside in Oregon high above a flowering springtime apple orchard. An obstacle was a swift-flowing river flooded with mountain snowmelt. No problem. Budz stripped down, waded right in (see page 7) and scaled several hundred feet up a steep cliff to get within range with a load of Hevi-Shot. Next mission?

After a couple of fresh setups, this late-season Alabama bird finally made his way into D. J.'s gun range.

ELLIS: I'll tell you, the best turkey hunters I know are the ones that tag-out quickly on either the first or second day before moving on. Sometimes they'll just kind of hang back depending on what their goal is. But those guys are the ones that have been out in the woods since February.

BUDZ: Yep.

ELLIS: They're scouting the land and been sitting in there every morning. The turkeys might not be gobbling but the hens are yelping. Things start to green up, the light increases in the morning, and they start hearing a bit of gobbling. Those are the guys that have done their legwork. On opening day they go straight to the birds. If I'm in a new state I'm sitting on a high point listening for birds gobbling. Those guys are already down there on top of the birds because they've been in there for weeks getting after them.

When do you sit and when do you run and gun?

BUDZ: If I know where a bird is and I can get in close enough to him in the morning, I have no problem sitting if I have confidence it's going to be good. Sometimes there's never a peep—you've seen strut marks or sign of dusting or whatever, but nothing else has worked. Those are the two ends of the spectrum. When it's really good or really bad. That's when I sit. But other than that, when it's questionable, when I don't have any intel, if he's changed up and he turns and starts going away, you just don't sit there. It's not like driving down the road and you have a flat tire like, *Oh, I need to stop and change the tire.* You take the time you need. First thing in the morning there's so much going on that by the time you figure out that the bird's going away or shutting up—you can't just hammer him with your call the whole time—it's too late.

So you must be ready to pivot.
BUDZ: Instantly. You have to have your finger on the pulse of the situation. David said it: do an end-run and get in front of him, *changing* the cadence. Go to a mouth call or a slate or a box, *changing* your calling, changing up completely from what you did before.
ELLIS: That's a good point.
BUDZ: I *love* to run and gun. If I had my choice I would much rather run-and-gun hunt than sit. But I start off sitting and I start off the old classical way. I have a couple of old-timers I guide: "I won't shoot a bird until he's gobbled." The other one says, "I won't shoot a bird unless he's gobbled and strutted." I've told both guys: "I want to hunt with

I'm not going to be able to get the job done because I don't feel confident with my weapon. It's doing what's right and what's right for the turkey and making the cleanest kill possible. A lot of people do not think. They think they can put a bead on that gun and grab a three-and-a-half-inch magnum load, not knowing that their gun doesn't chamber a three-and-a-half-inch shell. But they throw it in there. It's a wonder more people don't kill themselves. Or they try to kill a turkey with an improved cylinder or modified choke. . . .

You sound agitated.
ELLIS: I take it personally. This is my passion. Anyone who goes into the woods to hunt turkeys

> Instantly. You have to have your finger on the pulse of the situation. David said it: do an end-run and get in front of him, *changing* the cadence. Go to a mouth call or a slate or a box, *changing* your calling, changing up completely from what you did before.

you, I really do. Oh, yeah, because I'm going to pick up a lot of your scraps." [laughing] I mean it's a war and I will take advantage of every opportunity I can to get 'em. *Golly.* [more laughing]

Let's talk about the actual hunt. As you go about preparing for a typical hunt, what are the key elements?
ELLIS: Okay, No. 1 for me is you have to know your gun—my gun is my girlfriend. I have to know how she's going to perform whenever I'm out in the field. And that goes back to patterning your gun. It is my biggest pet peeve. I mean, I dislike it when I hear—from new hunters or people that have been hunting for a while—"Oh, yeah, I bought a box of No. 5 XRs [Winchester Long Beard shotshells] and I shot a couple times and, well, I'm doing all right." Doing *all right?* That would be like me going out with a bow that's not sighted in and wondering why I didn't kill a deer.

should take it seriously. If you cannot at least get the basics down, you know, pattern your gun and know what your best maximum yards would be if it comes to that, you shouldn't be out there. Calling and dressed in full camo all the way from your head to your feet. There have been times when I've hunted with guys who didn't have masks—they can put paint on. That's fine. A hen gets in close enough to you and she can see the white of your eyes. [makes sound] Your camo, your weapon, your shells, those are the main things.
BUDZ: I wear a turkey vest and I've got everything I need in that vest. I carry an extra mask and an extra set of gloves in one pouch to my left side. In the blind hit me in the head with a hammer and I could still find every single thing in my vest.

What's your favorite shotgun or shotguns?
BUDZ: A buddy of mine was so off, he couldn't hit the ground if he fell. On a trip to South Dakota

he needed a Merriam's for his Grand Slam. After missing several birds he switched guns and finally got two beautiful birds. After we got back to Florida, he stopped by one day and handed me his Benelli and I said, "I can't accept it." He said: "You don't understand. I'll never shoot it again. I'm giving it to somebody. I want to give it to you." I said, "You can't do that—you and I are friends." He said, "It would mean a lot to me." After going back and forth I finally accepted his gift. I had had a Black Eagle, a three-inch, all-black, which was my bread and butter. Now I have his camo Super Black eagle and it has killed so many birds for me and my clients that you could fill a truck.

So the unexpected gift keeps giving.

done that for two years, just to change it up. It was fun shooting four toms last year with a .410. I tell you it did as much damage as a 12. It was incredible—*incredible!* But I felt that pressure again of having to accomplish something. It's like back then when I knew if I didn't get Connecticut, I was going to have to go back to *Connecticut.* And you're hearing it from all sides. You're having to stroke the checkbook every time the credit card bill comes in.

How about you, D. J.?
ELLIS: Favorite gun right now is my Benelli M2 20-gauge. It's very light when we travel around as much as we do and it's easy on the shoulder. It's got an Indian Creek choke with a construction of

> Some people complain that with tungsten there's a lot of expense. You know, it's 40-some bucks for a box of five. Yeah. [pauses] I spend $500 on flights; $400 on hotels; $250 on meals; I spend $1,000 on licenses for three states—you think I'm going to balk at $40?

BUDZ: I just started shooting a Thompson/-Centerfire one-shot break-open gun. It's nice and safe. There's something to be said for one shot. That's all you get! Think about it: How many times do you get more than one shot? I mean, they're big old fat 20-something-pound birds. But when they want to get out of there, whether shot at or not, they're gone. And maybe a guy if he only had one shot he'd pay a lot more attention to it. Up till now most of my birds have been taken with that 12-gauge Benelli three-and-a-half-inch Hevi-Shot, blended. Yeah, I messed with all the different gauges. I got through that pressure of the Super Slam and then before I finished in 2014 I already said, "Okay, next year I'm going to start getting my four Grand Slams with different weapons each year.

Including bows?
BUDZ: Crossbow, recurve, compound. And I've

0.555-inch, I think. I'm shooting a T.S.S. No. 9. that I hand-load myself. I feel very confident with that gun. I shoot it five or six times before season starts because I have that issue when the turkey comes in everything around it goes white. Now I use a red reflex sight: Docter Optics with a little red dot. I take that cap off and I just put that red dot on the turkey. You can leave both eyes open. Once he crosses paths and I pull the trigger, he's done. Knock on wood, I have not missed a turkey since I put that red reflex on.
BUDZ: No sights. I've had so many people mess up with sights—fogged up, batteries dead, wasn't turned on. I won't have anything to do with them. A friend of mine did some work with Carlson and they made a choke for Hevi-Shot and it's incredible. If somebody doesn't take advantage of it and shoot it and practice with it—look at what it does to paper at different yardages—shame on them.

You know, I have *so much* gear and so much technology that I guess I reached a point when I can get away from it completely. I just want to be away from it. I put a second bead on my little 20-gauge. I'm taking more kids now and I just say, "Line up those two dots and you're going to be okay." And you call him in nice and close and you have him strutting stop still and give him a little cluck and he lifts up nice and pretty—you do everything to set the kids up for success.

You've seen it all—are these new loads worth the money?
BUDZ: That's the new frontier. Everybody's coming out with all these turkey chokes and ammunition. The guns really haven't changed that crazy much. But with the chokes and the loads nowadays, it's incredible. They're doing these turkey-shooting competitions and you look at what choke and load won, the number of pellets that hit the target just five years ago and what they're doing now. It's just night and day. It's insane what they're doing with that stuff. Some people complain that with tungsten there's a lot of expense. You know, it's 40-some bucks for a box of five. Yeah. [pauses] I spend $500 on flights; $400 on hotels; $250 on meals; I spend $1,000 on licenses for three states—you think I'm going to balk at $40? It's the least expensive thing they will spend on their entire trip. And they want to get down and nickel and dime it. You drive a Ferrari and you don't want to put the premium fuel in it? It's just insane. If you put it in perspective and you look at the numbers that way, what is your argument? I shot three-inch Federal copper-plated buffered No. 6 shot for years. When they came out that was cutting edge. But, heck, that goes back 20 years.
ELLIS: My tungsten loads are about $12 per shell—making them myself.
BUDZ: Making them yourself. So if those were available in factory loads they'd be about twice what Hevi-Shot is.
ELLIS: It's just like if you're a professional golfer you're going to play with a ball you can control—such as a Titleist Pro V1X. They're not going to

play with a ball they can hit straight but they can't work it left or right. With my loads I can put 325 pellets in a 10-inch circle at 35 yards. That's ridiculous. *Ridiculous!* For me, it's knowing that when I put my dot on that turkey's head and pull the trigger [snaps fingers] he's done. Unless I mess up he's not going to fly off. It's that confidence factor, knowing that I'll be successful and knowing that I'm going to do what's right for the turkey.

Are you still sold on Montana decoys?
BUDZ: Oh, my gosh—1,000 percent. I will also sometimes lop the tail off a bird and cut as much meat off as I can, then toss it when it gets a little gamey. Give me a flat golf course and I will go straight at a bird—no ifs ands or buts. I say that but I also say in the same breath it's the last resort. I do not run through the woods with it. It is not my first choice but I am fearless when it comes to using a Montana tail because I've had so much positive reaction. When it works right it will *blow your mind.* What's the percentage of it working? Far less than half. But when it works. . . . For elk I have a cow elk silhouette. I shot my biggest elk last year, 370 inches, with a bow. I had my Montana decoy. It was a bull and he walked through a window that a cow had walked through. I drew back as he went through, he stopped and looked at me, and I drilled him. Had I not had that decoy those cows would have blown out of there. He would have blown out as well. I know for a fact I would not have had a chance.

What about for setups?
BUDZ: Two hen and a jake Avian decoys are my standards right now.

And your use of decoys?
ELLIS: I don't use decoys that much. I do the fan trick, though. I don't want to carry the extra weight. If I have kids along I'll take them. Sometimes decoys work really well and sometimes they don't. But for me it's more about getting in the right setup and getting to a place where you have a little cover between you and the turkey so that

when he does pop up he's looking for a hen and you have a good shot. If I have a stubborn field turkey or turkey that is in the distance and you have the ability to use a fan, I will. But like Jeff said, I don't go tramping through the woods with a fan on the back of my neck! I'll sit there and hold it up and wave the fan and typically that turkey will puff up, look up, and come to you. But it's very rarely that I do it. I'm a low-key kind of hunter. If there's a lot of people out I'll try to avoid a lot of calling; I don't want people to know where I am. I try to get that turkey before somebody else does. I have decoys out, you know, I'm pinged automatically. If you're fanning around other hunters that's just stupid. I'm one of those guys who just goes where the wind blows whenever turkeys are around.

Blinds. How important are blinds and when and where do you think they're useful?

ELLIS: This year I bought my first blind because I'm taking my son hunting for the first time. He can't sit still—he's got A.D.H.D. like his daddy. They are useful. They have a place. If I wanted to kill a turkey with a bow I'd probably use one. Otherwise I don't have much experience. Maybe Jeff could chime in.

BUDZ: I started working with Double Bull back in 1998 when I lived in Boulder; they were in Fort Collins. That was when people were skeptical of them: "Oh, you'll never shoot a deer out of it." Now they're commonplace. Now every other hunter has either hunted out of a blind or wants to. But David said it: kids, archery. I would add filming, bad weather. You know, for me, here in Florida, when I have my guys, I'll put a pin on a map and say: "Go sit there. Put your decoys out. Call if you want to. But sit there and stay in that blind." Twenty minutes after fly-down, guess what's right there in front of them? If I have a choice, I'm personally not going to hunt out of a blind because I want to go, go, *go*. But if need be—

oooh—I have no problem with it. I've put a blind out in the middle of a golf course and crawled out of it with a Montana decoy and gone at a bird. I've *picked up* a blind and walked it at birds. No matter what I do, I'm always pushing the envelope. Calling more than most or not call at all in different situations. Once I put out 16 decoys. It looks like a goose spread! But, boy, when they saw it, it was like they had never seen that before: they cannot resist the party. I always try doing something different. When I travel I go into areas and ask people in that area how they hunt turkey here. And I'll do exactly the opposite because I figure those birds are locked into what the locals do. That's for sure.

What essentials are in your vest? We touched on the "turkey grab bag" earlier.

BUDZ: Yeah—one of everything—and there goes the gear list. With phones nowadays you don't really need a G.P.S. although I still have my Garmin. Slate call, mouth call, box call, tape, Ziplocs, rubber gloves, paper towels, lighter, compass, gloves, face mask, protein bar, apple, bottle of water. I'll go all day. If I'm traveling maybe one real good decoy, maybe a hen. And then some thin Montana decoys, a pop-up strutter. I have a Spyderco knife on me at all times in my pocket and three in the truck just in case I lose one. I couldn't imagine not having my Spyderco. And I'll probably have a Havalon with me to breast-out a bird real easy. Back in the truck I always have a scale and a tape measure. Ziploc bags ready for prep once I get back. A pen—sometimes you have to sign your license upon kill. Mosquito repellent. Cough drops—probably the most unusual thing I have in my vest is cough drops. I keep them in a film case—now there's a blast from the past. How many film cases do you see around these days? Everything's digital. I have two. I've got chalk in one and I have Halls cough drops in the other. After the season I throw them away because they've gotten all saturated and stuck to the wrapper.

FACING PAGE: "Nothing in the world tops a gobbling eastern," Ellis said, "from the time he pitches off a limb to the time he gets near. This Alabama beauty did just that and was tagged in March 2016.

Flavor?

BUDZ: Cherry. When you get a little bit of a tickle in your throat and you start coughing. That's the last thing you want when it's dead calm and you can hear everywhere [makes clearing dry throat sound].

ELLIS: I have pretty much everything he said. I also I keep a pair of clippers in my vest, so I can clip branches if I need to. There will be a time when you start calling, a bird gobbles, and I already know where I'm going to go. But I can't find that right tree and there's that one branch you just can't break. Clip it real quick and throw it off to the side. I also use it to clip any sticks and roots that are right in my butt where I'm trying to sit.

and you can't move a muscle. Now that root is raping you. So I carry one of those low camo chairs. I don't fly with them but I drive with them. My gosh, I own 15 of them for each one of my camps and anyone who hunts with me. They're so comfortable.

ELLIS: If you're planning to sit still you have to have a good seat. If you don't you'll go numb. You're done. It's unbearable. The one moment when that bird comes in and you have to kind of lift up just enough to get your blood back in your butt so you can sit down. I have a little inner tube with a cover that I blow up only part way. It's like sitting on a little air biscuit and it is absolutely perfect. Awesome. Love it. I can sit there for hours.

> I have slept on rocks. I've eaten bark. Done all this stuff.
> Sat on the most comfortable tree—I thought—until an hour later
> when your bird is close enough that you should be able to
> shoot him and you can't move a muscle.

Another thing I always keep with me are baby wipes. I know it sounds girly. But as much as you walk out there, if you start trying to wipe your butt after taking a dump with plain old toilet paper, you'll get dingleberries. And I'm telling you [chuckles] the worst thing you want to happen is get a nasty raw ass out there. Oh, it's the best feeling. Knowing you're going to go walk another 10 miles and you're clean. You don't have to worry about wearing your butt out. Because, I mean, 15-plus miles a day. You want to stay healthy.

There you go. Handy hygiene tips for the wild turkey devotee.

BUDZ: [laughing] Not on my vest but with me nowadays is one of those turkey lounger chairs. I have slept on rocks. I've eaten bark. Done all this stuff. Sat on the most comfortable tree—I thought—until an hour later when your bird is close enough that you should be able to shoot him

How many calls did you normally carry on the quest?

BUDZ: A gobble shake tube—we both missed that. My mainstays? I have two mouth calls: raspy and then a kee-kee purr single-reed in my mouth at all times and several more in my vest. Slate to start off with. And a box call when it's windy and I want to reach out there. And a gobble. That's it. Pretty simple stuff. They each have their specific time that you'd want to use them.

ELLIS: I stretch my own mouth calls. I make my own. I have different calls for different sounds— just like if I was competition calling. I usually run one call. It's usually a combo cutter, the one I was running earlier today. I can purr, cluck, kee-kee— anything I want. Then I run a slate call and a crystal call. I don't carry a box call just because I use that box call for all my strikers. I can get different sounds out of different strikers if I want a higher, more raspy call. With that crystal I can get really

loud and aggressive. I can reach out and cut through the wind and get that bird to gobble, get him to shock-gobble. Otherwise I'll mouth call. If I'm close enough, all I'm doing is real soft clucks and purrs [twittering sounds] and scratching the leaves. I do carry a crow call and a pileated woodpecker call.

BUDZ: A coyote call—a Drury Brothers coyote call. I've used that for shock-gobbling for years. That's my mainstay. I'll use that before I use a gobble. Only if he's far enough away; if he's close he's going to shut up and run!

ELLIS: You know, if you have a bird that's hung up and he's not gobbling anymore, you don't want to call because you don't want him to know you're there. You're afraid if you call and he gobbles you won't know if he's coming this time or not. The best thing—if you've been working him for a while, say, 30 minutes and he's not doing anything—well, if you resume your calling and he gobbles, he might come. But he might not. You might be in the same boat. Trying blowing your crow call or that pileated woodpecker [makes staccato uplifting put-put-put-put-*puuuut* sounds]. If he gobbles [vigorous gobbling sound] then you know he's like *right there*. So maybe you can wend your way around and get a little bit closer. And then change your calls and maybe sound like a different hen. Now he has a straighter shot. There's nothing between you and him. He'll come to you. So these are the kind of tactics you've got to work into your repertoire as you build your turkey-hunting arsenal.

How did you learn to call?

BUDZ: I hate to date myself but I bought a couple of cassettes and then after that I just got out in the woods and I would try to be around birds in the fall and winter, flocks of birds, just watching them. If you can see them interact with each other and then hear them, you go, *Wow, they really do make those sounds.* Then all the sounds and all the birds and a flock—they don't shut up. I mean they're always doing something. But I just tried to be around them as much as possible and not be

"In May 1999 I drove overnight to this public spot in Utah that someone had recommended," Jeff Budz recalled. He found lots of elk but no turkeys. Tired and disappointed, he took a nap in his pickup truck. "I woke and started driving off," he said. "As I crested the ridge I glanced back. There was a flock of birds where I had just been! I scrambled back just in time to get this Merriam's."

afraid. Right from the beginning I said: "I'm going to call. I'd rather call and mess up than sit by a tree and never make a noise—and never hear or see a bird." Again, there's enough information out there from people who know what this stuff sounds like. You can get these calls and mimic them and pretty quickly you can become proficient enough to be in the woods.

David, did you have a calling mentor?

ELLIS: I didn't have a mentor. Didn't have YouTube back then. It was trial and error. I started off running a friction call. Randy Rose taught me how to run a friction call. I'm left handed, too, so

it was the opposite of everybody else. As far as mouth calls goes it was just practice—figuring out how to open your jaw and huffing from your diaphragm. My mom can tell you stories for days about us going to the grocery store and her knowing right where I was at because she'd hear me in the egg aisle running a turkey mouth call.

"And now ladies and gentlemen, for your entertainment in the egg aisle"—I love it! What does it take to get good?
ELLIS: It's just practice, practice, practice. I don't put my calls away come the end of turkey season. I clean them up and leave them in the refrigerator and pull them out every once in a while and go to the bathroom so I can hear the sound bounce, you know, resonate in that room so I can hear myself. I work on it. I stretch new calls; try different side tensions, back tensions; different cuts; different latex thicknesses—all those things. It's an ongoing thing. It never stops.

In which circumstances do you stick with one call and when do you use multiple calls?
ELLIS: All right, so if I have a turkey that is hung up and I've been calling softly to him and nothing's happening, sometimes it takes the sound of two turkeys. Maybe if I pull out a slate call and I run a mouth call, maybe yelp on one [makes sound] and cut while I'm yelping, and kind of flip it back and forth, sometimes that'll bring him in. If I have a turkey that's really close, I'm not going to use a call that requires using my hands, of course, so I'm either purring or clucking softly on a mouth call. Soft yelps. I don't want to get too loud. I don't want to get too close. But you know sometimes it takes two calls to do the job. Sometimes it means calling going away from that turkey that's gobbling, sounding like two hens going the other way to get him to think he's got two chances. That might be what breaks the ice.

Anything to add?
BUDZ: D. J. nailed it. I try to start off simple. There's standards. I mean, you don't wake somebody up at 5 in the morning and go, "HEYYYY— GET UP!"

I don't know, Jeff, word is you can be quite the drill sergeant.
BUDZ: Besides that. [laughing] When you start out in the morning you start out nice and soft with the slate call and then you work your way up. My goal is to get him from a slate to a mouth call. And I go slate and get an answer. Slate—get an answer. Slate—get an answer. This is over time. Then I go to the mouth call. If I get an answer I give it to him again. And if I get another answer then I put the slate away. I don't touch it because I want to be hands free. Then I have two diaphragms I keep in my mouth. I just change up all the sounds if need be and there goes the chess match. I don't sit. Well, I say that, but in West Virginia there I was and the season closes in 10 minutes. It's just before 1 and I was like: *I can't believe it. I'm not going to get a bird.* Then I called and he answered. *You've got to be kidding me.* And I hit it again. And here he comes marching up the mountain. And I couldn't believe it. Shot him three minutes before the close. Rarely do I sit by a tree. I usually go to a ridge, you know, and do a really loud box to get way out there.

Of the 49 states that you covered how many birds did you take in the morning and how many later in the day?
ELLIS: I don't even know. Probably half. It depends what you're talking about; in some states you can only hunt until 12 noon. There were some states that I got in there early and killed 'em, but if I was in a new area it took a little leg work to find 'em. It wasn't until about 10 o'clock that I got my bird. During the U. S. Slam there weren't many

FACING PAGE: A New Jersey native eastern bird harvested in May 2015 on the Wharton State Forest Management Area. "He was another tough one that took me a couple days to finally figure out," Ellis said. The gobbler was sporting a double beard and now is a beautiful mounted masterpiece in his Florida Panhandle living room.

times when I had a bird first thing fly right down into my lap and pulled the trigger. I would much rather do a little bit more hunting anyway. So if I could stall it I would.

BUDZ: I would say that during the Super Slam I killed far more before noon than after. And I used to keep track of it. On all those birds I have recorded they ask for a time. So I could look it up. But I've always killed more birds before noon. If you broke it up into probably three times a morning—sunrise to 8, 8 to 10, 10 to noon—I bet I killed more birds in the 8-to-10 realm than at fly-down. I mean, fly-down is the classic. You hear

Under what conditions do you find turkeys most challenging?

BUDZ: Well, there's always a lull every spring when it's dry and high 80s and they hit a rut. They won't gobble. They might gobble once in the morning and once at night from the roost, literally, but they just won't do anything else.It usually takes a storm to change things up. Years ago I was hunting in the Talledega National Forest in Alabama. I hadn't heard a gobble in days. I woke up at 2 a.m. to a horrible thunderstorm. Most people wouldn't have been as excited as I was. "Please let it be clear in the morning," I mumbled as I fell

> I woke up at 2 a.m. to a horrible thunderstorm.
> Most people wouldn't have been as excited as I was.
> "Please let it be clear in the morning," I mumbled as I fell back
> asleep. It was clear and I scored a thumper that wouldn't shut up.

him in the tree. You talk to him. He gobbles. He flies down, struts and walks in. That's what everybody shoots for. But that's not realistic most times. That's not the norm, it just isn't. But having to work around a little bit, knowing the lay of the land, being attuned to the land and to him, and maybe moving a little bit, that's what to expect. I sit down for an hour or so at first light and then, okay, time to move.

ELLIS: Hey, if you can find a bird gobble around 10 o'clock I call it the death gobble because he's away from his hens. If he gobbles three times in the first two minutes he's by himself [makes series of gobbling sounds]. He's looking for that hen. If you can get in the right place and you can make those calls, he's done. Ten o'clock has always been my magic hour.

back asleep. It was clear and I scored a thumper that wouldn't shut up.

What's your approach in the rain and the wind—stay home?

ELLIS: Honestly, I despise it. If I'm out West and there's no going home to take care of things, I'll hunt, but it's terrible. The rain I can deal with because I can work into that, you know, as long as it's not windy. I don't like killing a turkey that's wet, as I said before. I'll kill one. There's options. Once the sun comes out you can hang him up and fluff him up and the wind will dry him out.

BUDZ: They dry out crazy quick in the sun.

ELLIS: But the wind makes conditions just miserable. You can go hunt a field if you can find a good field. But you can't hear them and I just don't like deer huntin' turkeys. You call to them and, heck,

FACING PAGE: This handsome Ohio tom taken in March 2013 was the third on Budz's best wild-turkey run ever: 10 toms from 10 different states in 13 days (10 actual days with a loaded gun and three days when he wait impatiently for two states to open). He is often racing to the next state with the latest bird still warm in his cooler.

they might hear you, but you can't hear them. If you're somewhere where you spent the money and you're going to be there, the best strategy is to hunt a good open area. Because typically turkeys don't like places where there's a lot of movement; they get real skittish. They'll be in open areas where they can see. That's your best bet. Otherwise use the day scouting. Move around. See what you can from the road. Maybe a farmer will help you. But I'll hunt in the rain. I got me a little umbrella made for a deer stand. If it rains hard I'll screw it into a tree. If it's a big storm usually you'll know before you go into the woods. You know that you're going to get into it. But if it's some little pop-up shower I stand under that umbrella and in maybe 20 minutes it's all gone. I fold it up and put it back in my vest. You didn't get wet. I do keep a little rain jacket but it doesn't breathe and I sweat too much.

BUDZ: I love when it's rainy and windy. You have to be a good still hunter. But neither keeps me out of the woods

What do you do with henned-up gobblers?

BUDZ: Get in front of them. Watch for a pattern. As I said earlier, you show a bird—a flock, a tom— that's done the same thing on two consecutive days, once he's in trouble, twice he's dead. Pay attention to that kind of stuff. That's part of your scouting. In most situations you're trying to talk to *her*. You're trying to piss *her* off. So if she comes to you, he's following. He's not leading the flock. He's a follower. So you either get in their way or you piss her off—kee-keeing or boss hen or different tactics. There's ways to do it. "Oh, he's with all these hens. Oh, he won't gobble. Oh, he won't leave the hens." That happens more often than not. So you better figure out something and make it work. If you say "I'm only going to hunt on days when they gobble or days when they're by themselves and they're going to come right in," forget about it.

What's the heaviest gobbler you ever killed?

BUDZ: Twenty five and a half pounds in Iowa.

Jeff in back of his friend Cameron Dean, with gun. Budz guided Cam to a single-season Grand Slam. No big deal? Cam is totally blind. "SO STOP WHINING!!!" Budz said.

Longest beard?

BUDZ: Ahhh. Probably 12 inches out of Texas.

Spurs?

BUDZ: Inch and three-quarters in Florida.

How about you, D. J.?

ELLIS: Heaviest—26 pounds in Georgia.

BUDZ: *Ohhhh.* Why didn't you ask him first? Because now he's going to one-up me on every one of these. [laughing]

ELLIS: No, no, no! Just the weight, just the weight. The beard was right at 12 inches—12 inches plus a couple of hairs. And then spurs, an inch and a half.

Who's the best turkey hunter you've ever known?

BUDZ: Being from Illinois and then going out West I had never been around a lot of turkey hunters. I knew the big names from their articles and books and TV shows. . . .

I don't necessarily mean famous. I mean personally— an exceptional hunter you've known personally.

BUDZ: I've got a couple of close buddies that are just predators. And that's what I think I am. I'm a *predator*. I make no pretense. I do not mince words about it. I am a predator [enunciates each

word slowly]. Gary Odenbaugh and Lee Britt and I—we won the World Turkey Hunting Championship in 2015 and came in fourth in 2016. They're both really, really good turkey hunters. I've got another buddy down here, Casey Ward—he's a *great* turkey hunter as well. But I don't care what animal it is. I mean, if you're a predator, you're a predator. You go and you figure it out. Show me a picture, tell me something, give me some intel. Sasquatch? Let's go. [laughing]

What characteristics do your friends share?
BUDZ: Physically, all three of them are in great shape. All three of them understand animals and understand *directions*. I don't care where you are.

all made sense. It's about sitting tight and being quiet and understanding. If that turkey responds, if he gobbles, he knows you're there. Just give him a little time. And so I've killed a heck of a lot more turkeys because of what Ron has taught me. And he's killed a pile of turkeys. He's a licensed guide. He's got his pilot's license and goes out West every year to hunt elk. He's distinguished among his peers. He is very humble. That's the one thing I most admire in Ron: this is a humble guy. He loves getting kids involved. He's been my mentor.

Jeff, you've been active in the wild turkey world a long, long time. How has the sport changed in 30 years?

> Over a period of time it all made sense. It's about sitting tight and being quiet and understanding. If that turkey responds if he gobbles, he knows you're there. Just give him a little time. And so I've killed a heck of a lot more turkeys because of what Ron has taught me.

Close your eyes. Spin around. Which way is north, south, east, west? I know people who couldn't find their way to save their life. It's a package. Being a predator is a package deal. You've got to be attuned to a lot of things at once and put it all together. Those three guys are as good as it gets.
ELLIS: Two people. One, of course, is my grandfather, who carried a lot of natural instinct, I guess, from our Indian culture and heritage. Our family has been doing it for so long and it's been passed down. And then the other guy I was telling you about is Ron Collins. He grew up in West Virginia and hunted those mountain turkeys. Before I met him I had never hunted a turkey in the mountains. He taught me a lot, took me under his wing. It's just about patience, you know. Before then I would get up and go hunt a turkey that I'd hear gobble somewhere else, after this one shut up. But then I'd hear the first turkey gobble back where I was last sitting. Over a period of time it

BUDZ: The biggest change has been in the technology: more sophisticated calls, decoys, clothing, gun chokes, shot, loads and on and on—everything we talked about earlier. Culturally, you know, I think the National Wild Turkey Federation has been a good reflection of trends over the years. It's a great organization. Last year I took my girlfriend Jenny to the national convention. Our first night we get back to the room and shes said, "I can't believe that there were whole families dressed in camo!" Years ago there was mostly a bunch of redneck guys. Now everywhere you look there are some really nice, well-kept women, *professional* women. So that's changed. Now it's about the family unit. And before it was just guys getting away. Heck, guys? We're a dying breed. Forget about us. It's not only about us anymore. It's about the family—wives, sons, daughters. I am *really happy* to see the kids excited about turkey hunting. And not just little boys; little girls, too. I think that's pretty cool. Otherwise we have a dying sport. But the big news if you're someone that's new to turkey hunting is now there's a hundred-fold—a thousandfold—more technology than what it used to be. Heck, there used to be a couple call companies: Primos, H. S. Strut and Quaker Boy. And now there's countless call makers. There's every gadget, every widget, every anything you could ever imagine is out on the market nowadays. And it's the same old turkey, you know, it's the same old turkey.

David, where do you see the sport of turkey hunting in America heading?
ELLIS: Well, since I'm the young lad here, the younger buck, Little Grasshopper, with my new

Agreed, but I would say the earth is overrun by too many people and strip malls rather than becoming "more civilized." Many years ago I had the opportunity to interview an extraordinary man named Ted Hughes. He was the Poet Laureate of England. He was an avid salmon fisherman and had done some some bird shooting. He told me he believed that fishing and hunting connect us with the real, living world in a way that nothing else can and that non-fishers and non-hunters can never understand. He said it's our meditation, a spiritual communion with ourselves deeper than our ordinary selves. We need and crave it to literally reconnect us—internally and externally—to who we really are.
ELLIS: We're in danger of losing the whole picture.

> It's about the family—wives, sons, daughters.
> I am *really happy* to see the kids excited about turkey hunting.
> And not just little boys; little girls, too. I think that's pretty cool.
> Otherwise we have a dying sport.

wife and my stepson, he's all into video games. I've tried numerous times to get him out to see and enjoy what God has placed on this earth and he has no desire whatsoever to do it. I think the more civilized we become, the closer we come to losing it. And we're seeing it now. There are a lot of people in this world that would love to see guns go bye-bye away. The threat to our second amendment all goes back to: we don't have enough people in this society that really want to go out and do the things that we value, that we share, that we *love* so much. I will stop whatever I'm doing if there is a kid that wants to go hunting; I'm gonna take him. Because they're the future of this sport and what I value so much for my kids and my kids' kids. We have a great system of public lands all across the country open to hunting. But when money becomes involved things can be taken away quickly.

I don't get it. My dad was a physician and we had Super Nintendo and Nintendo. But I would rather be out there on the lake fishing with my brother than inside. If there's daylight I can ride my four-wheeler, I can fish, I can do whatever I want. That's what I did. But I think we are losing that. For parents if you have kids and you can get them out there, then do it, because ultimately that is the future of something that we hold so dear. I would love it if everybody could experience that passion and desire that I have for the springtime woods.

Speaking of reconnecting with our primitive selves, how you like to eat your wild turkey?
ELLIS: I like to cut the breast meat into little chunks, marinade them in Creole butter for like six hours. I take a wok pan and put some peanut oil in it. Then I take the turkey out of that Creole butter, drop them in some wheat flour and drop

This gorgeous Gould's turkey came from the high mountains of central Mexico in April 2008. "The outfitter didn't have a blind," recalled Budz, "so I made my own out of sticks, leaves and grass. I can't describe my excitement when my Rage broadhead dropped him at 17 yards." Closing in on 100 Grand Slams, he experiments with various bows and guns.

them in the hot wok. They are perfect. Those nuggets are as good as Chick-fil-A. Even my wife likes them. [laughing]

BUDZ: There are so many people that hunt that just can't travel with the meat. I save every scrap. Last spring I made 83 pounds of jerky. This spring a little less. I'll give you some at the house tonight. It's 100 percent wild turkey. Turkey nuggets are

great, seasoned and cooked hot and fast in good clean oil. You can't beat it. I do this casserole with some cream of mushroom soup on top of the turkey and then I put pepper jack cheese in and I put Stove Top Stuffing dry on top of that. Foil over, put it in the oven cooked at 350° for an hour until it's bubbly and then it's lights out. It's a whole meal by itself.

Finally, gentlemen, now that you have each completed the U. S. Super Slam, what is your next challenge?

ELLIS: I might go to New Zealand and shoot some Merriam's. Eventually I'm going to Mexico to hunt the Gould's turkey. I have no desire to go kill an ocellated turkey in the Yucatán Peninsula—it just looks like a peacock to me. There's no passion for that. There nothing driving me to do it. But I'm going to go for round two on the Super Slam. A lot of the states I hunted I ended up killing two birds. I'm starting next year on the West Coast. I'm going to hit some of the harder states first: tag-draw hunts. I'm not going to go as fast, though. I want to take my time and enjoy it. I want to have an agenda, you know, planning where I'm going. It's something to look forward to each year—just like having a vacation with your family. So I'm going for 49 again and see what I can do. I just love it. I love doing it. But I'm not going to hunt the same exact areas I did the first time unless I have to. Like Nevada is a tough state to hunt whether it be Paradise Valley or wherever. You gotta know somebody to get your tags. Then I'm going to New Jersey and probably Delaware and work my way around, wherever I decide to go, wherever I can get tags and get after it.

BUDZ: I think since my standard has been to cut against the mold, now that I'm turning 50, I might have the time to have a kid and focus on family stuff. I've chased turkeys for so long and, as you know, I'm pushing to finish the 100 Grand Slams sometime in the next two years. I'll still get four Grand Slams every year. I think I've got 15 different weapons lined up. And I'll probably go back to some of the states I haven't hunted for years to share the woods with some good old friends.

FACING PAGE: The climax of David Ellis's U. S. Super Slam journey. This turkey made No. 49. His good friend Michael Yingling handcrafted this commemorative turkey call and gave it to David to celebrate his final state.

Tony Hudak

HOME:

Noxen, Pennsylvania

OCCUPATION:

Independent carpentry and masonry contractor

FIRST WILD TURKEY:

1986, Pennsylvania

COMPLETED U.S. SUPER SLAM:

2016, Hawaii

Benny—Tony Hudak's Labrador retriever—and Tony after a successful fall hunt in Susquehanna County, Pennsylvania, in October 2012. Ben located and split the big flock. Tony was able to call several birds back into range and harvest this jake.

OMEWHERE ON A LAVA MOUNTAIN overlooking the Pacific are what's left of Tony Hudak's scuffed and tattered dozen-year-old Danner snake boots, left as a nod to the gods, the foggy late-winter day in 2016 when he leaned against a Koa log and killed a wild Hawaiian turkey to complete his Super Slam.

When Tony was only six years old, he had his own .410 shotgun and a pocket full of shells, jumping out of his father's pickup with his young cousin Frank, the same age. Both were six years too young to even have a license. But that was the way of life in rural Pennsylvania back then. Everyone fished and hunted. There were 100,000 acres of public lands nearby to explore. Tony shot squirrels and rabbits, and, as he recalled with a laugh, shot *at* grouse and pheasants. He wasn't fast enough.

When young Tony wasn't hunting or scouting State Game Lands 57 with his dad and cousins or fishing Bowman Creek for native brook trout, he was playing baseball—pitching and sometimes playing third—and dreaming of making the Big Leagues. He followed the Yankees.

Dad got his deer every year. They hunted from home, driving an hour or more before daybreak on weekends during November and December, and returning home after dark. "We'd be right back at it the next day," Tony said. "Days long, nights short."

Today 51-year-old Hudak makes his living as an independent building contractor. He and his crew do mostly residential concrete flatwork. They build foundations, chimneys, decks, home add-ons. When he's not on a job site he is up late at night paying bills, writing contracts, figuring estimates. Spring is one of his busy times. Tax refunds turn into home-improvement projects. Spring is also turkey season. Tony doesn't tell his clients when he's going out of town dressed in camo. "They don't need to know," he said.

Tony carries on his late father's tradition of deer hunting in the fall. He hikes in miles over steep, rocky ridges to where scattered but enormous whitetails live. He doesn't get one every year. He likes the solitude. It's his special place.

Over the years Hudak has hunted goats and elk and big cats in the Rockies, and hunted deer in other states in the East. But nothing compares to the thrill of chasing wild turkeys.

"Having had the opportunity to do it all, there's nothing else," he said. "To some guys, shooting a rutting buck with a bow is the pinnacle. In my eyes, it's turkey hunting."

I drove north from Wilkes-Barre and turned off the state highway at a large roadside sign: NOXEN VOL. FIRE CO. RATTLESNAKE ROUNDUP, JUNE 16–19, RIDES FOOD FUN MUSIC.

Damn, I mused, *just missed it!*

Up the paved Pennsylvania country road I took another left and passed the Whistle Pig Pumpkin Patch: a worn red barn with a hand-lettered cardboard sign offering fresh spinach and lettuce. I passed white-painted porches festooned with American flags. Five or six circuitous miles later on a gravel mountain road I came to a lone house, bright and neatly trimmed with flowers. I pulled into the driveway.

"I guess this is one way to keep the relatives from stopping by unannounced," I said, shaking hands with Tony Hudak. He was holding Ben, his 11-year-old chocolate Labrador, by the collar. Ben was straining and whining to get a good whiff of me.

"He likes new people," Hudak said.

All your life, since you were a little boy, hunting has been a big part of your life. Aside from the obvious—the meat or the exercise or anything philosophical—what continues to draw you out there?

TONY HUDAK: The mountains. Hunting brings me into the mountains. I wouldn't be here otherwise. I guess it's the challenge of hunting these mountains, whether for turkey or for deer. With turkeys I think it's the one-on-one challenge that pulls me—you know, it's me against him. Whereas, you know, with pheasants it's you and the dog and the birds and maybe four or five guys lined up, which is great and I love it. But when I'm hunting for turkeys in the spring—or in the fall even but especially in the spring—I'm doing it alone.

What do you most love about turkey hunting?

HUDAK: I don't know—a lot of people have asked me that. And I don't know if I can really pin it down to just one thing. I guess first and foremost it's the scouting. The time I put into scouting, spring and fall, is my true turkey season, more so than the actual time I get to hunt and pull the trigger. That's just anticlimactic. My season leads up to that day. After putting in six weeks of effort, a lot of times I'm done the first week or even the first day of the season. So the one-on-one challenge, definitely, and the time that I spend scouting the birds and figuring out where I need to be. This can be somewhat repetitious in locations, year after year. But you still need to get out there and pin them down. When I was guiding I would have 120, 130 gobbling turkeys located before the season.

When did you guide?

HUDAK: From 1999 to 2008.

And you continued doing your construction work here in Pennsylvania?

HUDAK: Oh, yeah. I guided for a lodge in Pennsylvania about an hour north of here, and I also held a guide's license in New York where I freelanced. We're so close to the border. But I've done more turkey hunting on my own there.

What did you learn from your guiding experience?

HUDAK: I learned that people can be very demanding. Because they're paying for a service they expect instant results. I guess that expectation can be linked to a lot of things in the world but you know it comes right down to hunting. It's something that's supposed to be fun. I realize the guy's

days and by God you'd better make it happen.

Did it sour you on the sport?

HUDAK: It didn't sour me on the sport—it soured me on people because it made me really see what was out there. Nothing ever happened where I got soured toward the sport but there were times just like now in my business when you might pick up a customer who's not the most pleasant customer in the world, for one reason or another. Turkey clients were the same way, just on a smaller scale.

Did the revelation about the demanding side of human nature and today's desire for instant

> I guess first and foremost it's the scouting. The time I put into scouting, spring and fall, is my true turkey season, more so than the actual time I get to hunt and pull the trigger. That's just anticlimactic. My season leads up to that day.

paying money. I've spent a lot of money myself to hunt turkeys. But in my case it's been different because I didn't have somebody to lead me around the woods, right?

Did that surprise you, that attitude of expectation?

HUDAK: Yes, it did kind of hit me at the beginning of my guiding career. I never thought anything of it because I was so used to hunting with other people—friends or family. You know, you just went out and you did it. And if you killed one that day, great. If you didn't, we'll get them tomorrow. Whereas, these people were like [slaps hands together] "We want it now." And it's like, *Well that's not how it goes!* You know, we've got three days and there's a darn good chance we're going to get close to making it happen. But you've got to have patience. And some people just don't have patience. I saw that a lot. They were just there paying X-amount of dollars coming there for three

gratification make you a more reflective hunter or a better hunter—or was it something you just wanted to get the hell away from?**

HUDAK: I don't know if those encounters made me any better, because I think the way I looked at it was that I understood the sport. They didn't. So, regardless of how this works out, for three days or four days or longer, I'm going to give you 110 percent. I don't think it made me a better hunter; it just made me understand people better. Over the course of time you learned how to deal with it. It was just like any problem in any business: something comes up. We've been down this road before we got it right.

You must have guided a few decent guys!

HUDAK: Absolutely. The majority were. But there's a sour grape in every bunch—there always is. I made a lot of friends—some really good friends, I feel. The thrill was when you put them in the driver's seat to tag their first bird and you know you were the driving force to get out there. Because they're relying on you. Ninety-nine percent of those guys that came for the first time didn't have a clue what they were doing. So they relied on you for the setup. They relied on you to move their gun barrel. They relied on you to tell them when to the pull the trigger. So when you have to pull all that together and it works: success. It was very gratifying for me when that happened, especially with young kids. I don't know how many I took into the woods over the years—not everyone got a bird but a lot of them did. I called up their first bird and helped them get their first bird. Maybe it was even more gratifying for them because I got them started on the right foot.

When you were young there weren't many wild turkeys in Pennsylvania. Do you remember seeing your first?

HUDAK: Nineteen seventy-one. I was six years old. Not far from here there used to be a truck dealership out on one of the highways and my father was a customer. He was in the process of buying a new truck for his business and we were out there one night and he went to test drive a truck and I went with him. And we're driving up the highway and there's this turkey standing in this guy's field along the road. I'd never seen one before. My father said, "Look at the turkey!" It was a big hen, just standing there. I'll never forget it. In fact, not too long ago I drove by there coming home from somewhere and there's a house built there now in that field and all the trees are grown up. You can't see a turkey there today if your life depended on it. But at that time that turkey stood out just like, you know, a statue.

And after seeing your first wild turkey did you start looking for them?

HUDAK: Maybe I did. I don't know. My father never shot a turkey because there just weren't that many around and, again, as good a woodsman that he was he still didn't know what to do to get one—nobody did. Very few guys around here did.

Tony Hudak looking out over the hills of northeast Kentucky after tagging a three-year-old longbeard in April 2015: state No. 46. *The finish is near!* he thought.

I had an uncle who was a pretty good hunter. For the most part those guys back in the '70s, they didn't know how to hunt turkeys.

When did you start hearing about turkeys being more abundant—when hunters began talking about them?

HUDAK: In the early '80s, somewhere in there. I got my first license in 1977 when I was 12. That was the law here in Pennsylvania. And my father and I would go a few times—the whole gang would go, everybody went— but there just wasn't the birds. We covered these ridges. We were all over the place. But we never found one. Nobody ever got one. It was mainly a scouting mission for the upcoming buck season, but everybody was toting a shotgun and a box call in case we got into some turkeys.

A Silver State Rio Grande gobbler taken near Yerington, Nevada in March 2012 for Tony Hudak's state No. 33.

So this was in the fall.

HUDAK: Yes. Pennsylvania didn't have a spring season until 1968 and the spring season was not that popular yet, so it was mainly a fall hunt for most.

When did you kill your first turkey?

HUDAK: That's a good question—I knew you were going to ask me that. It was sometime in the 1980s. Yes, because I went in the Marine Corps after high school and I came home and hunted for a week or two and I got a hen turkey in the fall up in Lackawanna County. There was a guy that had some property up there. I met him at a sports show. He was in the logging business and he invited me up to hunt with him and I went up several times with him before I finally got one. I came home the one time—it was in November. I may have come home for buck season. It was the last couple days of turkey season and I got in touch with him and went up on a Saturday and, by God, I finally got one!

What did you think of it?

HUDAK: I was hooked. I was ecstatic. And then I got another one the next year. But till then I still hadn't killed one in the spring. When I killed my first one in the spring which was—I don't remember exactly—that's what did it.

What was different?

HUDAK: A lot of things. There was the gobbling. The whole thing, you know. Plus I killed him on my own. It was a jake. It's just—*here we go!* It was the second to the last day of the spring season and there were three of them. I called them in. They came in strutting, gobbling, just like they're supposed to. I picked one out and *BOOM!* the sickness started right then and there. I was hooked.

You said your uncle knew something about turkey hunting. Did you ever talk with him about it?

HUDAK: Oh, no. He took it all to the grave. He was really secretive. He wouldn't even take my father and he was married to my aunt—my dad's sister! Yeah. Lived right over the hill here. And they were close in everyday life. But, no, I had no turkey mentor. I figured it all out on my own, hunting with a few friends from school, you know, and none of us really knew what we were doing. We were just trying to figure it out and learn it ourselves and that's what we did. A couple of us all killed our first birds like that. On your own that's how you learn—you learn by doing.

You remember any particular mistakes you made?

HUDAK: Not being patient enough. I know that. The biggest problem I think we all used to make as a group was that we didn't set up on a turkey where the turkey wanted to go. I've learned that over the years that you've got to make it easy for that turkey to come to you. Not make it easy for *you*—you have to make it easy for *him*. I don't care where you're at, whether you're in Texas or Oklahoma or Pennsylvania. You got to make it easy for him. That's why I think that my success rate went as well as it did over the years. Because you learn. You go into an area and you figure out the terrain and you get a bird to gobble. Now it just comes natural. He's going to come right there and I'm going to kill him right there. And nine times out of 10 that's what happens.

But the average beginner doesn't know that.

HUDAK: I didn't know. None of us knew. We were kids. I think our biggest mistake was, you know, we'd get a turkey to gobble—somebody was good enough to call and make one gobble or one would be gobbling on the limb in the morning and you'd go in there and, *Wow—this looks like a good spot.* And it's dawn. Everybody finds a tree or if you're out by yourself you find a tree. It didn't work and that was the reason: I wasn't where he wanted to go.

Once you gained experience with turkeys here in Pennsylvania and felt confident about what you were doing, when did you start thinking about hunting other states?

HUDAK: The Catskills. We hunted state land and it was just crazy. It was so much fun and you learned from your experiences up there because, especially in the spring, you'd call one up and maybe you moved or you missed or whatever happened and you didn't kill the bird. Who cares? There's going to be another one 500 yards down the ridge. You just go down, crank up another one and start all over again. That's how it was in the fall, too. There were turkeys everywhere. Flocks everywhere. So you learned because you had a lot of opportunity to make mistakes and learn. Plus you had Sunday hunting. New York State then had liberal bag limits. It was a no brainer. We spent a lot of time there. You could camp on state land. It

> Who cares? There's going to be another one 500 yards down the ridge. You just go down crank up another one and start all over again. That's how it was in the fall, too. There were turkeys everywhere. Flocks everywhere.

HUDAK: Well, New York was the first state. I first went with the same group of friends from school. We all just decided to do that one year. I'd say at that point I had killed a dozen turkeys or so in Pennsylvania, somewhere there, and it was in the late '80s after I was out of the Marine Corps so it would have been '87, '88. A couple of those guys petered out. They didn't want to be traveling, you know; they found other things to do and so forth. I mean you're out of school and you're starting out in life, but anyway I stuck with it and a couple of other guys did too. So New York was really my learning curve. There were so many turkeys up there then through the late '80s and into the '90s.

Where were you?

was just fun. At that time turkey hunting nationwide wasn't as popular as it is today. So you didn't have hunter pressure. We would go up there for a week in the spring and not see anybody else on state land. If a turkey gobbled he was yours if you wanted to go for it. That was when I really got my feet wet.

When did you head outside the Northeast?
HUDAK: Well, the first trip we took out of state besides New York was South Dakota. Janine and I went to South Dakota in 1995 right before we got married.

Did you drive?
HUDAK: We flew to Rapid City and we stayed in one of those silver trailers called an Airstream in

FACING PAGE: A nice Montana Merriam's wild turkey—April 2002: state No. 9. Tony hunted both Montana and Wyoming on this trip with nine friends. The party killed 18 birds. The subspecies is found in America's Ponderosa-pine and high-prairie West, and was named in 1900 in honor of Clinton Hart Merriam, first chief of the U. S. Biological Survey.

some guy's backyard. It was cold and there was no shower. Yeah! That was the first time the spark was lit in me to kill a Grand Slam; that was when I wanted to do it. The Wild Turkey Grand Slam was starting to become popular. It was in all the magazines and *blah, blah, blah* it caught my eye and, of course, I was really hooked at this point. We went out there for like four or five days total. I didn't get a turkey. The weather was terrible. It was snowing and it was just nasty. It was cold but we made the best of it. We came home and then we got married a few months later that August.

And you hadn't scared her away. . . .

kept rolling like that every year with different guys: "Hey, I want to go get my Merriam's in Wyoming" or wherever and off I'd go with them. That kept happening. So by 2007 I had about 20 states under my belt without really thinking about it, you know. And in 2008 I shot a bird in a couple more states, Utah and New Hampshire that year, and by 2009 I had 23 states. I had planned to go to Louisiana in April and then I was going to go and hunt New Mexico and Colorado. At that time I said to Janine and to some of my friends, I said, "You know, if I could kill a turkey in 25 states I'd have half the states—wouldn't that be cool?" Yeah, yeah, that would be cool. So I went down to

> At that time I said to Janine and to some of my friends,
> I said, "You know, if I could kill a turkey in 25 states
> I'd have half the states—wouldn't that be cool?"
> Yeah, yeah, that would be cool.

[Janine, listening in to keep Tony honest, laughs.]

When did you get the idea of tagging a bird in all 49 states—the Super Slam?

HUDAK: I really didn't wake up one day and decide "I want to do it." I think what it was, I ended up finishing my Grand Slam in '99. I went to Chihuahua, Mexico in 2000 for the Gould's turkey to get a Royal Slam and I did that. Well, to kill a Royal Slam at that time that was the pinnacle of it all and I did it. As time went on a friend of mine that I worked with—he liked to turkey hunt but he wasn't addicted but he liked to go—he said something about going down to Georgia to hunt turkeys or South Carolina: "Let's go down there someplace." So we went. The following spring we went to Georgia and I killed a turkey. He ended up not getting one. And then Janine and I went to Virginia a few weeks after that because I always wanted to hunt in Virginia. And we went down there and I shot a nice bird. Well, it kind of started,

Louisiana and I killed a turkey; he was 24. A few weeks later I was scheduled to go to New Mexico. I told Janine, "You know what, if I go out there and if I get one in either state, I'll have 25 states. I'll be done. That will be nice." I killed two turkeys in New Mexico the first morning—which was legal. So I had my 25th. But I still had a Colorado tag in my pocket and I had two or three days to kill. I thought, *Oh, what the hell, I'm going to go up there and see what's going on.* So I drove north into the middle of a big snowstorm and one thing led to another but anyway I ended up in Colorado in the afternoon and then the next morning after the snow stopped I called up and shot this turkey. So I had 26 states. I came home and I told Janine, I said, "Well I did it and I exceeded it by one state." And she said: "What's stopping you now? You might as well just go all the way."

So you're responsible for this nonsense. . . .

JANINE: In a round-about way! [laughing]

A beautiful native Oklahoma Rio Grande wild turkey tagged in April 2003. "He shock-gobbled at an airplane passing directly overhead," Tony said. "Big mistake!" The long-legged subspecies evolved in mesquite, oak forest and prairie habitat.

HUDAK: That was our conversation. I remember that I didn't really jump right on it. I thought, *I don't know—I don't know.* Then it just kind of kept happening. I'd go here for a hunt or go there for a hunt and before I knew it I was over 30 and then I said, "You know what? You just have to keep going. You've got to finish this. You can't stop at 32."

How many years did it take to get to 49?
HUDAK: From the time I really started focusing on that as a goal?

Yes, from the time—Janine made you do it.
HUDAK: Seven years [laughing]

It's interesting that almost all the hunters who have reached the Super Slam are in there somewhere: seven or eight years. What was your last state?
HUDAK: Hawaii. That was this year in March.

Over those seven years was there any particular order to the states you hunted?
HUDAK: I would always try to combine at least two states on a trip. Yeah, but it didn't always pan

OVERLEAF: Hudak had this hefty three-year-old longbeard scouted and patterned during the 2013 pre-season. He slipped in close on the season's second day in April and dropped the hammer on the gobbler right after fly-down. Scouting is his real season. Tony scouts audibly in the spring, listening for gobbling, and looking for food in the fall—acorns, beechnuts, grapes.

A very vocal gobbler from the Catskill Mountains in New York—May 2005. "This bird had the longest gobble of any bird I've ever heard, so I named him "Ole Long Gobble" in pre-season, Tony said. "I tagged him later that season."

out. But there were oh, I don't know, six or seven times that it went right and I hunted two or three states on the same trip. You fly to someplace and then rent a car and go. No particular order, although I did take the advice of biologists if I wasn't sure where I was going. I would contact a biologist in that area and ask how's the hatch been the last couple years, how are the turkeys doing. Were several times when they would say, you know, if I were you I would wait another year— or "I wouldn't come for another two or three years because we just don't have the birds right now. Not to say you couldn't come here and kill one but you're coming clear from Pennsylvania, I don't know." That advice did come into play a few times.

Of your 49 states, how many birds did you take

during the spring and how many in the fall?
HUDAK: Forty-one in the spring and eight in the fall.

You enjoy fall turkey hunting.
HUDAK: I love it.

Tell me about the experience and why you like it.
HUDAK: It's an even bigger challenge than the spring hunt. In springtime the tom is basically giving himself up by gobbling—whether it's daylight or any time of the day he's telling you where he is. Whereas in the fall it's pretty much a boot-leather type of season. You gotta do your scouting. Here I scout about a month before the season starts. So I do have birds located. I know what ridge they're working. It's all based on food sources. In the fall their living pattern is survival

mode. They're not looking to breed. They're not looking to do anything else but to survive and survival means food. So in the fall, September and early October, I'm scouting for turkey food. I'm finding food sources. Whether it's acorns dropping, beechnuts, wild cherry, grapes, whatever that particular area harbors, that's what I'm looking for. That's where they're going to be. They're going to go to the food sources. And then, you know, in certain years when I would hunt longbeards only it's even that much more difficult. You're looking for food sources but then you've got to visually look for the birds or the signs of those longbeards—and they do lay down a different type of sign than a flock of young birds. You have to know how to read it. And if you find their sign they will generally stay on the same ridge. Longbeards in the fall are very habitual. They'll roost in the same area. Their travel patterns are the same. And if you can figure this out your chances of success are good but to call one in can be very difficult. I've done it in the fall a lot in New York because, as I said before, there were just so many you could experiment and learn and try different things. I remember the one year we split up nine longbeards in New York on a Saturday morning. The rule of thumb in the fall is when you split up a flock of birds, you sit down and you call one of those turkeys back to that location. Well, mature birds in the fall are not as gregarious as young birds are—they are in no hurry to get back together. We sat there to learn. We sat there all day Saturday and I sat there all day Sunday and not one of those nine birds ever made a peep in a day and a half. We didn't kill one. Never heard a peep. We called to them: gobbler yelp, gobbler cluck every so often. Not a peep. So it just goes to show you how challenging it can be. When you hunt the fall flocks of hens and poults, those young birds don't want to be separated from their mother hen. They will come back a lot quicker and they're normally very, very vocal which makes it exciting. Sometimes you have three, four, five different birds coming in from different directions at the same time—makes it fun, especially if you have a

Benny the Lab taking a well-deserved nap after splitting a group of longbeards in the West Virginia mountains in October 2014. Ben did his job, but Tony couldn't seal the deal when one of the gobblers came to the call.

client or friend with you to help in the hunting part of it. So I like it because it's way more challenging than the spring hunting is. It's a whole different sport and I think you have to exhibit better woodsmanship skills than you do in the spring. You know, you see these guys carrying bags of decoys, pop-up blinds, stools, coolers and everything out into a pasture in the spring. They plant everything there and sit there all day waiting for a turkey to come by. Now, you can do that in the fall if you know he's feeding there or he and his buddies are feeding there. But I don't hunt that way. I'm on the ground going from the time I leave the truck in the morning till the time I get back at night or if I kill a bird, whatever comes first. But I do not just wander. I know where I need to be based on my scouting. It's the same strategy. I still do the same scouting. My preseason scouting is my season. When I'm actually carrying a gun I'm there to finish the deal.

And in the fall you use a dog.
HUDAK: Yes, Benny [Tony's Labrador] is trained to follow the sound of the flocks, locate them and split them in a bunch of different directions—which he learned to do on his own—and then we move in there and sit down in that scatter location

and call a turkey or two back, depending on how many people are hunting. So it's still the same strategy, it's just that I let the dog do the work as far as getting close to the birds, run after them and split them up. I trained him to do that. He wears a tracking collar. The first couple years I took him he didn't have a collar at the time and I knew he was right on those birds but I didn't know where he was at the scatter site. So we had a difficult time. He would always come back to me, but I didn't know where to set up. So I guess I told Janine we needed to invest in a collar for him so I know where. Then, once he started chasing turkeys, then it was easy because I could watch him on the screen of the receiver and I knew where he was and how far away. His arrow would go in loops on

When you were chasing the Super Slam?

HUDAK: Yes, he split up a group of longbeards one day. I did call one up but I just couldn't get a shot and I had to let him walk. So it was a little bit disappointing because this was a state I still needed at the time before I'd finished the Slam and he had done everything that I needed him to do and I just couldn't seal the deal. I really wanted to have one of my states accomplished with his help. We tried. We were down there several times for a few days. We stayed in a motel and he had his own bed and it was great. But I'd choose the fall season. If I had to make a choice—if the Pennsylvania Game Commission said: "Look, you know, when you buy a license you have to distinguish whether you're going to hunt for fall turkeys or

> So it's still the same strategy,
> it's just that I let the dog do the work as far as getting close
> to the birds, run after them and split them up.
> I trained him to do that. He wears a tracking collar.

the screen. That's when I knew it was split because he would just run in circles and just kept getting them all out of there and it would tell me how far he was—you know, a couple hundred yards or whatever. Once I got that all figured out with him and knew what those loops were on the screen, then I knew where approximately to go look. You would always find a location where the birds had been feeding: scratches on the ground. If there was snow it was easy to find. Then we would set up and start calling them back.

Where is fall turkey hunting with a dog legal?

HUDAK: It's legal here in Pennsylvania, New York, Vermont and through the Virginia states. Benny was in West Virginia with me to try to kill a turkey down there.

spring turkeys. You got to make up your mind when you buy your license." I'd go with fall turkeys. All the way.

While you were pursuing the Super Slam did any feelings of competitiveness surface? Were you thinking about other hunters who were trying to accomplish the same goal or was it strictly personal?

HUDAK: I wasn't looking at it as a competition, from my point of view, however, there was a guy who kept kind of making it be competitive by sending me pictures and notes and emails about running here and running there, killing in all these states. I didn't look at it that way. I had never even met this guy or shook his hand, so how could you be competitive with somebody you really don't know? I wanted to do it at that point. I was dedicated to

FACING PAGE: Merriam's gobbler taken in October 2013 on the San Carlos Reservation in Arizona: state No. 40.

it and I knew it was going to get done one day. But at that time I didn't know of any other people who were at it or how close people were. How would you know unless you knew them? He was the only guy that I heard from. He got my number through a friend of a friend in Vermont. So I think there was some competition on his part but, no, not on my part. I mean, what's the difference if you're number five or number 50? You still did it. Who cares what number you are, really?

Were you ever discouraged to the point where you thought, *Oh, it's not worth it?*
HUDAK: Not to the point where I was ready to quit. You know, I'd go for stretches—how many times did I hunt Rhode Island, four times? Janine

think anything major.

Once you started fanning out and really going for the different states, when you got to a state that was unfamiliar, how did you find the birds?
HUDAK: It would depend on where I was. I did quite a few of my birds on public land. In those states my hunts were based on recommendations of biologists. That didn't always work out. One biologist in Vermont sent me to a piece of public land—said it was the best in the state. Janine and I went up there. I hunted hard for four days in prime time for turkeys and never heard a bird gobble. Didn't see a track in the mud. Nothing. I went on his recommendation. We had the maps and everything. We went up there blind. That was

> A lot of places that are key are these big-game outfitters that have a 20,000-acre lease in New Mexico or Wyoming or wherever where they hunt elk or deer or antelope. They don't hunt turkeys.

was up there with me once or twice. Where else? West Virginia. I mean, there were many states where I hunted several times where it just doesn't happen the first time you go. So, you know, I don't think I got *discouraged* but I think I got *frustrated* that I'm going wherever I go and put in 110 percent every day and it's not happening. Why isn't it happening? I think that was what got me more than discouraged. Just like mad at my own self that I wasn't getting it done.

Did the whole quest thing put any strain on your marriage or your business relationships?
HUDAK: [laughing] Not on my business because I would never tell anybody where I was going. It was none of their business. I think it was a little tough on Janine at times when I was gone. For her to handle her part of life: the house and the dogs and everything she has to do every day but I don't

early—14, 15 years ago—but I learned from that experience that these guys don't always know what they're telling you is true. You can look at harvest reports from that particular state, county reports, which I did on the computer. Then it was just a matter of boot leather. If you feel you're in the right place. Now, in the spring, back to the point of where these turkeys are they're going to give themselves up, it's a lot easier. You can walk out on a nice ridge in the morning and say, "God, there's got to be a turkey gobbling some place because it's just too nice for one not to be here." And if you hear one you're in the game. Now there were states—Connecticut's one. I went up there twice before hunting just to scout. Spent two weekends up there scouting. Found sign. Heard some birds gobble. Went back in the middle of the season and killed one right off the roost the first morning. But I base that success on two trips pre-season to get

A long-spurred old warrior taken at Willow Point, Louisiana, in the wildlife-rich Mississippi Delta in April 2009: state No. 24. "I hunted him for four days," Hudak said, "and finally tagged him on the last morning with two hours left to hunt." His spurs were long enough to hang him from the sign—a true "limbhanger."

it done. And I was on public land. Otherwise, how else would you know where to go?

How about in the West with such vast wildlands?
HUDAK: A lot of places that are key are these big-game outfitters that have a 20,000-acre lease in New Mexico or Wyoming or wherever they hunt elk or deer or antelope. They don't hunt turkeys. I hunted with a guy in Utah who was a lion hunter. He didn't know the first thing about turkeys. But he knew where they lived. When it came time to hunt he kicked me out of the truck in the morning and said, "See you later." I'm on this huge piece of B.L.M. land and I have to figure it out. So it just comes down I think to instinct. Maybe a little bit of help from local sources and

state or county officials, you know, and that's what they're supposed to do is to give you some insight when you go to their area. But they can't pull the trigger for you. It still comes down to having woodsmanship skills, figuring it out, doing some scouting while you're hunting and applying your best abilities.

What was the most difficult state for you?
HUDAK: West Virginia.

Why was that?
HUDAK: Well, I hunted strictly public land over the course of three years. Benny and I hunted in the fall a couple times and then I was running down there in the spring by myself, sleeping in the

A big corn-fed Illinois gobbler—April 2010 and state No. 28. Hudak hunted the famous Pike County area out of Brock Campbell's camp. During afternoons Tony enjoyed some fine hunting for morel mushrooms—delicious with wild game.

truck on the interstate near my exit and going from there. I would leave here at 9 o'clock at night and drive all the way get down there at 3 in the morning. I did that every weekend. Why? I don't know. Again, it was based on a biologist's recommendation. My friend from Tennessee who had hunted there told me it was a good area of the state. The area just said TURKEY all over. If you look at the terrain, if you look at the ridges, the hollows, the little hogbacks, it just screamed turkey. Were there birds there? Yes. Were there birds in great numbers? No. Should I have moved to a different location over the period of three years. Probably. But I didn't because I was too bullheaded. I kept thinking *it's got to happen.*

You were invested.

HUDAK: Yes, yes! I spoke to a couple local guys in the parking lot on the state land and you know I asked one guy one time I said, "Are there *any* turkeys here?" I said I was serious. I said, "Are there *really* any turkeys here?" And he said, "Well, I bow hunt here for deer in the fall and I see them and I hear them." He was a nice enough guy and he didn't hide nothing. He said, Yeah, there's turkeys here." So it was very tough. I put on a lot of miles. It was 242 miles from here to where I parked the truck, and I'd drive down every week and I'd drive back.

You did eventually get one in West Virginia.
HUDAK: Yeah: 2015, second to the last day of the season.

What was the trick—was it in a place where you had hunted before?

HUDAK: I had been through there. It was on a Friday. The season ended on a Saturday. I went down the night before, Thursday night. Same ritual: Slept at the welcome center for a few hours, then drove in and hunted this one side where I had heard birds earlier in the season. Nothing. It's big country. And I made my way across the county road. I made my usual loop through there. I had been through there just the Saturday before. Friday he gobbled—there were two of them, actually. Both gobbled and it was over in about three minutes. After all those years. All that driving and all the time down there. Miles walking. It came down to—I'm not kidding you—three minutes from the time I called a couple times and grabbed him by the leg. Three minutes. So, you know, West Virginia was state number 48 and it was far more gratifying to tag that turkey than it was to tag the last one in Hawaii.

What was the most challenging bird you never did kill?

HUDAK: A bird in Rhode Island. He was a state-land bird but he would roost on a piece of private property right off the state line up behind this guy's house. There were three of them, three gobblers, and I hunted them a lot and had them as close as 50, 60 yards one time but couldn't see him, so no kill. Had him right to the last day of the season; had him 60 yards but he wouldn't close the deal. Had to walk away. See you next year. So that group of turkeys, they were the toughest. They were the toughest I never killed out of state over a period of three seasons.

Did you ever purposefully pass up a bird that you could easily have killed?

HUDAK: Oh, yeah, many times, many. But, I mean, when I was going for 49, if it was a decent bird with a decent beard or whatever—pow! However, I let one walk in Utah where the guy dropped me off on the B.L.M. land. I got this turkey to gobble and he was down in this little

A nice California longbeard taken on a fall hunt near Paso Robles in November 2009. This bird was state No. 27. Two others just like him gobbled on the roost and strutted to the call just like springtime. Tony actually prefers fall hunting.

canyon and he only gobbled a couple times but I knew it was coming slowly because every time he got a little closer, a little closer. Well, anyway, I'm laying there on my belly on this little knob. Under a cedar tree watching down this bank where I know he's going to come up. And in the distance was a view of the Rocky Mountains. This was in late April, almost the first of May, and it was still snowcapped—beautiful. I don't know how far away the mountains were. Maybe it was 20 miles but they looked like they were right there and I'm laying there on my belly looking at this picture. My God, what a sight. And he comes up over this roll in full stride. He comes walking right to me: a Merriam's turkey with the white-tipped tail feathers, and it was a beautiful sunny day and he's coming right at me and I got this mountain behind him. He walked right up to me. I could've shot him easy and I couldn't. I let him go. I just thought: *this is too beautiful of a sight for me to ruin it*. I let him walk. He came up and stood there strutting, doing his thing, gobble-gobble, looking for me. I never took the safety off. He walked right past me about 15 feet around that cedar tree. I let him go.

What's the the weirdest or strangest place you

ever killed a wild turkey?

HUDAK: Michigan. It was fall and I was in the Upper Peninsula of Michigan. It was late October of 2011 and I got a fellow's name through a friend of a friend. He had property there that he leased for deer hunting and I called him up. That's how I found a lot of places. So I called and asked if he knew of any properties with turkeys. "Oh, yeah, sure," he said to me. "When do you want to come?" And I said at the end of October. "Yes we can work that out." Anyway, I go up there and he takes me the first morning to this horse farm. Pull up in this guy's driveway. Guy's house is there. "Listen," he said, "it's fine to hunt here—don't

third morning I got up and it was 20° outside and he drops me off. I know where I gotta go now but I know the turkeys are there, so I made my way to get into that hay ring, pulled some hay over myself, and laid there on my belly and stuck my gun barrel out where I know the turkeys are going to pitch down. I was warm as toast. I was there about 15 minutes. And here comes the horses—six of them.

Oh, no!

HUDAK: They came right to the hay ring. They're eating the hay. Some of them are nibbling on my boots. They're biting me on my arm. [laughing] This is the truth. And I'm trying to get them out

> Failure—we all face it. Turkey hunters have to expect to fail. You're not always going to succeed and you have to expect it to take a lot of your time and energy. Focus—you've got to be focused on what you're going to do.

worry about nothing" He said this is a horse farm. There's pastures, there's some stables. "You'll see everything. Just don't cross this fence, don't cross that fence to stay on the property. The turkeys are going to be roosted to the west here. That's where they always are—I seen them here a few days ago." Well, I go out there. I don't know where I'm going. It's dark. You don't know what to expect. I'm standing there by this gate kind of concealed. There are some weeds and things there. I don't know where to go up because I don't know what's going on. I gotta let it get light. Well of course they don't gobble but they start pitching down into this pasture. I couldn't get 'em. They went and did their thing. I chased them. The second morning I moved in there a little closer. Still didn't get them. That night and I saw where they roosted. They came back to the same trees. So while I was standing there looking at the trees, I said, "Tomorrow morning. I'm going to be in that hay ring." The farmer had a hay ring there for the horses. So the

of there. It's starting to get light and I don't want to make a commotion, right? I don't know what to do. So I pulled my phone out of my pocket and I sent a text to Dean, the guy that dropped me off. I said is there any way you can come back here and get these horses out of here? I told him where I was and I said I'm in the hay ring. He writes back: OK. So I'm thinking, you know: *The rancher is out of this pasture every day filling these hay rings. These turkeys are used to seeing somebody.* It took him a while to come back but pretty soon I see him coming across the pasture and he walks right by me and came in and pushed the horses away and got them down into another pasture somewhere. He told me later he got them down to another place, closed the gate and he just kept walking.

Perfect!

HUDAK: He didn't stop to talk—nothing—just made a big loop. I heard his truck start up way off by the barn and he left again. It got light. Actually,

Delaware bird No. 30—April 2011. Nonresident hunters must take a one-day turkey hunter safety course in person.

one turkey gobbled from the tree even though it was fall. They pitched down and there I am in the hay ring. But one, he went around me before I could get on him. I just came up out of the hay like Carlos Hathcock [legendary U. S. Marine sniper during the Vietnam War] and I powdered him. To me that was the strangest place because of what it took to get the turkey.

What a story.
HUDAK: The horses made it interesting.

What would you say are the most important considerations that a hunter needs to think about when he or she is seeking to get a bird in all 49—things that perhaps people don't think about up front that, with your experience, you now know they should think about.

HUDAK: That's a good question. I think first of all I think they have to consider the fact of disappointment or . . . what's a better word?

Failure.
HUDAK: Thank you. Failure—we all face it. Turkey hunters have to expect to fail. You're not always going to succeed and you have to expect it to take a lot of your time and energy. Focus— you've got to be focused on what you're going to do. You have to really want to do it. Like anything else that's difficult you have to commit yourself.

Is it as much a mental challenge?
HUDAK: Oh, absolutely. But you can't let it get you down. Like I said, I never got down. I just got frustrated because I knew I was giving it all I had and it wasn't working out, regardless of where it

was. But, boy, you can never lose confidence. [Above Tony's desk is a framed art print of a wild turkey with the phrase: Success is the place where dedication and preparation meet opportunity.] The other thing that's a huge consideration is the expense. What is it going to take? I don't care whether you drive your own truck like some guys do or you fly or you do both. I did both. But you have to consider what it's going to cost you financially, physically and mentally, because it takes a lot.

Ever figure out what completing the Super Slam did cost you in dollars?
HUDAK: I never kept track. I never even thought about it. I have no idea.

Having hunted in all 49 states where turkeys live, do you have any favorites?
HUDAK: Oh, yeah. I have already returned to a couple. North Carolina, Maine are two of my favorites. What's interesting about North Carolina is there's just so much game down there: turkeys, deer, waterfowl. They have no winters really to speak of. They keep their predators under control. And the habitat is just perfect for anything to live there. So there is always a lot of good gobbling turkeys. It's just a fun place to hunt. It's an action-packed place to go and when I do go I look forward to it. Maine is so different. Maine is a sleeper state as far as turkey hunting goes. It's well known for its bear and deer and moose, but it's a sleeper state as far as turkeys go. But the nice factor up there is that private property can be accessed as long as it's not posted. You can park your truck and go and it's perfectly legal. So it opens up an enormous amount of area for you because it's so vast to begin with and people are accepting. Hunting is a way of life in Maine. So you know you don't get out of your truck and walk across a field and have somebody out there screamin' at you to get off the property. They know that they don't have it posted. They know it's legal for you to be there and that's fine. And there's just so much room to hunt—that makes it fun. You're not worried about crossing property lines and there's turkeys there. It's a good place to be.

How about your least favorite state?
HUDAK: Rhode Island. It's so small to begin with but private property access in my experience anyway was nonexistent. I pounded on doors. I called people. But over the course of years I was never granted permission to hunt on any private property. It's not a welcoming type of atmosphere to hunters up there. Maybe it's more anti-hunting. So you're restricted to the state lands, of which there are generous amounts. However, they're not only for hunting. There's bird watchers. There's horseback riders, mountain bikers. There's motorcycle riders. There's an enormous about of activity on those lands any given day of the week. You have until about 6:30 in the morning to kill your turkey; after that the gates open. So it makes it very, very tough to try to kill a turkey in an area where there's so much human activity. And I know

FACING PAGE: April 2014—state No. 42. Taken along the shores of Lake Norfork, Arkansas on public land, this bird came a long way to the call on a late-afternoon hunt. Wild turkeys are abundant on land surrounding the reservoir. RIGHT: Tony's Colorado gobbler in April 2009 made state No. 26. He took it on the morning following a snowstorm when the birds were vocal at daylight with clear skies and cold air temperatures—his first spring bird killed in the snow.

that was part of the problem for me, you know, why I wasn't being successful. There was just so many people. You can't have that type of activity level and do what I was there to do. Turkeys just don't deal with it. Now they're used to hearing and seeing people every day—don't get me wrong—but they're not going to respond to a call.

Nowadays do you find it most satisfying to hunt familiar places or do you still like to explore new places?
HUDAK: I like both. Especially here at home I still have a lot of places where I hunt turkeys year after year after year, but I'm always looking for a new

turkeys. I'm just out taking numbers because the way I look at it is for every gobblin' bird you hear there's four or five more that are gobblin' right at that same location. Years ago I had no problems coming up with 120, 130 birds that I heard before season. So you know you could easily say in that whole area, whatever that radius was at the time, there was probably 200 turkeys there. For the taking. So my secret is to just get out there and spend time in the woods ahead of time. Put in as much time as you can—even if you don't leave the road. Just get out there and listen. But you know time in the woods can't be taken away. That's where you gotta be. That's essential. That's absolutely essential.

> Put in as much time as you can—even if you don't leave the road. Just get out there and listen. But you know time in the woods can't be taken away. That's where you gotta be. That's essential. That's absolutely essential.

piece of ground or a farm or a new piece of state land. So for me it's both joys of the old haunts because they've been successful and I always look forward to a new place that could be successful.

How many days do you think you devote to turkey hunting each year?
HUDAK: Including scouting?
JANINE: Six months. [laughing]

Who said that?
HUDAK: Truth be told that's a tough one because I don't really keep track of it. All I can tell you is pretty much every morning before work I'm scouting in the spring for six weeks, plus Saturdays and Sundays. I don't know—100 days probably by the time it's all done.

What's your secret—what exactly are you looking for?
HUDAK: In the spring I'm listening for gobblin'

Let's talk about equipment. Let's run down a quick list. Your favorite shotgun?
HUDAK: Winchester Super-X II 12-gauge. I call him Thumper. He's got a 24-inch barrel. He shoots a Primos Jelly Head Choke and I have my shells custom loaded by Nitro Company out in Missouri with tri-plex loads of Hevi-Shot.

Do you use a sighting device?
HUDAK: No, open sights. I had some experience with a scope on Thumper. The problem was when I was going on some of these out-of-state trips wherever I was going I was getting in too late at night to check the scope. So I found it was more of an obstacle than it was a help. In a couple states—Mississippi was one—I missed the bird down there. I missed the bird in another state with that scope and it wasn't like that system to do that. It was a very reliable deal. But once I got the chance to check the scope, I found that it was off, from being in the plane. So I got rid of it.

Do you ever use decoys?

HUDAK: No. I don't have anything against them but they can hurt you as much as they can help you. In a lot of locations, especially here at home, I use the terrain to my advantage. That turkey that's coming, he isn't going to see that decoy before I kill him anyway. So it's not going to help me one bit carrying a decoy around. It's all based on set up and that turkey—I don't want to see that turkey at 100 yards. I want to see him at 30 yards, 35 yards when he pokes his head up over the edge. That's where I want to kill him. So that decoy means nothing to me. I'm not a field hunter. I don't sit on the edges of fields in a pop-up blind with decoys out. That's not me. I'm on the go and I like to hunt them in the woods. I can control the turkey a lot better in the woods. They can see in the field, obviously, their vision is so good. He doesn't *have* to come to my call. He can step out at the edge of that field 200 yards away look over there: *Oh, there's nothing there for me.* People say, well, that's where a decoy comes in. But I don't want to be sitting on a field anyway. A lot of guys like to hunt that way. That's fine but that's not me.

What would I find in your turkey vest if I were to dig through it?

HUDAK: [laughing] Well, first and foremost, besides my turkey calls I carry a good first-aid kit and a snakebite kit. I think that's very important. I don't carry many calls—although a lot of guys do. I always carry two pairs of gloves, face mask, chalk for my box call, plenty of water or Gatorade and some snacks, a pair of brush pruners and usually a rain suit. But I don't carry around as much as I see some guys carry. I don't carry a seat—I sit on the ground. That's pretty much it. There's not a whole lot in there. When Benny hunts with me in the fall I have more of his stuff in my vest for him than I do for myself: his blanket, his snacks, his requirements for the day, some of his medicine.

Which calls do you normally carry?

HUDAK: Mouth call and box call. I carry four mouth calls in a small container and keep them clean

Maine gobbler in May 2010: state No. 29. "Big-woods hunting at its finest," Tony said. He took this bird while hunting with friend Orin Young: With its tradition of public access, Maine offers a lot to the traveling turkey hunter.

every day. I change my box calls up sometimes, not that one makes a difference in any different area than another—it's just personal preference. I have a small collection just for sound and I change something up once in a while. I do carry a crow call with me and a woodpecker whistle. An owl hoot I do with natural voice when my voice is tuned in the spring. And that's pretty much it. I don't overload myself with a bunch of calls or paraphernalia. I try to keep myself a minimalist.

Do you have a go-to call?

HUDAK: Just my mouth call. I use a three-reed, two-reed latex top-reed prophylactic. I have them made that way special. It gives me the sound and the rasp I'm looking for. That's pretty much been my go-to call for about 10 years. I killed about 25, 26 states with that particular style of call.

Did you notice any difference between regions of the country in the way the birds responded to your calling?

HUDAK: No. A turkey's a turkey. Some of the subspecies—the Merriam's and the Rios are a little bit more, shall I say, accommodating. You know, especially the Rios, I have found that they will respond to a call and come a lot farther, come a long

"One big Wisconsin gobbler!" Tony recalled. A real "Hoss" at more than 25 pounds, this big boy was carrying one-and-three-quarter-inch spurs and a 11½-inch beard. In May 2014 the traveling hunter from Pennsylvania watched him go to roost the night before. The next morning he chalked up state No. 45, where one in five hunters tags a bird.

ways to the calls than these eastern turkeys. Right here in the Northeast part of the country are the toughest turkeys you'll ever find. Not necessarily only Pennsylvania but New York, Connecticut, Virginia. Everybody says they're very tough turkeys. So you go to Texas or you go to New Mexico you hunt those different subspecies that make you a quick hero. But I don't change my calling.

Do you remember approximately how many birds you took in the morning and how many later in the day?

HUDAK: The majority were killed in the morning. However, I do enjoy the states that offer all-day hunting—not all do, you know—but the ones that do I would never ever pass up an opportunity to hunt for the last two three hours before dark

where it was legal because it's a very active time for the birds. But to answer your question, I would say in the vicinity of six to eight were killed in the late afternoon out of the 49.

Do you alter your strategy or tactics beyond morning?

HUDAK: No. Early morning is spent getting in tight on a bird on the roost. If I have one gobbling or two gobbling or whatever, I try to get as close as I can to him to minimize the chance that something can go wrong after he hits the ground. I want to be as close to him as I can. I want to shoot him as soon as his toes hit the leaves—at least that's how close I want to be. Sometimes you can't always do that. But I have tagged a lot of turkeys in Pennsylvania and around the country by doing

that, by getting as close as I can to them. Once those birds hit the ground things start happening. They may go with their hens, they may go to another hen, they may go somewhere else. My method is just the run-and-gun method. I stay with them, I try to stay in front of them, I'll out-call them, out-run them—whatever I gotta do. But I'm not a sitter. I want to go all day.

Rain and wind.
HUDAK: Hummm. Two nemeses. What do you do?

Go home?
HUDAK: No, no—I love to hunt the rain as long as it's not a downpour. It's a great time to hunt

because it's so windy your sound isn't going to carry as far. I will definitely use a box call or an aluminum friction call to get the sound to carry. And call more often. If you can't hear them they won't hear you.

What do you think is the most common reason that birds hang up? And how do you solve that problem?
HUDAK: Well, normally they'll hang up in my opinion for one of two reasons, one being the terrain feature. Maybe there's a barbed-wire fence. Maybe there's a small crick bed or a blown-down tree. You can solve that problem in areas where you can spend time scouting before season by knowing what's there. And so when you get to that

> If I have one gobbling or two gobbling or whatever, I try
> to get as close as I can to him to minimize the chance that
> something can go wrong after he hits the ground. I want to be
> as close to him as I can. I want to shoot him as soon as his toes
> hit the leaves—at least that's how close I want to be.

turkeys. They will move to the more open areas, not necessarily to a field. Yes, they will go to a field but if you're hunting timber turkeys like we have around home there are no fields. They will congregate on a log road or maybe a little clearing in the woods that was timbered years ago or some place like that. And I feel they do that simply because it allows them to hear better. When the rain's hitting the leaves, hitting the foliage—whatever time of the spring it is—of course they can't hear as well. So I think they go to the more open areas to where that's not happening. They can hear a little better but they can also rely on their eyesight more to see what danger could be around. The wind is very difficult. I find that the birds will be in a low-lying area more so on windy days—down in a hollow, down in a crick bed or a swamp, in a canyon out West—wherever you might be. I try to head for the low spots, and call more often

area during season you call a bird and it gobbles and you say, "Okay I got him coming." Well, wait a minute, there's a crick bed between us and I got to get across that crick before he gets there because he's not going to cross it. He's gonna hang up. I relate that back to knowing the land you're hunting. Now, if you're out of state your first time in a place you don't know, you may not have the opportunity to scout that property, to know that there is an obstacle there. The other thing is the reason they hang up a lot of times is improper setup which comes back to what I learned many years ago. You're set up in a spot that a turkey can see from 100 yards away and he hears a hen there. He's going to stand there watching until that hen steps out. Well, that hen obviously isn't going to step out because it's you. You're set up improperly. Your setup is the most important decision you're going to make that day. It's more important than your job or a decision at home or anything else that day. I've said that to different guys 100 times and I'll say it again. Your biggest problems are obstacles of terrain and obstacles you've created by setting up in the wrong place.

Do you have a particularly memorable single turkey trip?
HUDAK: I have lots of them. Hawaii was special because my wife was with me and, you know, it was the culmination of the whole thing. So I'll never forget it and it was the end of the whole quest. But there were others. West Virginia was one because I finally tagged that bird. It was very gratifying to take that bird even though it was number 48. It wasn't the end but it was the last of the lower 48 and I worked for that one. I think about it every day. And there's other places that I've gone with friends and so forth, you know. Montana and Wyoming were memorable. Ten of us went there to hunt for four days and we all shot turkeys. It was a fun trip. So that's one I think of a lot. It was a good time, shared it with friends, and we got what we went for.

Who's the best turkey hunter you know?
HUDAK: Dale Englehart. He's a local guy. He's an excellent woodsman, first off. I still say that woodsmanship is 85 percent of being a good turkey hunter—it's far more important than practicing your calling or being a good shooter. You got to be a good woodsman and Dale is an excellent woodsman. He thinks like a turkey. He was a professional caller for years. So his calling abilities and his abilities in the woods are astronomical. He just knows what that turkey is thinking, where he's going to go, what he wants to do, and where he's going to show up. I guess I could say I've probably learned a few tips from him over the years when we hunted together. It's been quite a few years since we've done that only because of families and life and other obligations. He's still at it and teaches those tricks to his own son, who I understand is becoming an excellent turkey hunter as well. I would have to say out of all the guys I

know—and I know a lot of them—he always stood out as the best I knew. By far.

Have you seen changes in the sport over the years that you think are important or notable?
HUDAK: In the past 10 years or so I've noticed a decrease in gobbling activity here at home in my areas that I hunt. Now, some say that our bird numbers are down a little bit and that could contribute to that, but I don't think they're down that much that it's decreasing the gobbling activity. I hear from too many local hunters that come to me that call me or I see at a restaurant or whatever: "What's going on with the turkeys? I'm not hearing them. I'm not seeing them strutting? What's going on?" I really think that they have changed their ways and I think it all relates back to human pressure—or credit predatory pressure. We have more predators now right here in Pennsylvania than we've ever had. Even as recently as 10 years ago.

What are after the turkeys?
HUDAK: Fishers.

Really?
HUDAK: Yes. They introduced fishers here a few years back. And right now there are so many that now we have a trapping season on them. I see them all the time. I see their tracks in the winter, you know, I see them live when I'm scouting.

They can certainly go get the turkeys in the trees.
HUDAK: Exactly. So between fishers and our bobcat population and coyote population and raccoons—and the price of fur is down so guys aren't trapping like they used to—it all adds up. It all has a downhill effect. I think the turkeys gobble less to avoid attracting predatory influence. They've kind of learned from nature to keep their mouths shut and ones that don't are in somebody's belly. I see it here. My gobbling count went from 125 birds, as I said, to right now I can't break 30 for the last three years and I'm still putting in the same amount of scouting time in the same areas. So that's a pretty good measure: 100 birds it dropped. I keep ac-

count of it. It dropped 10, 15, 20 birds every year.

Do you have a favorite book about turkey hunting?
HUDAK: *Turkey Hunting Digest* by Jim Spencer. He lives in Arkansas. I have a couple of his books. He's excellent, in my opinion, he's excellent. He was a contributing writer to *Turkey & Turkey Hunting* magazine with a column in there called "Bad Birds" which were all personal experiences of turkeys that gave him trouble over the years. Some he killed, some he didn't. He just has a way of putting his thoughts into words in a way that you can relate to, with a little bit of color. You can almost picture what he's telling you and his story, and with a little bit of humor but professional at the same time. Kind of hard to describe but I think he's my favorite.

Eating a turkey—do you have a favorite recipe to cook wild turkey?
HUDAK: Well, I leave that all up to Janine. She prepares it a few different ways.

Chef Janine?
JANINE: Scampi is the way Tony likes it best—a lot of olive oil and a lot of butter. Because the turkey breast has muscle around it I take off that first layer and cut it up into small pieces. I soak it in salt water to get the gaminess out of it and then I just put it in the butter and olive oil and garlic and at the very end in seasoned bread crumbs to mop up the butter and oil. And a little parmesan cheese on top. I also do a barbecue. French onion soup mix is good, too—it tenderizes it nicely in a Crockpot.

What is your next turkey challenge?
HUDAK: Well, there's a few states I want to revisit. I'd love to go back to the Black Hills.

Make sure you have a shower this time.
HUDAK: Yeah, yeah, yeah! We were there twice already. It took two trips to kill a bird there. But anyway I'd love to go back there again and to Missouri. There's a bunch of states that I want to

revisit. We've already done that this year—we were up to Maine and Massachusetts. Those are two places I wanted to go back to so that's kind of on the bucket list as far as maybe six or eight states that I'd like to revisit. But the World Slam is next: the ocellated turkey in the Yucatán in 2018. In the meantime, I've kind of resolved myself to pursue the Canadian and the Mexican Slams as well, which really isn't that much. Two turkeys in Canada will complete that. And aside from the ocellated turkey would be a Mexican Rio Grande turkey to complete the Mexican project. I already have the Gould's which I took in Mexico. I think I'm going to pursue that and have all the titles. You know it's a goal to strive for, to reach for, and why not? You have to have a goal. You have to have something to go for.

Do you still have the fever?
HUDAK: I still have some turkey hunting to do but not with the fever or the drive that I had before I finished the Super Slam. Obviously, I still want to be successful when I go. Anybody who says it doesn't matter isn't telling the truth. Florida next year—I'd like to get another Osceola or two to bump up my Grand Slam list a little. But right now the slam titles in Canada and Mexico are what I'm pursuing. It's really only four turkeys and I would have it complete and that I think would be the true pinnacle. The fire is still lit, bright as ever, and hopefully it won't go out for a long time!

3

Rob
Keck

HOME:
Edgefield, South Carolina

OCCUPATION:
Director of Conservation for Bass Pro Shops

FIRST WILD TURKEY:
1963, Pennsylvania

COMPLETED U.S. SUPER SLAM:
1997, North Dakota

IVE MINUTES FROM THE PRE-REVOLUTIONARY WAR small-town center of Edgefield, South Carolina near the Georgia state line ("Home of 10 Governors"), I drove through a golf course and took a left up a driveway next to a front-yard pond where, I learned, wood ducks landed. I rang the doorbell at the front door of a large, modern home. The man who greeted me was tall with a firm handshake and a bass-baritone voice; more than once he has been told he would be good at voice-over commercials. He was dressed in a sharply ironed tan safari shirt displaying the red and yellow logo of Bass Pro Shops.

OPENING PAGE: April 2016—Edgefield County, South Carolina: It's all in the family when it comes to turkey hunting and enjoying the outdoors. With a little coaching from Granddad, Rob Keck's five-year-old grandson Hank furiously worked a push-pin call to get this bird into range for Heather, Rob's daughter and Hank's mother. ABOVE: December 2005— Washington, D.C.: Rob Keck and his wife Susan presenting a decorative turkey call to Supreme Court Justice Antonin Scalia, who was an avid hunter who was the keynote speaker at two National Wild Turkey Federation Conventions.

The birds were still flocked up. Even though the North Dakota prairie on this spring day looked and felt like winter, the toms were gobbling. They were strutting. The draws and the hollows were still filled with snow drifts. The birds had dropped down from the giant gray cottonwoods, but the hunter couldn't do a thing with them. The hens had lured them away. He got close several times, maneuvering around the landscape, using every call and tactic he knew.

Late in the day he headed back toward where he had watched them come off the roost this morning. He reached into his pocket and felt for an ancient arrowhead; it was with him all the time. He pulled it out and rubbed it. If there was any magic in that flaked rock, he wanted to conjure it now.

The hunter feared that all the turkeys had gone by. He was on bare ground. No timber. But there was a little depression where he was able to set up. He called and a bird answered—a straggler. He could see the top of his fan. When the gobbler came around the side of the hill he was looking for a hen that wasn't there. The turkey raised his head and the hunter squeezed the trigger. As the load of No. 7s found their mark he was filled with a rush of emotion. He broke down. This 49th-state turkey had been a long time coming.

It was beginning to spit snow. Light was fading. And then the hunter knelt down beside the turkey—as he did with every kill he made—and said a prayer of thanks to God for allowing him to be in this sacred place, to take this very special gobbler. He reached into his pocket and touched the arrowhead again. He slung the big bird over his shoulder and stood there for a moment, looking out across the darkening prairie.

The hunter wasn't just any hunter. He was Rob Keck, the man I had traveled to South Carolina to meet, and what he did for a living in 1997 set him apart from every other hunter in the country. Rob was the C.E.O. of the National Wild Turkey Federation. The organization was a small, essentially regional group when Keck, a young schoolteacher in Pennsylvania, was hired in 1978. By 1997, guided by Keck's leadership, the N.W.T.F. had grown into one of the top hunter-supported wildlife conservation organizations in the country. The men and women of the Federation—legions of devoted volunteers backed by professional game biologists—had played pivotal roles in bringing back the wild turkey.

When 13-year-old Rob killed his first wild turkey back in 1963, there was no talk about getting a Grand Slam. Certainly no talk of a Super Slam. The species was still absent from

many states. Pennsylvania didn't even have a spring season—he had to go south to Alabama to kill his first spring gobbler.

By the mid-1990s, following the expanding arc of turkey populations, Rob Keck had killed a bird in 48 states; only North Dakota remained. But North Dakota did not (and still doesn't) issue turkey-hunting licenses to nonresidents. Keck, of course, knew that the Standing Rock Sioux Reservation allowed nonresidents to hunt for deer and turkey. He had heard stories of hunters coming off the reservation being ticketed, fined and the bird or its parts confiscated by state game wardens. He couldn't take a chance. As head of the National Wild Turkey Federation, the last thing Keck wanted was getting caught up in controversy—much less accused of hunting illegally. When the governor appointed a new executive director of the North Dakota Game and Fish Department, Keck reached out. The director assured Keck that it would be legal for him to come hunt the reservation. He even loaned Rob his truck.

When the hunter picked up his Rio-Merriam's turkey, he had a two-mile hike back to the truck. The sky was darkening and it was snowing. He increased the pace of his steps.

"That feeling of the weight of that gobbler over my shoulder with his head hitting me in the back of the legs," he told me, "is a feeling I'll just never forget."

As he hiked down a ridge and through the creek bottom he ran into a herd of bison. He didn't realize he was on the tribe's buffalo range, although he knew the land belonged to Keepseagle, one of the Sioux tribal members, who had earlier told Keck where he had seen turkeys. He didn't think much about the bison—he was used to walking through pastures filled with cows.

In the distance he could see the truck on the skyline and the outlines of two men. When he got closer he recognized one as George Keepseagle, who introduced Rob to the manager of the buffalo range.

"Man, we were worried about you," Keepseagle said.

"You are so lucky," the buffalo biologist added.

"Why is that?" Keck asked

"Because there was a hunter in here this past week, just a couple days ago, and he was killed by one of the cow buffaloes. When they've got their calves, they are really, really mean."

FACING PAGE: Spring 2002: This picture of Rob Keck was used to promote *Turkey Call* television on The Nashville Network. It was the first hunting program to air successfully during off-season. Before then only fishing shows during spring and summer.

I followed Keck out his back door and across the yard to a fabricated-steel shed the size of a small airplane hangar. The walls were covered with turkey skins and fanned-out tails, and dozens upon dozens of hanging beaver traps. And there was Rob staring out from a framed cover of *American Trapper* magazine!

There's a mystical quality to your Dakota story. Have you always been interested in Native American lore and mythology?

ROB KECK: I always have. I had an uncle that collected arrowheads and all types of Indian artifacts and his collections were of great interest to me. There was something special about Indian lore. I grew up in Lancaster County, Pennsylvania, close to where a very prominent tribe, the Susquehannocks, lived along the Susquehanna River. Penn State and Franklin and Marshall College were conducting a survey along the river at Washington Boro and the researchers allowed me to be part of the dig down there. I was in college close to the area being studied and between classes I participated in digging out some of those fire pits. The numerous artifacts discovered there were magical to me.

Have you ever found loose relics while hunting?

KECK: I'll never forget when I found my very first arrowhead. I was turkey hunting in Alabama. I held it in my hand, admired its symmetry, and wondered if the Indian that napped it had taken a turkey or deer with that point. As I looked at it I thought, *Boy, would I love to communicate with that man that crafted that point out of a piece of flint.* And shortly after I picked up that point and rubbed it and put it in my pocket, I killed a turkey. That experience has happened again and again and again—it happened right up until this very season. Each time I'd find a point, I'd kill a turkey.

Some people would say you must believe in ghosts.

KECK: I don't believe in ghosts, but somehow I do think there's some kind of a connection there that has tied me back to the Native American that crafted that point and hunted here thousands of years before me. It just seems like it's far more than a coincidence. I've got lots of arrowheads in that one frame. [Looks to picture frame on wall.] There might be two dozen points. Every one of those has a story that goes with it: finding that arrowhead and, shortly after, killing the turkey. And it's just been amazing to me because it's happened in a variety of states, not just here in South Carolina or in Alabama. It's been in the Midwest and the West. Heck, in New Mexico I picked up a bird point and 30 minutes later arrowed a six-by-six elk.

Coincidence?

KECK: Maybe it's just a coincidence. Who knows? But it's sort of funny how many times it has happened. A few years ago, when my good friend Rick Collier from Pennsylvania was down here to hunt with me, we had hunted about 10 miles west of town all morning. Never heard a turkey gobble. It was 11:30 and we're walking back up the hill towards my truck, on this red clay road. I happened to look down and I see just the shape of the back of a point. I said, "Wait a minute," and I reached down and dug out around that piece of stone and pulled from the red clay a perfect point. I rubbed it off and cleaned it. I said: "Rick, you've heard me tell stories about this. What do you think this means? We're going to kill a turkey." So I put it in my pocket, got in the truck and drove down the ridge. Right where the ridge dropped off into a big hollow, we stopped and I called. I hit the call and

a turkey gobbled in the bottom. It was the first gobble of the day. I told Rick to get right there, down in front of me. I hit the call again and about that time I could hear the bird drum and saw the top of the fan coming up the hill. That longbeard walked right in and Rick killed it. He said, "Let me touch that arrowhead again." He held it and then I put it in his pocket: "There you go."

Native people everywhere believe there is an inherent spirituality to the hunt.

KECK: I think one of the most moving experiences I've ever had was one where I got to see the Zuni perform the honor given to a dead animal after a kill. I had heard about the ritual before but that it was a very private thing. After I had visited with Nelson Luna, the game manager there on the reservation and in charge of the turkey program at the Zuni Nation, I offered him an idea. The reservation is in New Mexico, real close to the Arizona line. Nelson had told me about the incessant need that they have for turkey feathers, which are used for their prayer sticks that they bury monthly. That need was part of the conservation problem that they had—why turkey numbers were so low. Members of the tribe were killing the birds throughout the year for their feathers. And so I said, "Let's try something." At the time we were moving a lot of Merriam's turkeys onto the Zuni Reservation and were asking them to please don't hunt them out of season, but it wasn't working.

What was your idea?

KECK: I said to Nelson, "If you let me come and film this ritual that you do to honor a dead animal, I'll send you all the turkey feathers that you're ever going to need." I said, "I'll put out a nationwide request through the Federation that when somebody kills a turkey, they should save all the feathers and send them here to our office and we will send you boxes of feathers. I asked Nelson to run it up the flagpole with the tribal council. It took a couple tries before the tribal elders okayed it. They held a lottery for one lucky tribal member to be the hunter to be filmed. We met up with everybody in Zuni and on that day of the hunt we had a small crowd. We had the hunter, the biologist, Nelson, the medicine man of the Mudheads, the No. 2 medicine man, my camera man and myself. Six people. That's an entourage. That many people create its own challenge when you're turkey hunting and trying to keep everybody still. It was the end of the turkey season and they were not very optimistic about being successful. Turkey numbers weren't really great and they said the gobblers were done gobbling. I reassured them we'd have success: "Don't worry—we're going to find one." It wasn't long after daylight that I had heard a turkey gobble, way off in the distance. We went in his direction. He had flown down and was now quiet. I hit the call and a hen responded, so we set up. She came right on in and her response to the calls and her mood was really unique. Instead of me copying her calls, she copied mine. I sort of led the way. And as I'd make a call, she would imitate *me*.

Had you ever experienced that before?

KECK: It was one of the few times that this had ever happened. This was really amazing to me. I mean, I would double cluck and she would double cluck. Man, I'd do a series of nine hen yelps and she was right back with the same. With all that turkey talk going on, way off in the distance a turkey gobbled and I said, "Yes!" As the gobbling picked up and got closer, I could tell there was more than one bird—possibly three. It wasn't long before I hear a turkey drum and here they come down through the Ponderosa pines. Three strutters and they came in to the hunter and he took his bird. Success! That was cool. And we got good footage. But what I really wanted to see now was how this ritual was going to take place, and how this honor was going to be given to this bird that we've just taken the life of. The medicine man, he took the turkey and the first thing he did was face the bird to the east, as they do with all their dead. This was to allow the dead bird to watch the rising sun. Then he said a prayer and with his hand moving over the top of the bird, moving the hand along the neck and over the head out over the beak and up to his mouth, showing the transfer of life from the bird to the Zuni. Then he moved the turkey to the side and marked the spot where the heart of the turkey would have been and the No. 2 medicine man dug a hole that was about three inches in circumference and maybe six inches deep. He then took and laid the turkey back down and he took a leather satchel which was around his neck and from it took cornmeal and ground turquoise and sprinkled it over the head and neck of the turkey.

What did these gifts represent?
KECK: This was to give honor to the turkey with the cornmeal representing sustenance to the Zuni people. The Zunis were an agricultural tribe and that cornmeal had provided food for the Zuni for hundreds of years. The turquoise being a precious gem showed the tremendous respect for the bird. Then they held the turkey upside down and spread the legs and gutted it. They laid the gut pile to the side and laid the turkey back down. With his knife, the medicine man took and plucked a feather, cut a piece of the heart and cut a piece of the webbing between the toes and then took a piece of pine straw and swabbed saliva from the bird's mouth and placed it all into the hole and covered it. This ritual represented planting for new growth, so that they would have more turkeys in the future. Then the turkey was laid back over top of the filled hole and another Zuni prayer was offered. Then we went back to the gut pile and we all knelt down around it. I was completely blown away by what happened next. The Zunis are known for carrying their animal fetishes. Every one of the Zuni men had their animal fetishes around their neck which were kept in a leather satchel. The animals they carried were all predators. After another prayer the medicine man, kneeling opposite me, presented to me a bear—a grizzly bear fetish. It was carved out of blue turquoise. The medicine man said: "You are now one of us. You're a hunter!"

November, 1973—Short Run, Lycoming County, Pennsylvania: Young Rob and his father on a successful hunt, not far from where Rob killed his first gobbler 10 years earlier.

Magnificent!
KECK: I was so honored. And to be accepted that way. I mean, it was off the charts special. Talk about blowing your skirt up. Man. Every animal that they celebrated was a predator and each represented a different point of the compass. The grizzly bear represents the West, the blue of the mountains, the blue of the Pacific Ocean. I think it was the coyote to the south, I think a wolf to the east, and a mountain lion to the north and then the eagle hovering over top. After they finished the prayer, they all took their animals and nosed them into the gut pile to let each animal feed so that you would have strength, and the next time you would hunt that you would have that power and that ability and that skill to kill the animal that you were after.

March 2012—Crockett's Plantation, Bamburg County, South Carolina. Decades after 1973, Dad's last wild turkey.

Rob, let's move to a fundamental question: why do you hunt?

KECK: I hunt because it's been a lifelong passion of mine that I've held, since I was a small kid—from the very beginning. I remember watching my dad, my granddad, my uncles heading out into the field, literally walking out the front door of our home, to hunt ring-necked pheasants and rabbits, squirrels and quail. Then there were special stories about turkeys in the mountains. That passion has just grown with me to the point where it's who I am. It's all about the love of sharing with family and friends the specialness of nature—whether it's hunting turkeys, whitetails, wood ducks, sheep, and moose. Those are things that I connect to.

Where did it come from?

KECK: It's just been part of me. Maybe it was simply God-given. It was certainly inspired and fed by those who were around me. It always was something very special, above and beyond all the other things that I was exposed to in life. So I followed that passion, followed that dream. And I still to this day love to hunt, to take people hunting, and I hope that I can continue to do that until my last dying breath.

Let's hope that's not anytime soon.

KECK: Let's hope not! But, if so, the good Lord has given me far more than I deserve.

What is it specifically about hunting wild turkeys that you love most?

KECK: It's the gobble—not the gobbler—that makes turkey hunting so special, so unique. If you took the gobble out of hunting turkeys you'd take out what inspires millions of people every year to go do it. And so in connecting with that gobble, putting calls out to that gobbler, you reverse the tables of nature. Instead of you being the hunter, you become the hunted. And that fact, that I'm the hunted, is the thing that connects me to the bird and his gobble connects me to the call. Watching a strutting gobbler is awe-inspiring, something that was imitated by Native Americans in their dance, in their rituals, and it does the very same to me. There is a specialness about it that nothing else compares.

What do you remember about your first turkey?

KECK: I'll never forget it. It was on the weekend John F. Kennedy was killed.

November 1963.

KECK: It was Friday afternoon, I was in science class—seventh-grade science class—and the loudspeaker came on in our classroom and told us about the passing of the president. As tragic as that was and still is, was the fact that the next day I was going to join my dad, my uncle and my granddad to go to the huntin' camp to hunt fall turkeys.

Where was that?

KECK: Lycoming County, Pennsylvania, up along

Pleasant Stream and Sullivan Mountain. I hunted with my dad that morning and we were on one side of the creek; my uncle and my granddad were on the other side. We heard them shoot, multiple shots and Dad told me it sounded like it might have been a flock break. Dad and I had seen a flock of turkeys at a distance but could not catch up and get them scattered. About midday Dad said, "Let's head back to the cabin—those guys if they killed anything they should be there." They had. They left a note telling us exactly where the break point of the flock was. We went up on the mountain, just above the old narrow-gauge railroad grade and that's when I had my very first wild turkey encounter with a gun in my hand and learned that I could actually call in and kill a wild turkey.

How old were you?
KECK: Thirteen.

It is something you had anticipated?
KECK: Well, obviously, from the many, many, many stories that I'd heard from Dad and Granddad, I was excited. I knew that killing a turkey was very special—because at that time, very few people I knew had actually killed wild turkeys. There weren't that many wild turkeys around at that time. And, you know, even though my dad and my granddad and my uncles were inspirations, they weren't highly skilled at turkey calling and hunting. They were still learning themselves. So when I heard those shots that morning and knew we were heading to the break point, the location where they had shot and after we read that note, my excitement built beyond belief. We got to the spot where they had left a marker indicating break point. Dad moved 100 yards over to the west of where I was positioned and I took out the Louis Stevenson box call that I got for Christmas when I was eight years old. After about 30 minutes of running that call, I heard a turkey answer me—a coarse gobbler yelp—and when he came into range, I was waiting with my hammerless Savage single-barrel 12-gauge and I got my first chance ever to look down the barrel at a longbeard, there

on the edge of the mountain laurel up on the side of Sullivan Mountain. Watching this turkey come in to my call is a sight I will never forget. That experience was the hook that launched my lifelong love affair with the wild turkey.

Over the years, as you've called in turkeys for beginners and watch their excitement, you must in some way relive your own first experience.
KECK: Well, there's no doubt about it. There's nothing like the first of anything—but especially with my first turkey that I called in and got to kill. I do relive that first experience vicariously, through other people that I take, and of course each year I get a chance to take many. I still get just as excited chasing turkeys as I did way back at the very beginning. That excitement hasn't lessened for me one bit. It just gets to be more exciting. In fact, at the end of each season, I go through withdrawals—almost like I can't believe the season is over. I don't want it to end. And it's especially true when you end up on a really good note. But it's also true if you end on a sour note because, man, you want to *make it happen*. And as we all know it doesn't happen every time that you get him in and you get a chance to kill.

Probably a good thing it doesn't.
KECK: And that's why you don't want to win this game every time. The turkey wins more times than the hunter—that's just the way it should be. That challenge, that uncertainty of the outcome of a hunt, is what builds mystique and appreciation of the bird. Losing to that gobbler is what makes it so *special*. As much as I feel confident that I'm as good a turkey hunter as there is out there, I also know that the bird's going to win some days. And that is a good thing.

Were your dad and your uncle your early mentors in the woods?
KECK: Yeah, I learned from my dad, granddad and my uncles but also by reading *Pennsylvania Game News* magazine and watching *Call of the Outdoors* television. That was the longest continuous-running

outdoor show on network television, a local show in Lancaster on channel 8, and periodically call maker Louis Stevenson would be on the show running his turkey calls. That's where I got the inspiration to become proficient with a call and that's where I got the want, the desire to get one of those box calls. I was always glued to that set watching, learning. Another thing that was a key was the Eastern Sports and Outdoor Show in Harrisburg: one of the biggest of its kind, and it's been running forever. As a little kid I'd go to the show with my dad. There were just a few vendors of turkey calls back then, but they would take time to show me how to call. I just didn't want to go anywhere else at the show. Those call makers were mentors that gave me inspiration and also instruction in calling.

Looking back to your beginnings in the 1960s, what's the one vital piece of advice you'd give to a young Rob Keck?

KECK: Patience. Patience is one I would give to any level of turkey hunter when he's asking, *what do I do in a certain situation?* I think most times most hunters don't give the bird enough time to work the call, to respond. Maybe they've been in a situation where they had a prior experience with a turkey that just ran over the top of them as soon as they hit the call; they think it happens that way every time and, of course, it doesn't. That element of patience is something you can't buy at Bass Pro Shops—it's something that you have to really learn.

How did you learn that lesson?

KECK: I thought that I learned patience early on but it was only through the years I began to realize I had no idea what patience really was. Patience was something that I had to experience, I had to learn. I remember hunting with my great-uncle Bill, who at the time had a broken leg. He wasn't mobile, so we sat longer than normal, listening to a turkey gobble off in the distance—a bird that we'd normally have gotten up and gone after and repositioned on. Instead, we sat. My patience was challenged. But we got the bird. What I learned

was that by giving the bird time, a gobbler that answered my call, he would eventually come on his own time frame, not mine. So patience is the kind of thing that is hard to describe. It's hard to tell someone how long should you sit at that spot. But if you think you're ready to go, give it another 15 minutes.

Frank Woolner always advised the opposite with ruffed grouse, saying facetiously that boots— not guns—killed grouse.

KECK: Yeah, well [laughing] you're talking to a runner-and-gunner as well. But let me tell you, there's a lot of those turkeys that don't say anything when coming to the call. And it's different when you're chasing grouse. With turkeys we're actually trying to call them in; with grouse you're moving trying to flush them—two different scenarios completely.

How many turkeys do you think you've killed?

KECK: I know exactly how many, and I'd like to think I've probably taken as many birds as any turkey hunter has ever taken legally. But quite frankly it's one question that I don't plan on publicly giving an answer to in terms of numbers, for two simple reasons. One, focusing on the number of kills puts the spotlight on the wrong target and secondly, it provides fodder for the anti-hunting element, especially in the media. There is nothing wrong with talking about achievement, and I, like many others work hard to take long-spurred and bearded gobblers, but I think that today we've emphasized way too much about the importance of the number of kills, number of slams, the trophy aspects of the animals, the number of inches, trying to equate it with maybe a baseball player and the number of hits that he's had or a football player and the number of touchdowns that he's had. Maybe we should think more in terms of the number of trophy experiences instead of the number of dead turkeys. The number that possibly is more important is the number of birds that I called to the gun or bow for kids, first timers, family, friends and business associates. That number of memories is huge.

How should success in a hunt be measured?
KECK: To me, it's very simple. If we want to pass this tradition on, if we want people to really enjoy the experience of the outdoors, to me, you have to focus on the experience itself. I like to say a trophy experience is far greater than a trophy bird. So much in our outdoor media—whether it's on Outdoor Channel, whether it's in major hunting magazines—it always seems like we look for the biggest buck, the longest spurs, or the longest beard. What we really should be talking about is the biggest *experience*—the experience that sticks with you for a lifetime. And that's where our focus needs to be. I think that if hunters do that they

a big party. Carl Brown and I had a different idea on having fun and headed to Alabama not knowing where the heck we were going. I'd read a story in *Outdoor Life* magazine that talked about Alabama as the state with the longest spring season and the state that had held a season longer than any other. I looked at the dates and they overlapped with spring break. I was sitting there in the college library reading hunting magazines instead of doing what I was supposed to be studying for my classes and we just made a decision right there: We're going to Alabama—with no other information. And what a time it was. It took us a while before we finally found a place where we could hunt.

> If we want to pass this tradition on, if we want people to really enjoy the experience of the outdoors, to me, you have to focus on the experience itself. I like to say a trophy experience is far greater than a trophy bird.

end up enjoying the hunt more by far. You know, when you can look at beard length, when you can look at spur length, when you can look at the weight of a gobbler—it's incidental to the experience. Rarely, *rarely* do people go out there saying, "Okay, unless those spurs are inch and a half, I'm not going to shoot this turkey." Most times you can't even see those spurs if he's coming through tall grass or moving quickly or what have you. People that sit at a feeder or in a pop-up blind could do that more easily. But I think for myself— and I know for many, many others—we focus on that turkey: really outfoxing him with positioning or patience or camouflage or calls. Taking that bird in that way, your level of satisfaction—that needle goes way high.

Do you remember your first spring gobbler?
KECK: I killed my first spring gobbler in Alabama in 1969 during spring break when most college students were going to Florida to have a big time,

Once we hit the Alabama line, we pulled off the interstate and traveled down a dirt road where we saw a guy who looked like the Dodge Safety Sheriff sitting under a big white oak that was whittling on a stick. We pulled off the road and I asked the guy, "Any turkeys around here?" He said, "Yeah, but since they put the dam in, there are so few we don't even talk about them." I'm thinking, *Oh, my God, we've just driven 15 hours.* So we get back on the interstate. We're driving south-southwest and we get off at another place. We stopped to gas up and check the oil in our old Oldsmobile. We got out and I asked the guy, "Any turkeys around?" This was back when they'd fill your gas tank up and wash your windshield. He said, "Yeah, there were three gobblers in that field right across the road, just a little while ago." Our spirits went up. I asked where we could get a hunting license. He said: "Go on over there to the courthouse. The sheriff's office is down there in the basement." This was a Sunday. He said, "Somebody will be

there." He told us we could get a license and to hunt on "the reservation." I thought he was talking about an Indian reservation; what he was talking about was the Coosa Wildlife Management Area. So we went in and got our license. At that time it was $10.10 for a nonresident hunting license—called a "trip license." I asked the sheriff, "Where's this reservation the man at the gas told us about?" He said, "Oh, he must be talking about Horse Stomp camping area on the Coosa Wildlife Management Area. I said, "How do you get there?" He said, "Boys load up and just follow me." So the sheriff led us down there and took us right to the campsite where we put up our tent. And that's where I ended up killing my very first spring gobbler. In fact, I killed two turkeys on that trip. Those were my first spring gobblers. On that trip we met an old turkey hunter named J. D. Prickett. This colorful man, chewing Black Moriah plug tobacco and driving a Volkswagen van with an interior literally hanging full of turkey beards, really impressed upon me the understanding of the power of a green plot in spring. I hung on to every piece of turkey advice he'd offer and then he took us on a scouting trip. We snuck to a saddle on a little ridge overlooking Weogufka Creek, all the while humming the theme song of ABC's *American Sportsman* TV show. Down there in the creek bottom in a green field was a gobbler in full strut with a couple of hens. In that field the next day I killed my first turkey.

How many years did it take you to complete the 49 states?

KECK: Well, I killed the first bird in 1963 and my last state to take a gobbler was North Dakota—that was in 1997. I thought about the possibility of taking a bird in every state that had a season while I still lived in Pennsylvania before I moved to South Carolina in 1978 to work full time at the National Wild Turkey Federation. But at that time there were only 30 states that had turkey seasons—

so you weren't talking about 49. I had at that time a dozen or more states that I'd already killed turkeys in. Having traveled on the turkey-calling circuit all over the eastern half of the country, a bunch of invitations were extended to hunt in some pretty darn good places. After Alabama I had hunted in Arkansas, Florida, Georgia, New York, Ohio, West Virginia, Maryland, Mississippi, Louisiana, Texas and Virginia. So I thought, *Gosh, it would be pretty cool to do that, to kill a turkey in all the states that had seasons.* But it wasn't that I was in a rush to do it. I mean, it didn't feel like I was under some kind of a gun, that I was in some contest to accomplish that. And then once I went to work at the Federation and traveling and building chapters and dealing with turkey hunters all over the country, as you can imagine, I had invitations from many, many people in a lot of different places: "Come and spend some time with us. Our chapter is holding a cookout and a meeting. We can hunt. We can socialize. We can talk about the future of the Federation." So I had that privilege and opportunity as well. And I continued to add on states.

Although you killed your birds in 49 states over a span of many years, do you recall approximately how many were taken in the spring and how many in the fall?

KECK: I have been an avid fall turkey hunter—I grew up fall hunting. But the new states I was adding, I was doing that in the spring. The only fall one that was part of the quest was Arizona. I along with other Federation staff and board members were out in Flagstaff for a meeting with all of our chapter leaders. Through the help of some of the employees of Arizona Game and Fish and our volunteers with the Arizona chapters, they served as guides for some, yet for others simply sent them in the right direction where we might find turkeys. National board member L. A. Dixon from North Carolina and I paired up and I was lucky enough

OVERLEAF: Keck keeps a complete collection of licenses, tags, photos, news clipping and other memorabilia in stacks of three-ring binders documenting his turkey hunts from the 49 states, Canada, Mexico, Guatemala and New Zealand.

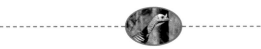

to be one of two hunters from the entire group that killed a turkey. It was pretty cool on the attention those two birds drew, since many had never seen a Merriam's wild turkey, certainly different than what a lot of guys from back East had ever seen.

Some hunters seem to put a lot of emphasis on the birds being all toms as part of a Slam.

KECK: I think every hunter has to find his own level of satisfaction. But I guess I go back to my statement that I think so many times we put too much emphasis on "it's got to be the biggest or the oldest, it's got to be an adult gobbler," you know, something that is totally off the charts. I come back and say, Look, it's all about the trophy experience. I can tell you that in a few of the states where I killed turkeys they were jakes. But some of the most challenging turkeys that I've had over the years have been jakes, especially some of those that we term many times as bull jakes. I've had gangs of jakes—let's say four of them gobble really good. They gobble to each other and they come so far but then maybe, just maybe, they won't come any further, because maybe there's a gang of adult gobblers somewhere in the area and they're afraid to make that last little move. I think that we've got to make sure that we never look down at somebody because they took a jake or took a bearded hen. I think if it's a legal bird, that's certainly the No. 1 criteria, but No. 2 is the fact that every wild turkey is special. I can attest first hand, that some of the most challenging or toughest birds were not longbeards. I've had people ask me, "Did you kill a good one?" I can tell you I have never seen a bad one.

Because of the span of years it took to achieve your Super Slam—with the range of the species expanding and the sport evolving—you must have used many different firearms.

KECK: During my early turkey hunting days my first gun was that single-barrel hammerless 12-gauge Savage that I took that first gobbler with. When I was 13 years old, I bought a Remington 870 pump with money I earned from mowing

yards. In fact, the first 100 birds I took were with that 12-gauge with a modified choke. After that, I found that in addition to that modified barrel I bought an aftermarket full choke and then an extra-full-choke barrel. Then I remember the day I got a semi-automatic Remington 1100 and had the barrel cut down and sleeved with an extra-full constriction. Through the years with the Federation, we produced a number of different commemorative and specialized turkey guns that I experimented with. Eventually I settled on the superb efficiency and light weight of a 20-gauge. A Browning Gold 20 accounted for a number of birds as well as a sweet pistol-gripped specialized Benelli 20 and a custom thumb-hole-stocked Remington 1187. Let me just sidetrack here for a moment. As turkey hunting evolved with the return of the wild turkey, and as more and more states were adding seasons because of the restoration success, there was a growing demand for improved equipment. One of those was specialized turkey guns. I'll never forget back in 1981 at the SHOT Show in Atlanta, where I visited with Remington Arms' Dick Dietz and I asked Dick, "What are the chances that Remington could build a short barreled, extra-full-choke 1100 or 870?" He laughed at me and he said "There's no market for that kind of gun."

And you thought there was.

KECK: Conventional thinking was use the same gun that you use for ducks and geese, but turkey hunters wanted a turkey-only gun. I said: "Dick. You don't understand what turkey hunters are looking for. They're getting their barrels cut off. They're sending them to gunsmiths like Mark Bansner in Adamstown, Pennsylvania and having sleeves put in them to make those barrels extra-full." I said "You're missing an opportunity." Dick continued to chuckle at the idea. Well, guess what? Within a year, Remington began producing an aftermarket 870 and 1100 barrel that was extra-full—and short. Up until that time the shortest barrel you could get for an 870 or 1100 was 28 inches. Well, now we got them down to 26-inch.

Custom barrels got even shorter than that. And then they began looking at the constrictions and they began producing interchangeable screw-in choke tubes. Eventually, I created the World Still Target Championship at N.W.T.F. with the goal of determining the very best shotgun, choke tube, ammunition and sighting device, all with the intent of making the cleanest kills and reduce crippling loss. As a result of these major changes in both turkey guns and ammo, I look back and really feel privileged that I had a chance to be a pioneer and have an impact in developing a lot of these different tools that are part of today's turkey-hunting gear. The short-barreled, extra-full-choke turkey gun was something that didn't exist before turkey hunting had its rebirth.

that loved to hunt in the mountains, and grew up hunting in the mountains, I was looking to reduce weight wherever I could. One of my mentors was Wayne Kochenderfer from Ickesburg, Pennsylvania. We called him "Kochie." He was using a 20. Another guy that was a champion caller—a guy that created the double slate and a lot of calls that really were the forerunners of what we use today—was George "Fritz" Fleisher from Millerstown. He was using a 20-gauge Franchi. And these guys were killing truckloads of turkeys. So two decades ago I started using a 20—and I never felt I was lacking anything. Since then I've inspired a lot of other people to go lighter and go 20-gauge. I then added a thumb-hole stock, a pistol-grip stock. You're looking at one to your right. [points to guns] There's a Benelli that has a pistol grip. In

> I asked Dick, "What are the chances that Remington
> could build a short barreled, extra-full-choke 1100 or 870?"
> He laughed at me and he said, "There's no market
> for that kind of gun."

Do you still shoot a 12-gauge?
KECK: As I mentioned, over the years I migrated to a 20-gauge. I am a huge fan of the 20 and in no way do I ever feel undergunned or a need to go back to a 12. With today's modern turkey loads and all the improvements in chokes, sighting devices etc. there is a real strong case for the 20-gauge turkey gun. In the early days, some guys thought they had to have a 10-gauge. Then a 12-gauge three-and-a-half-inch magnum.

Why, do you think?
KECK: They just had to have a big heavy gun, possibly to make up for poor calling or poor hunting skills. If they were weak in their calling skills, weak in their hunting skills, they wanted to make up for it by having a gun that they thought was a blunderbuss and could kill anything. Well, being a guy

that case is an 1187. I took advantage of the opportunity to really dress this thing up and had Remington build that thumb-hole stock in their custom shop. And then things like sights were added as well. I remember those new firearms, when they first came out of the box, they were shiny: glossy wood finishes on the stock and shiny bluing. Guys started spraying their guns. They put camo tape on them. And then the factory-dipping process came along. I'll never forget pulling my first 1187 out of the box and I took a spray can of olive-drab green paint and started spraying away. My wife said, "What are you doing to that beautiful gun?" I said, "I'm camouflaging it." She about had a fit.

Ultimately, what was your motivation to get a wild turkey in all the states?

KECK: Well, first of all, I've always been goal-oriented. Having competed successfully in sports, once you set a goal then you had to go out and achieve it. And I guess once I'd gotten to that point where I was at 48 I said, "Man, this is stupid if I did not finish it off." So just that innate drive and desire to finish something I'd started. My dad always told me, "Look, if you start something, you'd better finish it." This was just another one of those things that I said, "Well, I'm going to finish it." I also thought, *I'm in a position here where I can achieve something that I don't know if anybody else had ever done it.* For the most part, when I mentioned it, most people had never even thought about it. Most of them were still hung up trying to just kill a turkey, you know, and others were hunting maybe a couple states a year. When I told them I've killed one in nearly every state it was like it didn't even compute, they couldn't fathom this. Just to travel to 49 states is hard for the average Joe to wrap his mind around, let alone shoot a turkey in every one.

At the time, did you imagine that someday what came to be called the U. S. Super Slam would be a widely recognized feat and that other hunters would try to follow?

KECK: Yes, I actually I did, and the reason that I did is there were guys like Dick Kirby, who was a well-known call maker. He was always talking about how many Grand Slams he had killed; that was catching on. People asked how many Grand Slams I had and I'd say: "I don't know. I've never counted them. I don't think that way. I'm not one of those guys that has to put the numbers up like balls through a hoop or touchdowns or the number of hits." But in looking at how excitement was growing about Grand Slams, Royal Slams, World Slams, I thought the broader goal of a Super Slam would eventually trump all others. More people will want to do it when they finished all the Grand Slams and then a Royal Slam and then a World Slam—they're going to want something else to challenge them.

November, 1976—State College, Pennsylvania: Penn's Woods Products—at the time the largest manufacturer of turkey calls in the country—asked Keck to don buckskins and a coonskin cap. He called in a bird with a wingbone and shot it with a Vince Nolt, Lancaster County flintlock, all captured on film for the movie *Trophy and Tradition.*

You were in a unique situation in that traveling for the N.W.T.F. gave you exceptional opportunities. I wonder what kind of strain this maniacal quest puts on some personal relationships.

KECK: Well, there isn't any doubt that when you look at traveling to 49 states, logistically it's a huge challenge. You're going to drive there or fly there. Then you start adding the amount of time you have to devote, what it's going to take for you to kill a turkey, and maybe some place you go to you don't kill one and you have to come back. So you're looking at an expenditure of money, you're looking for a place to stay, you're looking to gas up a vehicle, buying a nonresident license—all those kind of things create stress on a relationship.

As I've always said, there's two things as a turkey hunter you've got to have: a good wife and a good boss, because without them at the end of season you will have neither.

When a hunter starts thinking about getting a turkey in a state far away from home, how does he or she know where to focus?
KECK: Network! As a member of the N.W.T.F., many hunters from different states exchange hunts with one another. Contact the turkey project leader with each state fish and wildlife agency. They can be very helpful. Today's social media allows you to easily connect with other turkey hunters.

But you were on your quest long before Facebook!
KECK: Well, as I was coming down to the last handful of states and traveling on my own nickel, I thought, *Okay, out of this trip where can I hit the most states with one flight and a rental car to get around?* That's how I did Idaho, Oregon and Washington all in one swoop. I killed a turkey in Hells Canyon with outdoor writer Ron Spomer; he did a story on that. And then I had been in touch with our turkey project leader, a biologist for the State of Washington and went over and met him at one of the fish hatcheries and he said: "I'm not a good hunter but I know how to catch and release them. I'll put you in the right places where they are." After I finished that I had a local chapter guy in Oregon that said, "Man, we would love to have you come visit." So I went down across the border and I was able to put all that together in just a few days' time. But it can become a challenge. You may have bad weather. You may have turkeys that aren't cooperating. It may take a lot longer than you anticipated. You may have all kinds of logistical challenges—not to mention that sometimes a turkey is just hard to kill.

Say a hunter does his homework and chooses a route or a circuit, how does he find the turkeys?
KECK: That's a great question. Before I go there I've usually made contact with somebody. I always start with the turkey biologist in that particular state. And if they don't have a specified turkey biologist, find the biologist or the director of wildlife management that could point me to a general area: this National Forest, that piece of B.L.M. land, this National Wildlife Refuge or this wildlife management area has a good number of turkeys. Then, armed with that information, I would go to, let's say, the Flint Hills National Wildlife Refuge and then I'd take off and drive and call, drive and call, trying to locate them. I had a variety of locator calls that I'd use, drive, stop, call and repeat. That's what I advise anybody to do, you know, certainly if you get out in the morning before daylight or daybreak and listen—you can hear them gobbling from the roost. They're higher up so you can usually hear easier and generally winds haven't picked up or late evening. But I just take off and ride. Also a lot of times you can spot them in fields, openings. They might be strutting out there with some hens. So I cover ground but I'm using my ears and my eyes to try to locate birds and then play off that.

With all your extensive travel, where would you say it was easiest to kill a turkey?
KECK: Texas. Over the long haul and over many, many trips, if I wanted to take a donor, V.I.P. or someone special and have a reasonably good chance of putting a turkey in front of him or her, I'd take them to Texas. But even some of the hardest turkeys are easy on some given days. When we were filming for *Turkey Call* television, many times I would go to a state at the very end of the season. One of the reasons is I wanted to get those old long-spurred boss gobblers on film. It was also a time of the season when the majority of the hens would be incubating, making those dominant birds far more vulnerable than earlier in the season. This same turkey at the beginning of the season was all henned up; he was virtually *impossible* to call, although he could be fanned more easily. At the end of the season, when he doesn't have any hens coming to him like the weeks earlier, this tough turkey now becomes an easy turkey. I found that even with what I consider the "easier"

turkeys—Rios and Merriam's—even when they're henned up, they're really challenging to call. So for me, the easiest turkeys usually come at the very end of the season or if you're really lucky, and it's a late spring the very beginning, right when flock breakup occurs. Those turkeys can be very, very easy as well. When you look at a state like Georgia, their spring season covers everything from coastal plain to the mountains. Peak gobbling on the coastal plain is different than the piedmont and it's different in the mountains. So in that state, where you go and when you go can determine how easy it's going to be at a given time. So to say one state is going to be easier than another—generally speaking, any state that has Rios or Merriam's is going to be easier than those that have easterns or Osceolas.

The flip side—difficult places?
KECK: I think some of the more difficult places have been places in the South where you're hunting flooded backwaters early in the season when the gobblers are henned up. Alabama would be No. 1 and I would say that for a couple different reasons. They've had a turkey hunting season longer than other states. Turkey behavior is in direct response to the amount of hunting pressure that they've had placed on them. If they're hunted longer and have been hunted harder they become more difficult to kill. So is the case for eastern turkeys of the Deep South. Then you add the element of lots of hens and you add the element of water and the birds become isolated on small islands exposed above the flood water, you are talking about the toughest birds to hunt. They're going to have to wade through water or fly across that water to get to you. Your ability to position yourself in a way to get that gobbler to come to you is a huge, huge challenge. Most times you have got to go to them. So if I had to say the most difficult state, I'd have to say in the South, Alabama—but I've killed easy ones in Alabama, too.

What do you consider the most challenging thing about hunting turkeys—the birds or the terrain?

KECK: Great question. Add "elements" to that challenge factor. I think that it's a combination of factors that adds to that challenge. Certainly weather can be a huge element, especially if you have high winds and you can't hear. Let's say you're hunting in Kansas. A 25-mile-an-hour wind to someone from Kansas is a breeze. When you get 40-mile-an-hour gusts it is hard to hear a turkey gobble even when you're really close to him. So that to me is probably the biggest challenge. Now, if you happen to be hunting that flooded backwater and you've got pockets, little islands out there, certainly the terrain adds a tremendous amount of challenge to that hunt. Or if you don't know the piece of land you're hunting and you have something like a fence between you and that turkey. Let's say he's coming in from 100 yards away but you can't see across that draw, that there's a woven-wire hog fence there. He keeps coming up and he's going back and forth, back and forth, and you wonder why is he hung up? Normally he would fly across, but in spring, when he's just tore up with your hen calling and he's trying to get there, he can't figure it out. It just seems absolutely impossible. Whether it's a creek, whether it's a fence, whether it's rock outcroppings or what have you—it could be a snow drift—those kind of things are challenges that you wouldn't normally have in flatlands.

How far will they come?
KECK: I called one in from over a mile away in California out at the Tejon Ranch. We were set up on an overlook with a video camera filming a scene for *Turkey Call* and for the fun of it hit a long box and this distant barely audible gobble rang back in response. I hit the call again and we finally located the tom far on the other side of this deep canyon. What was really cool was that as we watched through binoculars, you could see the turkey's neck stretch out and gobble, but there was delay in hearing it. So we began filming as I kept calling and in amazement we were trying to guess how far this turkey was. There were three of us standing there in the wide open—the manager of

the ranch, the camera man and myself. This turkey was unbelievably distant, but we kept the camera rolling and I just kept pouring it on loud with that big long box and all of a sudden the ranch manager, standing next to me, said, "Hey, Rob, that turkey is flying to us." And, sure enough, he flew across that *deep* canyon. He flew what we guessed was over a mile and landed right below us. I put the manager of the ranch right down in front of the camera, and called up that longbeard, and the manager killed it. There are other days in that kind of terrain when you couldn't begin to

in the spring, gosh, I don't even know where to begin. We had one that we called "Limpy" due to his infirmity of having a broken leg that had healed up. For five years he was always dragging behind the other gobblers that came to the call. We'd call to them and call them in, and as a result of him following way behind the others, his buddies would get killed. He always got away because he was way, way back, and the hunter I was guiding always shot the lead bird. Even times when we let the other turkeys come in he still just hung back out of range. We never ever did kill that

> I think some of the more difficult places have been places in the South where you're hunting flooded backwaters early in the season when the gobblers are henned up. Alabama would be No. 1.

think about calling that turkey. Attitudes of a turkey at any given time can change instantly.

Is there a single most-challenging bird that you actually never killed?
KECK: Gosh. Lots of them. [chuckling] You don't have enough recording time. I think every one of us that have turkey hunted any length of time have those stories. I mean, with me, it's been over 50 years, both fall and spring hunting, but I can't say there was a specific bird that was memorable. Let's say you've scattered a flock of birds in the fall and that old hen comes in close to—but not in—shotgun range and starts an old-hen assembly call. You cannot beat her at that. Those young turkeys are imprinted on her voice; they've been imprinted since they were in the egg. I can't tell you the number of times that has happened, when you think you're just about ready to make it happen, and she gets out there in front of you and all these birds are answering your call, but going around you, directly to her. They're going right to her and she takes them away. As far as an individual gobbler

turkey. And we knew it was him because he had that distinctive limp. It was like he had this magical aura about him that made him really, really tough to kill.

Are certain birds more predictable than others?
KECK: Yes, and probably one the great examples is hunting Rio Grande turkeys in Texas where there is a common isolated roost. Because of the very limited places where they can roost, you can predict where they come back in the evening and where they will be in the morning. You can almost set your clock on the time that they're going to come back into their roost. They may travel four or five miles out there during the day but let me tell you they're coming back to that roost. I make it a point not to shoot the roost because you want to keep that in your hip pocket. You've got to find places to hunt out beyond the roost trees. You want to keep those birds wanting to come back into this place where they feel safe to spend the night.

How about seasonal predictability?

November, 1980—Hollywood, California: Keck and country music star Hank Williams, Jr. on the Mike Douglas show the night Ronald Reagan was elected President. Rob said that minutes before they were on stage with Bob Hope, Ernest Borgnine and some soap opera stars, he put a Neil Cost Boat Paddle call in the hands of each guest and showed how to work it. Backstage the gobbler perked up to the noise, but when brought into the lights all he did was poop.

KECK: I think there's different times during the year that birds also become predictable, when you've got a specific food source—let's say January in Kansas. Let's say there's one corn field and it was harvested but there's always waste grain in there. There's no other corn fields in that area. You can predict that they're coming back. Where feeders are legal in some states—and they are in Kansas, Texas, Oklahoma—the turkeys become very, very predictable. So there are predictable roosting areas and predictable feeding areas. In the spring I watch the patterns of turkeys at times for maybe several days in a row; they've got a routine in where they're going to fly down, where they're going to meet hens. I call these places meeting

areas. Maybe up in the day I've learned that a particular turkey likes to go and strut on an open ridge and you'll find him there between 11 and 2 and I can just about predict that he's going to be there. I did that in Nebraska a couple years ago with a gobbler. I knew where and when he was showing up. He paid the price!

The strangest place you've ever killed a gobbler?
KECK: I would have to say that killing a turkey in a junkyard was probably the strangest place. In fact I've killed them in junkyards and in trash dumps on several occasions because—believe it or not—they just happen to be in the middle of good turkey country. One day I was hunting over in

Georgia with outdoor writer Aaron Pass. It's afternoon and he had told me about hearing some gobbling down in Butcher's Hollow. I looked the place over and I'm thinking, *This place is so grown up around here, the only place that's halfway open here is this trash dump.* So I hit the call before I even set up and a dat-gum turkey gobbled down in the bottom of that hollow. So I leaned back up against an old refrigerator and, sure enough, he was answering every call I threw at him. Eventually, before I could see him because the hill sort of broke down over, I heard him dragging his wings through tin cans and rolling bottles—the strangest sound I had ever experienced hearing a turkey coming into the call.

A bit different than rustling leaves.
KECK: Absolutely. [laughing] I've been in a junkyard in the middle of a bunch of old trucks and cars and watched a turkey jump up on top of the hood of this old fire truck. He jumped up there and was looking for me. I had shut up after he had started my way. He got up there and I clucked to him and watched him glide down off the hood of that truck and come right on it. That was in south Alabama, and I was hunting with my good friend Earl Groves.

Have you ever purposefully passed up a bird you could easily have killed?
KECK: Many, many times—while we were filming turkeys that would occur. In fact, people would say, "Man, I'd like to do a TV show with you." I'd say: "Look, let me tell you something. You have *got* to make sure that you don't *have* to kill a turkey. Because if you really have to kill a turkey, you're going to be really mad at me when the camera man doesn't ever give you the signal that you can shoot." Many times I was in that situation where I had a giant strutter come in and the gobbler really put on a show. I mean the light was pretty, everything about it was perfect, but the angle the camera man had wasn't right. Maybe there was some kind of an obstruction that wouldn't allow him to get the kind of footage that he wanted. I purposely

let him go and watched the turkey just drift off. I could've killed him a bunch of times. That happened numerous, numerous, numerous times. There were other times when I was looking at a gobbler that was maybe hung up and I had some subordinates come into me—legal turkeys, long-bearded turkeys. But I passed these up because I wanted the dominant bird that was out there with a hen. He wouldn't come. So in my waiting to try to kill him I ended the day having not squeezed the trigger.

Which turkeys give you the most satisfaction?
KECK: There's no question in my mind that at the end of the day the hardest turkeys give me the greatest satisfaction. To me, if you take an eastern and you put him in one of those difficult situations I talked about—like in flooded backwater or being henned up—that forces you to employ a number of different positions to move on that turkey. Or the number of times you've had to switch up calls. Those are the memorable hunts. Probably one that really sticks in my mind was one day that my daughter Heather and I hunted. There were actually four gobblers together, four good long-beards, and we worked them right from the roost. They flew down and started our way. I heard a hen call in the distance. They just veered off and went directly to the hen. We stayed on those turkeys and the amazing thing was those turkeys gobbled throughout the entire period of time that we chased them. We started at about 5:30 that morning. After a long, long chase of setting up and calling and setting up and calling, at noontime we came close to where I had the truck parked. I said to Heather: "I've got some crackers and some water in the truck. Let's get a bite to eat and let's just keep going. We can take the water with us." We'd set up and every time we'd set up another hen would cut us off and the turkeys would go in a different direction. And these were four gobbling fools. It was now 3 o'clock in the afternoon. We crawled to the edge of a two-acre field that was sparsely grown up in broomstraw. There they were—they were in the far corner.

When I hit the call they gobbled to us. And dang if I didn't hear another hen! She was up this logging road and they went straight to her. I said to Heather: "Okay. I'm going to put out the Montana strutter decoy. I've got a hunch they will come back to this field when they finish with that hen." So we patiently waited with the thought that when these guys come back and see that strutting decoy, they're going to come to fight. I kept looking down that logging road that came into that field and I said, "We're just going to give it some time." I heard them gobble and they milled around where that hen was and then I challenged them and gobbled with a tube. I switched up tactics altogether. I started challenge purring on the slate and, boy, did that light them up. They were double and triple gobbling and then I could see them way down the road—I could see those fans. I said: "Heather they're coming. We're going to even the score up *big time*. There's probably going to be a chance you can kill two with one shot and I want you to try to do that." As they were coming down that road they finally picked up on that Montana and, as suspected, I watched their heads' color change and they were in that very aggressive trot. They were now coming full speed. Heather was sitting shoulder to shoulder with me and I said: "All right. When those two on the left get their heads together and get in here just squeeze it off. You kill two and I'm going to kill two. They came in there and I just cut real loud. They stopped and ran their heads up. I said, "Kill him, Heather." *Pow!* She killed two with one shot. At the report of her gun, I smoked one of the two remaining birds, and as the other one was running off I hit my mouth call and started challenge purring. He stopped and started back. That was his fatal mistake.

All four?

KECK: We killed all four—something I'd very rarely ever do, but in this case there we had lots of gobblers from several good hatches in a row, it was the only day that season that I could hunt with Heather as well as hunt in South Carolina, and the bag limit was two a day and five a season, so we went for it.

What a story.

KECK: It was 3:15 in the afternoon. We just sat there. I mean we were literally just *wore out from almost 10 hours of chasing those birds.* But you talk about a level of satisfaction. Most people would have given up a long time before that. And to share with my daughter added another level of satisfaction. Heather's killed her Royal Slam with me. She's been to Mexico a couple times with me. But that hunt right there is one that we remember maybe most of all. We talk about it often. Those birds all had spurs of inch and a quarter to an inch and a half. All of them had $10^{1}/_{2}$- to 12-inch beards. These were old turkeys. And it was just so, so special. I don't know of any other hunt where I would have experienced that level of satisfaction.

How about crazy experiences, oddball circumstances that to this day leave you shaking your head?

KECK: I still lived in Pennsylvania at the time. It was probably 1974 or '75. Dad and I were up in Lycoming County, the next valley over from our camp, in Rock Run, and we got this turkey gobbling really, really well. He'd come so far and then it was like *what happened to it?* I waited and waited and waited to call. I'd get it fired up again and then it would just quit. Well, eventually I got him close enough—this is over a two-and-a-half-hour period—and I realized that he was catching green inch worms. I told Dad, "Look at that crazy turkey." I hit the call and he'd gobble and strut and then he'd be looking around and then he'd reach up and catch inch worms that were dropping down out of the trees. As long as I kept calling he kept coming. When I quit calling he was back to catching inch worms. It was comical. It was certainly different than anything I'd ever seen up until that point. It just added another element to marvels of the great outdoors. You would think, with it being spring time that sex is the only thing on that gobbler's mind, but it's not! No, by golly, some want to eat, too! [laughing]

From your experience, Rob, what are some of the more important considerations for a hunter seeking his or her own Super Slam?

KECK: The time factor is huge. I think you've got to decide in what kind of a timeframe you want to accomplish this. I've seen guys go after Grand Slams and slam dunks and everything else and they think they have to do it all within a certain parcel of time. And I'll be honest with you—I don't think they enjoy it nearly as much as if they spread it out. Enjoy it! So time, to me, is probably the No. 1 consideration. Decide what kind of a timeframe you want to do it in and still enjoy it. Secondly, you have to set a budget for yourself. Are

to develop some good, reliable contacts. I'd start with every game and fish department turkey biologist or chief of wildlife or possibly law enforcement. I've never found any that weren't more than happy to cooperate and help when you tell them what you're trying to achieve. Some of them will actually go out of their way and maybe even take you to the spot where you have the best chance.

What about a young hunter, a teenage boy or girl who's just getting into that turkey hunting—what advice do you have for that kid?

KECK: I love taking kids, teenagers or anyone that wants to learn about turkey hunting. I tell every-

> I told Dad, "Look at that crazy turkey."
> I hit the call and he'd gobble and strut and then he'd be looking around and then he'd reach up and catch inch worms that were dropping down out of the trees.

you going to drive to all these locations or are you going to fly and get a rental car? Maybe you fly to some and maybe have a friend pick you up. There's a lot of public land out there; I killed a lot of my turkeys on public lands. You really have to put together a plan that gets the most bang out of your buck, the most bang out of the trip. Try to take in several states in a short distance of travel. You know, for example, if you go to Rapid City, South Dakota, you could hit Nebraska, Wyoming, Montana, and the Standing Rock Sioux Reservation in North Dakota—all within a three-hour drive. Multiple-bird opportunities. You can hunt the prairie. You can hunt the mountains. Careful planning is a must and the old adage: prior planning prevents poor performance really applies here. So there's the time factor—and setting a budget. Making a game plan that makes a whole lot of sense is something to strongly consider. Then I would get on the phone, online, and any other resource in the chosen states and really try

body to dream big. Dream beyond your wildest dreams! Develop that passion that will commit you to follow through with that dream and say: "I want to do it. I want to do it *well* and here's what I'm going to do to get there." A lot of people just don't take time to plan. They don't take time to figure out: what's it going to take for me to do this?

Your top five or six turkey states?

KECK: Well, certainly South Carolina. As Dorothy said in the *Wizard of Oz*, there's no place like home. You know, hunting in a place where you've got family close by, having a place where you have intimate knowledge of the land that you're hunting, to me is extremely special.

Alabama is very special because my first two spring gobblers were taken there, and I love the challenge of those birds, not to mention it is the cradle of spring turkey hunting. This is also the state where I won the World Turkey Calling Championship. Another favorite is Kansas. I like

Keck's trophy room. Although Rob is known nationally as a turkey man, he is a longtime successful whitetail hunter.

heading there in the spring—but the late December and January hunt for the huge wintertime flocks may be my overall favorite. For the past 30 years, being part of the Kansas One-Shot Turkey Hunt has created many wonderful memories and friends. In Kansas, you see lots of turkeys and you hear lots of turkeys. And then places along the Rocky Mountain plateau: New Mexico, then up into the Black Hills of Wyoming and South Dakota with the Ponderosa pines where I can see a turkey coming a long, long way as they come to the call. California's Tejon Ranch where I hunted amongst oak trees that were so big it took three guys to get our arms around the trunks. Six hundred and 700-year-old oak trees. I remember filming a show with Kim Rhode—the only American Olympian to medal in six different Summer Olympic Games, in double-trap and skeet—watching

these birds come from a long, long distance underneath this canopy of oaks and beautiful flowers in a place that's only an hour out of Los Angeles. And my home state of Pennsylvania, where I grew up, to go back to a place where there were no turkeys when I was a kid, after having then been instrumental in restoring birds into that country where they were gone for over 100 years; to shoot a gobbler above the ball diamond where I played Midget Baseball, where there were no turkeys at that time, to come back and take a turkey there and have a farmer show me pictures of flocks of 150 to 200 birds. It's hard to pick out favorites but there's usually little things about a particular state that may make it a favorite over another. To me it depends on what day you ask me. There's days I like to be amongst the Spanish moss in the low country. But there's days I like to be at snow

line as the turkeys follow the snow melt high in the Rockies.

You have had so many rich experiences. Is it more satisfying for you to hunt a familiar piece of land or to learn a new place?

KECK: I always like adventure. I love going into a new place because the challenge is trying to figure it out. Yet there's certainly a comfort level you have when you hunt a place that you know well—I love doing that. It's always special to come back home, because there are always changes from year to year. Turkeys aren't always in the very same spot you found them in the year before. But when you're going to a place you've never been before, you're starting from ground zero. You got to figure out what's going on here. Where are the turkeys? Where do they roost? Where do they like to hang out? Where are they going to get water? Where do they like to strut when they don't have hens? So that newness, that excitement of not knowing, has to me always been a very important part of the challenge.

How many days do you hunt?

KECK: In the spring I approach 90 days. But I also hunt in the fall and winter. Over the course of a year, maybe 100 days.

You obviously hunt more than wild turkeys. We're sitting here in your den surrounded by mounts of deer, elk, wild boar, caribou—even a musk ox.

KECK: I'm a passionate whitetail hunter. I love big whitetails and I love calling them. Unfortunately they're not very vocal, like a turkey. If they vocalized like an elk or they vocalized like a gobbler it would be off the friggin' charts! Many times they just come. You've got sneakers and you've got chargers. If there's anything that compares to hunting spring gobblers it's hunting bugling elk in the fall. A lot of the tactics are exactly the same, just the noise that comes out of your call is different. You get a 900-pound bull heaving his sides and slobbering, looking right at you from 15 yards

away, and you've got a bow in your hand, that is a rush as well. Unlike quartering and packing out an elk, you can carry that gobbler out over your shoulder and then go hunt another one, if you live in South Carolina. Sheep hunting is very special to me as well and the thrill of a big bull moose stepping out in front of you is off the charts!

Pre-season scouting. What should a smart hunter do?

KECK: First of all understand when flock breakup occurs, winter range does not necessarily equate to spring range. Research that we did at the N.W.T.F. on eastern gobblers found that some of them—not all of them but some of those gobblers—traveled anywhere from five to 25 miles from where you saw them all winter to where they ended up in the spring. So that means if you pre-season scout really, really early, you're probably only going to get to know the lay of the land, because the turkeys could be miles from there when the season actually opens. So my advice is: You can scout early but the scouting that gives you the most information is the scouting that takes place just days before the season opens. And make sure that you're not only looking but you're also listening. I think to become a good listener you need to be a good hearer. Try to determine how many different birds you're listening to. Early in the season you'll hear more birds gobble than you hear at the end of the season. You may hear more gobbling from a particular bird but nonetheless it would give you some idea if the gobblers are there when your season opens or right before you're about to hunt. So it's important to know the place but also the birds.

Do you prefer to sit and wait or run and gun?

KECK: Let me say this. Back when I first came to South Carolina and turkey populations were still exploding, running and gunning was probably one of the most productive ways to hunt. And I love to hunt that way. When turkeys don't gobble but you know you're in the middle of good numbers of turkeys, putting the time in on your butt in a good place is critical to your success. So it really depends on the situation. If I'm in a state where that population is still sort of on the rise yet, and there's lots and lots of turkeys, I'm going to run and gun. But if I'm in a situation where maybe numbers are down, maybe they're not gobbling real well, I don't want to chance bumping those gobblers that are there by moving too much. You'll find that you're going to run a lot of turkeys off. You're going to maybe subdue some of the gobbling activity. So find you a place where you've seen activity, a lot of scratching or if it's a food plot or on some ridge where you know they like to strut. Go in there and sit. That element of patience I come back to is absolutely critical to your long-term success in turkey hunting.

Let's talk about how you prepare for a typical hunt. What are key elements?

KECK: First of all I want to know that my gun is *on*. I'm taking a shotgun that typically was built to wing-shoot by pointing and swinging through the target and now going to aim it like a rifle. I want to understand point-of-aim and point-of-impact on the target. I'm going to go pattern it. I'm going to know the effective range of that gun at different distances. I'm going to know that pattern. Because regardless of how good the place is, how good your calling is, when the moment of truth comes and you're trying to connect and kill the turkey, if that part isn't refined and understood, you'll be a very disappointed hunter. You know, I've seen that happen too many times with turkey hunters new and old who haven't taken the time to regularly do it every year before the season—even during the season—to make sure they understand the point-of-aim and point-of-impact. Then I go through my vest. I go through my calls. I want to make sure that everything in there is what I need. Not only calls, but tools that help me in the woods. I want to make sure things work. Like my ratchet cutter—I use the heck out of that thing and if it was weak or the blade was getting dull last season, I'm going to sharpen or replace it. I'm going through there to make sure my locator calls

are all in good shape, that I've got good rubber in my gobbling tube. And make sure that I've got fresh bags in there. You know, a lot of times when you make a head shot on a turkey and you've got a long way out of the woods and back to your truck or camp, where's the blood of that turkey's head going to go? On the back of your thighs. So I make sure I've got a plastic bag and a zip tie that I can put around the head and neck. I'm going through my vest making sure all those parts are there. One piece of equipment I've forgotten so many times is my binoculars. I've learned to just leave them in the back of my vest. A lot of guys might ask what I need with binoculars. Let me tell you, I couldn't hunt without them. So many times you come up over a rise and you see something out there. What is it—is it a hen, a gobbler or is it a jake? It's critical to know what you're looking at because sometimes you don't have a whole lot of time to react.

In the field where are your binoculars?

KECK: I don't keep them in a pocket or the back of my vest. I've got them on a harness around my neck so I just instantly reach down and I can see what's happening out there because it may be fleeting. Maybe it caught a glimpse of you as well. What was that bird I just saw? What was that animal?

What other gear do you check?

KECK: Making sure that my footwear is in good shape is critical—if I'm using rubber boots, I want boots that aren't going to leak. Repair holes and then make sure they fit well. It's like old Wayne Kochenderfer told me: There's two things in life you've got to have that are really important. One is a good bed and the other's a good pair of boots—because you're going to spend half your life in one or the other. So I'm making sure that I've got a good pair of boots. I like high boots. RedHead 16-inch Bayou Camo side-zip snake boots are my favorite. I want a tall boot that I can absolutely put my pant legs in, for a couple reasons. One is support. You look at all the pictures of old-timey hunters. What kind of boots are they

wearing? They're wearing L. L. Bean-type boots that came up to right below the knees. There must have been a reason for that. One of my reasons is because when I'm in tick country—and there are a lot of places today where that's a problem—I stuff my pants down in there and I rarely have a problem with ticks. Another thing I check is my Chapman chair. It's a little lightweight aluminum seat that I carry at my side that gives me elevation and keeps me up off the ground, but also is on an angle that props my knee up, so that I can rotate my gun off my knee. I'm going to make sure that those legs are all intact and my seat is good. Those kinds of things are really, really important. I just go through to make sure that I've got the right grit Emery paper, and that I've got the right cleaning tools like for a glass call that is going to roughen

tube that has ventilated holes, it's then considered an illegal weapon. In gun laws they've passed they call it an assault weapon—which is bullcrap.

Any sighting device you prefer?

KECK: Yeah, well, lots of different options out there. I'm a guy that simply likes good rifle sights. My 1187 was built in the Remington custom shop and it comes equipped with a front and a rear sight; I know exactly where to place them when I squeeze that trigger. The options are of course rifle sights, the red dot, or a low-power shotgun scope. People ask "what's the best?" I say, simply, "The one you're most comfortable with." Most importantly, know point-of-aim and point-of-impact on the target.

> I want to understand point-of-aim and point-of-impact
> on the target. I'm going to go pattern it.
> I'm going to know the effective range of that gun
> at different distances. I'm going to know that pattern.

that surface and the right kind of scrub pad to use on my slate, and that I've got adequate brown railroad chalk to chalk up my box call. Inspecting it all is part of getting ready for any hunt.

Favorite shotgun?

KECK: Twenty gauge 1187 with a thumb-hole stock.

Barrel and choke?

KECK: Twenty-four inches extra-full—I'm not sure what the choke constriction is. I'm actually using a factory choke in it although I've got an Indian Creek tube that does very well in that gun, too. That's the pistol grip 20 gauge Benelli there [pointing to gun] which I love. The only reason it's here is that Heather was using it. She likes it. But in the State of New York if you've got a thumb-hole stock or pistol grip, plus have a choke

What load do you normally shoot—or is there a normal?

KECK: I typically shoot 1.25 ounce of tungsten alloy No. 7s. There is no normal. I've taken birds with a light load .410 as well as quail loads, but at short distances. I think each hunter has to determine what the range is that he wants to shoot his turkey. That will help determine the load. Now that doesn't mean you're always going to get him to that spot, but you've got to know what's going to perform best at your average distance you choose. The average distance that I'm shooting a turkey is 22 to 24 steps. I want to make sure that the pattern is tight but I also want to make sure that it's going to open up enough to allow any kind of small human error. My choice is tungsten alloy 7s, because it's like a swarm of bees hitting the head and neck of that gobbler. I also know that

those tungsten alloy 7s are the same weight as a lead 5 so they maintain the same down-range energy as that lead 5, which means my range is good out to 40 yards and beyond.

What do you mean by error?
KECK: More times than not when people miss turkeys they shoot over the bird. When that happens it is almost always because they're not burying their cheek into the stock. And when they don't, they shoot over the top. They think they're looking through those sights properly but they're not.

What about shot size?
KECK: I like the most shot that's going to go the longest distance out there. My preference is tungsten

didn't hear me, and crippled the turkey. As soon as I saw that the turkey was hit but running, I just picked up my gun instinctively, pulled down, and squeezed the trigger as the turkey was going away. He said, "Oh, my God, how far away was that turkey?" I said, "Well, let's step it off." Seventy-three steps and I didn't catch him with just one pellet, I had several number 7s in the back of his head. Many people think a 20-gauge is less effective than a 12. I have never felt under-gunned *at all*. It's just the number of pellets you've got in there—certainly less than you have in a 12. I did a show with Federal Premium Ammunition called *The Federal Experience.* The host of the show, Tim Abell was shooting a 12-gauge Benelli and I was shooting my 20-gauge Benelli. I shot Federal

> More times than not when people miss turkeys they shoot over the bird. When that happens it is almost always because they're not burying their cheek into the stock. They think they're looking through those sights properly but they're not.

alloy No. 7 Federal Heavyweight or No. 7 Hevi-Shot 13s. A tungsten alloy 7 is the same weight as a lead No. 5—if I use a 5 I'm going to have less pellets than I do if I use a 7. If they're the same weight I'm going to take more pellets but have the same down-range energy. With my turkey guns, I feel very, very comfortable shooting out to 50 yards. I've killed some way beyond that. The reason is that often I play cleanup when I'm guiding people. I'll never forget one day I was calling for John Barton. We were down in Louisiana in the Atchafalaya River basin. At high noon we had five strutters coming to our set-up—something you don't often see with easterns. All five were strutting. It was spectacular. I told him not to shoot when the turkey was in strut. That is a no-no. "Wait until he's got that head up," I said, "neck stretched out to give you a bigger target area." Well, he didn't listen through the excitement of the moment or just

heavyweight 7s. He was shooting 6s. At a 40-yard target with a three-inch circle, I beat him three times, putting more pellets in each of those circles. He was in disbelief. I've converted a lot of guys from 12-gauge to 20, even 10-gauge to 20.

How about your use of decoys?
KECK: I grew up hunting in the '60s and '70s when nobody even *talked* about decoys. In Alabama, where I killed my first spring gobbler, decoys were not even legal—and I'm not talking about *live* decoys, which were not legal anywhere, just plain old decoys. The first 100 turkeys I killed, I never used a decoy 'cause I never knew anybody that used one. There were none on the market that I knew of. As decoys arrived on the scene and became more and more popular, more experimentation came about in their use. As time progressed, decoys became more and more lifelike. I'll never

forget the time in April when I was in Kansas, 27 years ago, when an old trapper by the name of Sonny Johnston invited me to join him and my good friend and N.W.T.F. president Glenn Harrelson one afternoon to hunt. Sonny said, "I want to show you this home-made decoy and how it works." He took the dried tail fan of a gobbler and fastened a small rectangle of wood to the base of the tail and glued an inverted hollow brass shaft to the wood at the base of that tail. He had an iron rod that he put into the ground and slid that tube down over top of it. The slightest breeze would let that fan move. It did the trick and two dead gobblers later that afternoon convinced me that fan could be deadly on toms.

Nice.

KECK: That's the first time I'd ever seen or heard about anybody using a tail fan. Well, I picked up on it and what I did I simply took an empty .300 Win Mag [Winchester magnum shell casing] and epoxied it to the base of the tail. I took an arrow, cut about a third of it off, left the threaded end on the arrow and added a field point to stick into the ground, then slid the shaft and fan down over the arrow. Same results as Sonny's decoy. Today you see lots of people using fans and in a variety of ways. It's one of my aces in the hole that I still use, especially on henned-up gobblers. One of my favorite decoys that does the very same thing is my Montana Strutter; I carry two of them in the back of my vest all the time. It gives me the silhouette of a tail and also adds the head [pulls it out of vest] and it's one that you use to challenge a turkey with. I've also taken and modified decoys. For example, when I'm out West and hunting Merriam's—although I don't think it makes any difference—I took and painted white the tail coverlets of the decoy, making it a Merriam's. Maybe I'm in Rio Grande country and then I'll just flip back over to this. [Turns over tail to differently painted, banded pattern.] And so I always, always have decoys in my vest, but I don't always use them. In fact, this past season, I probably used them less than any time in the last five years. Part

of it was the kind of response I was getting. Sometimes I use a hen decoy alone. Sometimes I use it in conjunction with a jake decoy. And sometimes in conjunction with the Montana Strutter. But there are just certain reactions at certain times that help me decide whether I'm going to use one or not.

Any special tips?

KECK: I do not use any decoys with upright heads. Upright to a turkey means she's alert. She's looking at something that she could be concerned about. For some of the subordinate gobblers that come into the call and they see an upright head, some guys wonder why they turn around and go the other way. It's because there's an element of fear. Do I use decoys? Yes, all different combinations at different times, but many times not at all.

When you do use decoys, what about setting them out as well as distance?

KECK: If I'm using a bow I probably want to set those decoys at 15 yards. I want them really tight. If I'm using a shotgun, most times at 20 yards for the simple reason that some of these subordinate gobblers when they're coming in, often they won't quite close the deal. They come just so far. So if I've got the decoy closer to me, then I've got a better chance—or the person I'm guiding has a better chance—of killing that turkey. If I do it at 15 my pattern doesn't open up as much so I want it out there a little bit further. But, you know, so far as your setup, one thing you'll find if you use just a hen decoy many times it will take *forever* for that gobbler to come once he's put his eyes on that sweet thing. He will strut and strut and some of them might take 45 minutes to come 100 yards. He's putting on the show because typically in nature the hen goes to the tom—not the tom to the hen. You're trying to reverse the law of nature. Now, if you want to speed things up and he's not a subordinate and he's willing to fight, then I'll throw that jake in there. When he comes he's going to come running. He's going to be on the trot. He's going to be in an aggressive posture much like you see that white one right there

May, 2004—Bull Mountains of Montana: This naturally white wild bird was the most nervous gobbler Keck had ever hunted. He and Tim Abell, host of the television show *The Federal Experience*, spied the unique turkey just before noon and tagged it just before fly-up time.

[points to mounted white turkey] and he's in that aggressive posture to come fight. That's the posture he was in when he came into this decoy right here [holds up Montana] after hunting him for *eight hours*. I tried everything in the book. That's the way he came and he came there to fight. I will tell you this: if you have a hen and a jake, a hen and a strutter, 99 times out of 100 he's going to go to that jake decoy. I always advise people—say the turkey is coming in from the right. The guy's got his gun on the turkey out here to the right. You've got to move it when he comes to the decoys. That turkey is going to pick up on your movement. I tell people—once we know that turkey is coming—put your gun *on the decoy* and let him walk to it. Don't let him see any movement. Lot of mistakes are made in that last little bit, the last 15 yards…because they move the gun. So, single hen decoy? That turkey is going to strut and take his

time and probably won't gobble any. He's just going to strut and drum, strut and drum. Put a jake out and you're going to get him to run in. Many times I'll just use the fan and I use that on henned-up gobblers.

Where did you get that bird?
KECK: This white turkey was taken on film in Montana. In fact, that ghost gobbler was featured on *The Federal Experience* TV show.

How unusual is a white turkey in the wild?
KECK: Very unusual.

Is it considered an albino in a pure sense?
KECK: He was mounted with albino eyes but he did not have pink eyes. You see that one black feather down there? He is simply a mutation—but there are albinos. I friend of mine who used to work for me, and is now the Deputy Director of the Pennsylvania Game Commission, killed one in North Carolina last year that was an albino. One of the problems a bird like that has surviving in the wild is, of course, when they hatch out white, predators pick them out in a heartbeat. It's hard for them to become an adult. That really makes it rare. I think there's probably a lot more that are hatched out than what you'll ever see but they don't live. What was really cool was at one time he had nine hens with him that were all normal, colored. This gobbler was like a ghost, I mean, just like a ghost.

What's your experience with blinds?
KECK: My style of hunting generally does not require the use of a blind. But certainly they have applications. If I've got a young kid, an inexperienced hunter or a first-time hunter, a pop-up blind is a good way to introduce them because they can get away with some movement that otherwise, if they were in the open, could not get away with. Also, if you decide that your style hunting on this particular day is going to be to one of those where you're going to sit at a food plot, put decoys out there and sit and wait for turkeys to come, you

can relax. Certainly a pop-up blind can keep you dry on a wet weather day hunt. Sitting in a blind makes it more comfortable because you can sit in a chair and relax. There are others that will carry a simple ground blind with five stakes or poles that they set up in front of them. They can work their box call or slate minimizing their movement getting picked up by the bird. I would advise a blind if you feel you need it. Growing up hunting in Pennsylvania with open understory in big timber, I learned that you can sit right in front of that tree without a blind and if you remain motionless, kill turkeys. Also, if you wear 3-D camouflage, the chances of you being seen are a lot less than you would ever think. You can get away with an awful lot. The thing is to minimize those movements.

What's your approach to clothing for turkey hunting?

KECK: I usually go to my closet [walks over to large closet filled with camouflage] and start looking. Is it going to be warm or is it going to be cold? In some places heavy clothing is absolutely necessary. In the month of January in Kansas, sometimes it's brutally cold and I've got to have boots that are well-insulated. But to me the main thing is I want to make sure that I choose camouflage that isn't faded out. I've seen some guys that wear the same camouflage day in and day out. It's gone through so many washings that it has a white glow. And that does just the reverse—instead of being camouflage, you *glow*. You stick out like a sore thumb. So make sure that your camouflage is good and crisp and has contrast to it. I also want to pick out camouflage that's going to blend into the terrain or the habitat that I'm hunting. If I'm hunting in the Southeast and the trees are starting to leaf out and you know the understory is coming alive, I want a lot of green. If I'm going to hunt, let's say, again, Kansas in winter, you're going to find me in a lot of grays and browns. So I'm going to match that habitat as best I can. It's got to be camouflage clothing that is going to be able to move when I move because sometimes where you start calling that turkey while sitting against a tree,

The Montana ghost gobbler mounted by Rob's friend, Callie Morris, stands sentinel in the trophy room.

you could end up 180 degrees from where you started when the bird finally is in range. The other thing that I usually carry with me is a cool overtop three-dimensional leafy wear camouflage that is cut so that it takes off any hard edges that create an unnatural silhouette. [Pulls on shaggy-looking featherweight camo jacket.] When you put on this thing—some people refer to as leafy wear, what have you—it just breaks up any hard edges and blurs your outline. So, matching to the habitat, matching the color of the habitat, making sure that it's comfortable and roomy, and making sure that if it's cold in the morning that you can adjust as it gets hot towards afternoon.

Do you wear a mask or face paint?

KECK: It really depends. Most times I'm using a mask. I always carry several extras in the event that somebody hunting with me might have lost their

Rob Keck has a vast collection of turkey calls, many custom-made, but said he uses only a few that have the right "ring." At a young age he won the Pennsylvania State Turkey Calling Championship at the Franklin County Fair Grounds in the 1970s, quickly followed by national and world titles. He is partial to slate calls because he can do more with them.

mask—or I may lose mine. I've always got a couple of them. I like a half mask. Some guys like to come the whole way over their head, but I want to be able to pull it down quickly or pull it back up just as fast when the occasion calls for it. With face paint I don't have to ever worry about pulling it down or pulling it off. It's just whether you can stand the feeling of that grease on your face all day, which to me isn't a big deal. I want to make sure too that I've got camo gloves that are adequate not only in fit but also extend up and over my wrist, because when you put that gun up and aim, often times your sleeve slides or pulls down your forearm. This helps cover that up especially if you're wearing a watch or a shiny wrist band. The flash of that watch could give you away in a second

when you're working turkeys in close. So I make sure I've got gloves that have extensions on the back. Back before they even built gloves with wrist extensions, I had them added by my seamstress wife.

How many different calls do you carry? Notice how I didn't ask you how many you own....
KECK: I've never actually counted—but the answer is many. [Chuckling and searching through vest.] Let's start with box calls. I always carry two boxes, a long box and then I always have a short box. [Demonstrates calling with each.] You notice two different voices? Sometimes you have to keep experimenting to see what that turkey's going to respond best to. You may start with one and have to finish with another. Both are high-pitched and

both can be used as locators or finish calls. The long box is my go-to box as a consistent locator and its sound carries further than any other. I've got two pot calls. One is aluminum, the other one is double slate on glass. I carry a variety of strikers, all of them producing different sounds and pitches. Here's the aluminum call. It's much, much more higher pitched. [makes sound] Hear how it rings your ears? If a call doesn't ring my ears, it does not go with me to the turkey woods. I've got lots of beautiful calls, custom calls that don't ring my ears. They sit on the shelf. People ooh and ah over them—I'll never turkey hunt with them though. They've got to have this ring. [makes sound] I'm looking, I'm experimenting all the time with those pot calls. Here's one of my slates. It's important to keep the surface roughed up a bit so the striker bites on contact with the surface of the slate or aluminum. I've always got conditioners with me to treat the surface of each pot call. I carry Emery paper, I've got scrub pads. [demonstrating cleaning] to freshen that surface. You want to keep your fingers off of the striking surface and keep it grease free. I know which peg works best under certain situations with different calls. I like a custom peg that is heavy and dense, like rosewood or cocobolo. I also carry a carbon graphite peg. [makes sound] I may want to use this one for just tree calling when the turkeys are on a roost. [makes sound] So I've got two boxes, two pot calls, a variety of pegs. Then mouth calls, I probably carry carry a half-dozen different mouth calls with different stretches, layers, cuts and thicknesses of rubber. There's a whole pile right there. I don't carry them in my vest. I actually carry them in my pocket. Those are downstairs on my nightstand in a special call case. I carry them with me most times throughout the year. I usually have a turkey call with me. Then I look at my locator calls and see, for example, my custom crow call. That one is my go-to-all-the-time kind of a locator call. It's the kind of call that doesn't matter whether it's at daylight or whether it's up in the day, it can bring a shock gobble when I need it. Maybe I've lost track of a turkey that I was working. He hasn't

gobbled in a while. So I wonder where is he? I'm contemplating making my move. He gobbled 20 minutes ago. And so I'm going to hit that crow call. [caw-caw-caw sound of crow calling] I want the call to be high-pitched and staccato. Those sudden bursts will make him gobble—not all the time but many times. Certainly that is an important call. When I'm out West, and when you can't get him to gobble to anything else, he will generally gobble to a coyote call. [Makes sound of coyote squealing.] That sudden high-pitch tears them apart. I mean, he's going to gobble to it. Nine times out of 10. And then lots of times when I'm trying to challenge that turkey I'll challenge-purr on my slate, my mouth yelper, and then I'll gobble on my homemade pill bottle tube call. [Makes vigorous gobbling sound.] I need to put new rubber in there; it's been sitting there for a long time. That's a high-priced call made out of a Brut cologne bottle and plastic pill bottle. [chuckling] I like to keep it inside the bell of the Brut bottle so the rubber doesn't get messed up. I always carry extra rubber with me when I need to change on that tube call. Another thing too is where you hold the box. You can change the voices on all these if you hold your thumb right there [calls] or move it here to different place [calls] I get a different sound. When I have a sense of what sound I'm looking for I'll be playing this thing like a fiddle. So it's not just the call. It's how you use the call that will give you different voices in trying to make that turkey respond.

Is there any such thing as a universal turkey call?
KECK: Probably more turkeys have died coming to a box call than all the others put together. It's been around longer than any call. It's been more widely sold and it's one of the easiest to use. It's one both the beginner and an expert can use. Most hunters with some practice can locate and call a turkey with a box.

What's your favorite?
KECK: I'm partial to slate calls. I love slate calls. So many things I can do on a slate. There are

things I can do on a slate that I can't do on the box and things on a box that I can't do on a slate. But if I had to pick one, I'd probably pick a slate call to take with me. But again, I'm looking for the key on a given day that a call is going to make that turkey work. And every day is different. Just like trout fishing—what fly pattern is going to work today? If you're a bass fisherman, are they going to take a top water or plastic worms or crank-baits? What are they going to hit today? What are they going to respond to right now, and I'm going to find that "right" call—and to do that you have to carry a variety. That's what I'm constantly looking for.

How did you learn to call?
KECK: I got that Louie Stevenson box call when I was eight and my dad showed me how to run it. I listened to my granddad. They both gave me a few tips. When I went to the Harrisburg show, turkey-call makers that I'd visit took time and showed me how to work that call. And then as years progressed I watched turkey calling on television. Then I started going to turkey-calling contests and in 1974 I won the Pennsylvania State Championship. Then I won the U. S. Open Championship and then won the World Championship. All along the way I was taping different callers and listening to the turkey sounds they were making. I'd talk to various contestants and watch them run their calls. I'd take a cassette tape recorder and tape different callers and try to mimic what they were doing. But I also went out and listened to wild turkeys or recordings of them. I knew some people that had domestic turkeys and I spent endless hours listening to those domestic birds. I'd sit there and I'd call to them and they would call back. That gave me an understanding of the rhythm, the cadence, the tone, the pitch and the volume—all those kind of things that are really critical to becoming a proficient caller.

In what circumstances do you stick with one call and when do you use multiple calls?
KECK: I usually experiment and try to find a call that he is going to respond to. If he's responding,

I stick to it. I try to stick to what seems to be making him move. If I can't budge him, I'm going to be digging in that vest to find something that will, hopefully. You've got to have that level of confidence. So many people go to the turkey woods and are beaten before they start because they think they can't call very well. Well, let me tell you, there's more to killing a turkey than just calling. Positioning is absolutely key. You got to be in the right place so that turkey feels comfortable coming in. So my decision whether to use one call or multiple calls is the kind of response I get back. If I don't get what I want, I'm switching off. I may end up using a half-dozen different calls. Sometimes you never do find the right combination.

What sound brings more birds to your gun: clucking, yelping, lost-hen or gobbling?
KECK: To me, yelping is probably the one that brings more birds to the gun than any other call. It's the call that most people can make when they pick up a box call. It's a two-note call, two-note sound. It's "kee" "owk." [makes sound] That's a yelp. It's something everybody can make. Clucks are a little bit harder for some people. [sound] It's not hard for me. I love to cluck on the slate. [makes sound] I cluck a lot but I'm really very proficient yelping with my mouth calls, getting really raspy high pitch and doing a variety of sounds by shifting the call around my mouth. I guess that's always been my strong call. It was my favorite call in competition calling and was *the* call that made the difference in winning the World Championship. When they'd ask for caller's favorite at the competitions I think I could yelp as good or most times better than anybody at that time in my career.

Is it true that you were the first one to use a turkey call in the White House?
KECK: Yeah. [laughing] I haven't seen any reporting that would dispute that! Of the visits I made while President George W. Bush was in office, I presented him with over a half-dozen different box calls. I'll never forget, while attending a White

House holiday party, Karl Rove said to me that I had created a real problem in the White House. He said the president kept one of those box calls on his desk in the Oval Office: "Every time he wants a senior staffer, he calls on it—one yelp for Dick Cheney, two for Condeleeza Rice, three for me," he said. "I want one of those calls so that I can answer him!" I think I was also the first one to use a turkey call in the Supreme Court.

That's even better—in session? [laughing]
KECK: No, actually it was in the chambers with Justice Scalia. Two times he was our guest keynote speaker at the National Turkey Federation Convention and on one occasion when I was in Washington I went by to visit with him and I presented him with a decorative turkey call. You know he

you were allowed to hunt only mornings. Today there are still, I think, 10.

And, irrespective of geography, if you had a choice to hunt any time of day?
KECK: If I were hunting early season I'd pick afternoons. I look back over the years we were filming turkey hunting and we had more afternoon kills on film than we had morning kills, which should tell you something. And it's simply because the gobblers were henned up early and when those hens go to nest and lay their eggs they're away from that gobbler he's more susceptible to come to the call.

Let's talk strategy. In hunting a roosted turkey at daylight what is your typical approach?

> I cluck a lot but I'm really very proficient yelping with my mouth calls, getting really raspy high pitch and doing a variety of sounds by shifting the call around my mouth. I guess that's always been my strong call.

was an avid hunter—in fact he died on a Texas quail hunt.

Of the 49 states—and, again, I realize in your case you reached the Super Slam over a great many years—do you remember approximately what proportion of birds you took in the morning as opposed to later in the day?
KECK: I know many of the birds that I took in the South were afternoon turkeys; I can't begin to tell you how many.

Significant enough that you remember.
KECK: Yeah. And because most of the times, you know, I was there early in the season. They were henned up and it took me all afternoon to finally get in position so I could actually kill one. Back when I started there were probably 15 states where

KECK: The first thing I want to say, roosted is not roasted. Many times you get a turkey on the roost and he gobbles his brains out. He flies down he goes the other way. When I've got one located the night before and I know where he is, I like to get as close to him as I possibly can with the thought that there's probably some hens close by and I know how they will cut me off if he doesn't get to me first when he flies down. So I'm going to get fairly close and when I say fairly close I'm talking about inside 100 yards—a lot of it depends on the terrain where he's roosted, the vegetation, because when they've got that high point where they're roosted they can see a lot of things happening underneath. When you're hunting early season and there's no leaves on the trees, boy, you get picked out very, very easily. Later in the season when the trees have leafed out you can get a lot closer and

get away with things you couldn't early in the season. Then I always try to pick a spot with my back right against a tree.

Where's your shotgun?

KECK: I've got my gun always up on my knee. A lot of people don't understand what "being ready" really means. This is so key because when he flies down you're not going to have a lot of chance to get in the shooting position without him picking you up—unless and you've got that gun, if not shouldered, at least pointed in the direction you think he's going to be. I see a lot of guys, they think they're ready and they're sitting there with their gun across their lap. Try it sometime. How

sparing on calling. When he hits the ground, though, I'm gonna pour it on. [rapid calling sounds] That's when my strategy goes to a lot of calling. He's just going to choke himself gobbling until he gets to within range and make that hunt short.

Do you differ your strategy or your tactics for the rest of the day after the gobbler flies down?

KECK: Yeah, let's just say he flew down and the hens cut me off or he flew out to some hens he heard off in the distance and he just ignores you. Then you gotta say: "What's my next move? What's my next step?" Obviously, when you reposition yourself you want to go undetected. Sometimes you have to go way out of your way because of the

> Forget the strategy of calling like a hen;
> he's already got hens. He's not going to leave those hens
> to come to another hen. But if he thinks somebody is
> encroaching on his harem, he will come to fight.

long does it take you to go from here to here to here? I'm talking about going from here to there. [Makes compact motion.] You never know when he's going to pitch down. When he glides down, I mean, it happens very, very quickly and you got to respond quickly. That's why I'm generally using my mouth yelper to tree-call to him, so I've got both hands on the gun.

How much do you call?

KECK: You can't call a lot. The more you call to a bird roosted in a tree, the more apt he is to sit there until he can see the hen that's doing the calling. I've seen what I call "Mexican standoffs"— that's what I refer to it as—and the hunter just wears his call out and the turkey's gobbling but he's wondering: *Where are you? I'm looking for you. I want to see and I'll fly to you.* And so I just want to give him enough that he's heard the hen, hasn't seen her but he thinks she is there. So I'm very

terrain. Maybe it's open understory. Maybe it's an open field. And you gotta loop around it to get where you think you're going to get ahead of him. Knowing where he is and where he wants to go many times is a big key. You're going to rely a lot on how you think he's going to travel. Maybe there's a grain field where those turkeys are going to. You may not get close to him to start but if you know where he wants to end up—I've done this a lot of times with turkeys that I couldn't get in on at all at the roost because there were so many hens roosted right there close to him. But I knew they wanted to go to this particular field. I may have been 300 yards away from them when I set up and he's still on the roost. But I know that the birds are eventually going to get there and so that's what I'll do—I'll wait. I may not do a whole lot of calling because one of the things those hens don't like is competition. When you start calling many times they'll end up taking him away. So I may not say a

thing at all. I may not call at all until they're almost on top of me.

What conditions do you find most challenging?
KECK: If you can't hear him he's tough to hunt. High wind is probably the condition I hate most, when the winds are howling 25, 35 miles an hour. I'll never forget a hunt with Kansas Governor Kathleen Sebelius (she went on to work under President Obama as Secretary of Health and Human Services). It was after the Governor's One-Shot Turkey Hunt at the end of the season on the Flint Hills National Wildlife Refuge. We were hunting public land and the place had been heavily hunted, and we had just one day to capture her hunt on film for our television show. We got in there early in the morning and did not hear a thing—not to mention the wind was already blowing probably 20. We tried a number of locations where the refuge manager had taken us and at midday broke for lunch. Our bad luck continued when the governor got a call from Topeka on a major issue that surfaced. As a result, she said, "Look, I can only stay till 4 o'clock—there's an issue come up at the state house and I have to leave early." So here we were at 2 o'clock and I had two hours to get it done. I'm thinking, *Oh, man, what am I going to do?* I asked the refuge manager where he had been seeing turkeys late in the day. He said they had been showing up over in this one particular area. I said, "Let's go." We went there and set up and I was hitting *loud* calls, I mean, I just yanked the volume up as high as I could to try to cut through the wind which had picked up even more. I couldn't hear anything in response. Just wind blowing. Now it was about 3:30. We'd been sitting there for, gosh, almost an hour and a half and I knew she was getting a bit impatient. I was *really* impatient. I knew my time was running out. I hit that call one more time and through that wind I thought I heard a gobble; we hadn't heard one all day. All of a sudden through tall grass I saw the top of a fan coming our way, tail blowing in the wind. I said, "Governor, get your gun up on your knee." She said, "Where, where?" I said, "Just point it slightly to your left."

She got it up and about that time here he comes and the cameras were rolling—perfect. He comes in to 20 yards. I said: "Let me get him out of strut. When he sticks his head up, kill him." He sticks his head up, she shoots—and misses. But the wind in this case was actually working to our advantage. He didn't know where the noise came from and he didn't see our movement. But anyway, he just stands there. I said, "Shuck another shell in the chamber." I had to help her, so I reached up and luckily for some reason he didn't see me and, of course, when she ran that 20-gauge pump back, boy, he really ran his head up. I said, "Put the sight on his beard," so she wouldn't shoot over the bird this time. She held on him and squeezed. The big gobbler dropped. Whew, we got it done and all on film. It was really, really cool because that bird had inch-and-three-quarter spurs, had a $12\frac{1}{2}$-inch beard and weighed 25 pounds. Here I was with a female governor on public land and we got her on film with just about 10 minutes to go before her newly unplanned departure—just enough time to get pictures and some cutaways. So the wind hurt us but then it helped us. As I've often said: in turkey hunting, you can go from the outhouse to the penthouse and vice versa in a mere heartbeat.

What strategy do you find most successful with henned-up gobblers?
KECK: Taking the challenge to the gobbler. If I can get in position where he can see a tail fan or a Montana Strutter, there's a good chance I can suck him away from even a dozen hens. Forget the strategy of calling like a hen; he's already got hens. He's not going to leave those hens to come to another hen. But if he thinks somebody is encroaching on his harem, he will come to fight—not every time but a lot of times he will. And so that fan becomes a really important part of the strategy, but the call is important as well: gobbling, challenge-purring, and gobbler clucking complete the package.

Given the choice of location, when calling to a bird would you rather be above or below?
KECK: Always above. But let me say this. I've had

situations where I had no option other than to be below and killed the bird, but generally speaking it's easier to call them uphill than downhill. One thing you'll find in turkey behavior: there are rarely any constants. The words *always* and *never* don't seem to apply to this game. I've seen them hang up on a ditch with a trickle of water in it, but I've called them across a mile-wide section of the Alabama River. I've seen times when it had been much more advantageous to be above but the property line was up there. You couldn't hunt up there so I got below and the turkey pitched right into my lap. So, if I got a choice, it's going to be above—but don't let anybody tell you that you can't call them from below.

In your experience, what are the most common reasons birds hang up and how do you solve it?
KECK: Turkeys can hang up for a number of reasons. Usually it's either a geographic or a physical obstacle, sometimes a fence, a hen, a creek or a place where he was spooked on an earlier occasion. If you're in new country and you don't know what all is out there and in front of you, a woven-wire hog fence, that's maybe 70 years old, stretched out off into the distance with sections that may not even exist. But if there's an old section standing between you and him, he hits that wire and he'll go back and forth, back and forth, with a fence he normally just walks around. You're calling. He's strutting. He's excited. He's gobbling. He can't figure out how to get there. I've lost so many birds to fences, it's unbelievable. I've also had some that get to a ditch and would not cross it, only to find out if I got to the other side he came right to me. So it's those barriers that to me, more times than any, will hang up the turkey. The more intimate knowledge you have of the lay of the land, the better to your advantage. A stone wall, a road, a creek, all those kind of things can serve as a place for that turkey to hang up.

Among what must seem an infinite number of hunts, what was your most memorable?
KECK: Oh, gosh, I've got a memory that lasts about 10 minutes, so I guess I have to go to one of the more recent hunts. I've had so many memorable hunts with my dad and with my kids, with special V.I.P.s—athletes, astronauts, secretaries of state—you name it. But one memorable hunt that happened just this year was with my daughter Heather and my six-year-old grandson Hank. He was five then. Hank loves the outdoors, especially turkey hunting. I gave him a pushpin caller that he perfected last year and he's always calling. Every time a turkey is there at their house and he sees it, he's calling me on the phone: "Paw-paw! There's a gobbler here with two hens." Anyway, before daylight we got into a blind I put up close to where the farmer had told me about seeing this turkey earlier in the week. This was a particular bird we'd been after for quite some time. As daylight broke we heard a turkey gobble once at about 250 yards right below a pond dam in a big chunk of timber. We saw two hens fly down. I was calling and I told Hank to call as well. He's pushing that push-pin caller so hard I could just imagine smoke rolling out from under the striker. It wasn't long after, the gobbler flew down and went into full strut. They all were coming our way. And to watch that turkey strut and catch the early morning light and share the beauty and the anticipation of what's to come, *wow*, and here's Hank: "Paw-paw, I see him—I see him coming!" Hank kept calling and I was helping him out a little bit. The more we called the harder the turkey strutted. He was following the hens and fortunately the hens wanted to come here, too. Heather was readying herself I said, "Watch your mom." Then Hank said, "The hens are right here in front of us." The gobbler finally got in there and when he stretched his head up Hank got to watch his mother take that turkey.

Is your daughter an experienced hunter?
KECK: Heather has already killed the Royal Slam. She's killed 40-some turkeys sitting beside me. She's killed some of them on film. But now to have her son—my grandson—witness that is certainly a memory I'll never forget and one that is special to them as well. When the gobbler stopped flopping,

April 2004—Aiken County, South Carolina: Daughter Carolyn Keck and Dad with her first turkey, an afternoon double on the Cameron tract. They planned to roost some birds and hunt the following morning, Rob said, but they couldn't pass up a chance that afternoon. Carolyn looked at her father and said, "Guess I don't have to get up early tomorrow!"

Hank turned to me he said, "Paw Paw, when's it going to be my turn?"

Who is the best turkey hunter you've ever known?
KECK: I guess the word "best" is somewhat subjective. The answer depends on your definition of the word best. He could be the most knowledgeable? Maybe best caller. Maybe the guy who killed the most turkeys. You know, *best* can be described in a variety of ways. I guess one of those that had as much influence on me as anybody I ever knew—and he was as good as anybody in the turkey woods—was Wayne Kochenderfer.

You mentioned Kochie from your early Pennsylvania years.
KECK: He was from Ickesburg and Ickesburg is in

Perry County and that was back at a time when Perry County was producing a lot of champion turkey callers like Chester Lesh, the Fleishers, the Rohm brothers, Harry Boyer; Dick, Chris and Scott Smith; Ron Zendt, the Earnests, myself and others. These were men, young and old, that won junior and senior, local, state, regional, national and world championships. Terry Rohm and I each won the U. S. Open and finished No. 1 and 2 in the world. A feature story in the N.R.A.'s *American Hunter*, called Perry County the Turkey Calling Capital of the World. The area was also noted for call makers. Kochie was a great guy to bounce things off about how to call and what callers would work best, and built some calls himself. When turkey season came in he was at his camp from a week before the season to a week after it

went out. He was just gone! He had a wife and a family but he'd been that way forever. He was very, very knowledgeable and had that extra sense about how to anticipate, how to set up, when to call, how much to call, what call was going to work. He was an inspiration to a lot of folks. He was a great storyteller, always humorous—always had a great story to tell. But if there was anybody going to kill a turkey out of a group of hunters, he was going to be the one. There's probably a lot of Wayne Kochenderfers out there today, but he was one of those earlier guys that made a great impression on me personally. He helped me an awful lot.

You've been hunting wild turkeys for 50-plus years. You have witnessed—indeed, helped steer—many changes in the sport.

they would say, "All you're doing is creating more hunters that are competing for the turkeys we want to hunt." I told them, "Yeah, there's more turkey hunters, but there's a whole lot more turkeys because of the work we're doing restoring them." Those guys were secret. They didn't want to share much. It was hard prying anything out of them—what calls they were using, what sounds they were making, where they were going, what their strategies were. Today it's wide open. You can go to the Internet. You can go to YouTube and find out anything you want about this sport. People don't have to show up at seminars and calling contests if they don't want. When I started calling back in the early '70s, if you'd announce a calling contest or a turkey calling competition, you'd pack the place. Thousands of people would show up.

> I think that baby boomers, as we age, must continue to put more back in terms of time of mentoring young people into new hunters. We have a great legacy to pass on: opportunities to hunt wild turkeys in places where they were gone for over a century.

KECK: First of all, the changes we've been discussing—the innovation in equipment: whether it was in the guns and turkey ammo; whether it was in the calls; whether it was in the increased knowledge of what calls were needed. From cassettes and eight tracks back in the '70s to DVDs today. Outdoor television and its impact on teaching hunters all kinds of outdoor skills, hunting skills, calling skills. And obviously the fact that when I started there were only 30 states with turkey seasons and today every state except Alaska has a season—and beyond: the Canadian provinces, Mexican states. I think there's been a change, also, in the secretiveness that was once prevalent. When I started with the Federation back in 1978, there was this core nucleus of old-line turkey hunters that didn't want to see new turkey hunters. When I was first at the N.W.T.F.,

Today not so much. They go to other places to learn about it. You've got another generation of turkey hunters that learned from Dad or Granddad. And, you know, the whole scene has changed. There's more wild turkeys, more places to hunt, more specialized equipment—things like game cameras and Thermacells. What's that got to do with turkey hunting? Let me tell you something. I remember back in the early days in the Atchafalaya River swamp with mosquitoes in clouds so thick, it didn't matter what bug suit you had on. They'd eat you alive. Today you can get back in there and turn a Thermacell on and you can sit and hunt comfortably. Once we were filming up in New York in May with Chris Kirby, I remember swarms of blackflies literally covering the lens of the camera. Today turkey hunters don't have to worry about bugs. So there's been a lot of

innovation a lot of change, a lot of opportunity that wasn't there 50 years ago.

Where do you think the sport is headed?
KECK: I think you have to ask yourself, first of all, where is hunting headed? Firearms ownership is under attack all the time. I think that it will be affected greatly by the upcoming presidential election. Just a change of one person on the Supreme Court could change the view of the Second Amendment and impact gun ownership. . . . Let's say my turkey gun, that gun sitting right there [nods toward shotgun] with a pistol-grip stock and the choke tube with holes. It's already illegal in New York—it might become illegal all across the nation. So I think that when you look at more restrictions, and a likely decrease in the excise taxes generated from the sale of firearms and the ammunition, you're looking at a change in conservation funding, and that change in conservation funding may reduce the number of wild turkeys that we've got out there, because maybe they won't be able to be managed properly because the money is not there. But I want to think positively. I really do. I'm always thinking, *what are my grandchildren going to have to look forward to?* America has learned how to deal with challenges, huge challenges, sometimes even when the future appears muddy and when you're in the minority.

Do you think America is becoming anti-hunting?
KECK: I think the general public still is very supportive of hunting. There has been some research that supports that as well. But you've got a very vocal minority that influences a very liberal media, and how we deal with that and being proactive, showing how professional management of our wildlife is absolutely critical to the health of wildlife. There are some positive changes in attitude. With the "locavore" movement, people that were maybe once against killing a deer are now thinking, *I want my kids to eat this natural meat*—deer, turkey or what have you. And so I think that by putting on a better face to the general public, responsible hunting will continue to grow, and

that turkey hunting will continue to be very, very special. It's a great way to introduce young people and women. Spring turkey hunting comes at a wonderful time of the year, when usually temperatures aren't too severe, a time when Mother Nature is blooming. And there's a sense of thrill and an accomplishment in successfully killing a turkey. It's not easy—it's not a fish in a barrel. It gives people from all walks of life a sense of having achieved something by actually calling this critter in and then having the choice of whether to take it or not with a gun or a bow. I think that our hunting community must continue recruiting young people, women, first-timers. I think that baby boomers, as we age, must continue to put more back in terms of time of mentoring young people into new hunters. We have a great legacy to pass on: opportunities to hunt wild turkeys in places where they were gone for over a century.

Speaking of eating, what is your favorite way to cook a wild turkey?
KECK: I look back to shortly after the turn of the 20th century and referencing E. H. McElhenny, when he was writing a book about turkey hunting, and he essentially said that if you ever eat fried turkey once, you will never eat a baked or roasted one again. I agree. Deep-fried turkey breast is my absolute favorite. Kochie popularized deep-fried turkey that he referred to as "shake and bake," not to be confused with the commercial breading called Shake and Bake. Kochie's advice was to cut that breast meat down off the keel bone in two big steaks, cutting across the grain into pieces the size of an oyster. Bread them in eggs and milk and bread crumbs. Deep fry to 375° in peanut oil or whatever oil works to your satisfaction and in five to six minutes the pieces will float to the top and you break it apart with your fork. You'll have to put a lock on the refrigerator door. People are going to sneak down in the middle of the night to get the leftovers because deep-fried turkey is just as good cold as when it's hot.

4

Clyde F. Neely

HOME:
Kingwood, Texas

OCCUPATION:
Personnel management consultant for oil and gas industry

FIRST WILD TURKEY:
1978, Texas

COMPLETED U.S. SUPER SLAM:
2012, West Virginia

 WAS SITTING ON A STOOL in a strip-mall bar in Houston called the Hoot County Saloon, beside a long-haul truck driver named Mike, waiting for my Styrofoam take-out tray from Gumbo Jeaux's next door. Specialty: catfish opelousas— two blackened fillets, topped with étouffée, and five fried shrimp served with dirty rice and mixed vegetables. $10.99. A faded sign at the other end of the bar read: NOT RESPONSIBLE FOR WOMEN LEFT OVERNIGHT.

ABOVE: Clyde Neely killed this rare Gould's subspecies at Durango, Mexico in April 2006. It scored 74.5 with a 14.0625-inch beard, spurs of one inch and .9375 inch, and weighed 27 pounds. The stunning bird was the No. 1 typical Gould's killed with a firearm until 2008 when one was killed that scored 74.75. Neely's bird is still the world's No. 2 typical.

"Wild turkeys?" Mike said. "Shoot—I just left 50 of 'em in my back yard."

"Where's home?" I asked.

"Pottsville, Pennsylvania."

"I'll be up your way in a few weeks," I said. "What do you do there?"

"Not much anymore. Used to make good money—80 grand a year running a Cat, diggin' coal. Good money. H'aint no more."

"Is that your 18-wheeler out in the lot?" I asked.

"Yep. Headed south to get me a Mexican wife."

I wet my lips with another sip of beer while looking up at a mount of a spike buck's head displaying a flared mouth with the fake fangs of a rabid boar.

The man I had flown in to meet was Clyde F. Neely, 68, oil-rig engineer and lifelong hunter who holds the distinction of being the only individual who has accomplished what he calls the ultimate wild turkey "Slam of Slams": Grand Slam, Royal Slam, World Slam, Canadian Slam, Mexican and U. S. Super Slam. He lives 23 miles north of Houston among the pines and magnolias of Kingwood, Texas, a sprawling community of meticulously kept Georgian brick homes that likes to advertise itself as "the Living Forest."

Clyde grew up in a small town in south Louisiana called Eunice. Farmers there raise rice, corn, soybeans, sugar cane—and crawfish. When the rice is out the crawfish are in. His father died when he was eight so he did not have anyone to take him hunting. He learned to work at an early age, bagging groceries for 12 hours a day, and then pumping gas at a filling station.

"I'm glad my mother did that," Clyde said. "It kept me out of trouble and it gave a me a little spending money. We had a roof over our heads and I had clothes on my back. But if I wanted to spend money, I had to work."

When Clyde was 16 his mother allowed him to start hunting squirrels. He progressed to deer hunting. But Louisiana whitetails were small. Not terribly exciting. After he started his career in the oil and gas business—at first offshore on drilling rigs and then on work-over rigs servicing and fixing drilled wells—he joined a group of hunters in a lease in north Texas. He had never seen such huge whitetails! Plus they had eight miles of the Red River with flooded timber where the mallards lit in like crazy. They built deer stands, from which Clyde watched with fascination the wild turkeys that came to the corn feeders below. They were easterns that had recently been introduced.

Neely spent years throughout the 1970s and '80s shooting sporting clays, hunting pheasants and grouse in the best places. He successfully pursued deer, elk, antelope, bear and cats all over the United States and Canada. He started turkey hunting because it was something he could do in springtime. He could stay at home and keep peace during the holidays.

"When I made my first hunt, I was hooked," he said. "It's addictive. It's something you do more alone than with any other sporting endeavor. So many times you're out there by yourself with nature. And you hear and see things that you don't at any other time."

When Neely turned 60 and was closing in on his quest for the Super Slam, he accidentally fell. It had nothing to do with an oil rig. It had nothing to do with dragging a mule deer off a mountain. He was cutting down a birch tree in his yard. The ladder slipped and he fell 12 feet to the ground, crushing two discs in his back. The examining physician at the Memorial Hermann Joint Center told him he had to have surgery. It was January. Neely had drawn a rare turkey tag for the coming season—it might take him two or three years to get another.

"Doc," Clyde said, "I'm fixing to go turkey hunting."

"What?" the surgeon asked, alarmed and incredulous.

"Can I put the surgery off—will I damage anything further?"

"I don't think so, big boy, if you can stand the pain."

"Then I'm going to put it off a couple months."

"I think you're crazy, but okay."

"Can you give me something?"

The doctor prescribed 750 milligrams of hydrocodone, an extremely potent opioid pain medicine. And he told Clyde that he was sending him to get steroids injected in his spine.

The first shot did nothing. The pain was so intense, Clyde recalled, that when he tried to leave his house in the morning to drive four miles to work, he couldn't make it. He couldn't sit still long enough.

Turkey season was only weeks away. His doctor explained that he was supposed to give Clyde only three of these spinal injections during the course of a year. Neely talked the doctor into giving him three in one month—after all, he'd be hunting exactly three states. With the second shot he was feeling a little better. After the third shot of steroids

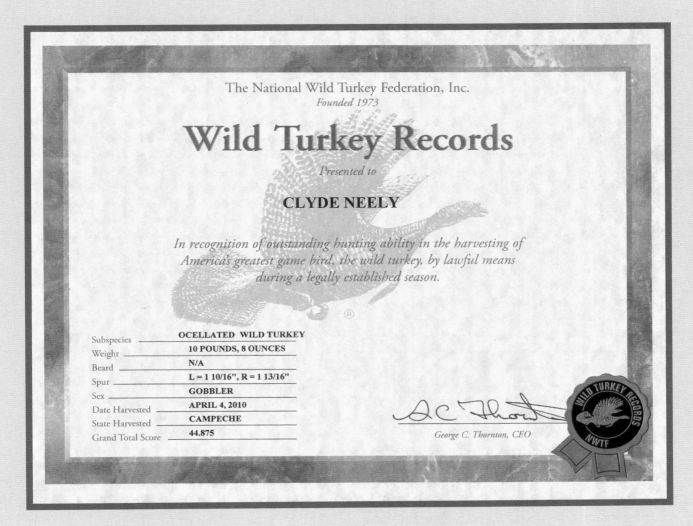

The National Wild Turkey Federation, Inc.
Founded 1973

Wild Turkey Records

Presented to

CLYDE NEELY

*In recognition of outstanding hunting ability in the harvesting of
America's greatest game bird, the wild turkey, by lawful means
during a legally established season.*

Subspecies	**OCELLATED WILD TURKEY**
Weight	**10 POUNDS, 8 OUNCES**
Beard	**N/A**
Spur	**L = 1 10/16", R = 1 13/16"**
Sex	**GOBBLER**
Date Harvested	**APRIL 4, 2010**
State Harvested	**CAMPECHE**
Grand Total Score	**44.875**

George C. Thornton, CEO

the daily pain was tolerable.

Neely flew north to hunt Delaware, Pennsylvania and Vermont. He could hunt only half a day anyway. He got up before dawn, came out of the woods at noon, got something to eat, collapsed on the motel bed and slept until the following morning. Then he got up and did it all over. He telephoned Memorial Hermann: "When can you do the surgery?"

"I can't do it Monday," the surgeon replied. "But I can on Wednesday."

"Okay," Clyde Neely said. "I'll be there."

He locked his gun, packed his camo, and headed home.

National Wild Turkey Federation recognition of the ocellated turkey Neely chased through the Mexican jungle in April 2010.

Clyde sat in his leather upholstered storytelling chair, discreetly spitting tobacco juice into a Lipton green-tea bottle. Behind him sat his U. S. Super Slam trophy. A display case was filled with turkey commemorative liquor decanters. Through a door I could see his prized mount of the Gould's world record he brought home from Mexico a decade ago.

I always enjoy listening to avid hunters and avid anglers talk about why we do what we do.
CLYDE NEELY: I've thought about this a lot. I love to be outside and I love to experience everything that nature itself provides. And I love the challenge of defeating an animal's own natural defenses and how they use them, because every animal is different.

That's interesting—you mean on its own turf?
NEELY: On its own turf, yeah, exactly. Because every animal I've ever ever hunted, has different ways of living and surviving. They all have predators. We're predators just like when we're hunting wild turkeys, and so they're always on the defensive. So for us to defeat them on their own turf, in their own world, is quite an accomplishment. I think that a turkey is unique—their eyesight, their hearing, everything about them is different than any other animal I've ever, ever hunted.

On another level?
NEELY: On any level. They are, in my opinion, the hardest animal I've ever hunted. They are the most difficult to defeat. They just have an innate ability to sense something being wrong. You can be completely camouflaged, completely still, everything and I've seen birds stop 200 yards away, and for no reason at all, turn around and go the other way. And I *know* they didn't see me. I *know* they didn't hear me. I had watched them for three days take an identical route and then, when I'm waiting with a gun, *boop*—and for no apparent reason they turn and disappear. "No, I'm not going to do that today." [laughing]

If you had to describe what it is about hunting wild turkeys that most captivates you, how would you define it?
NEELY: Every hunt is a different experience. Every bird that I've ever harvested and every hunt for that bird is a totally different experience. There's no two turkey hunts the same. Never! Never the same!

You've done many other kinds of hunting.
NEELY: I have, I have. I've killed elk, antelope, deer, I've killed bear and everything else, but turkey hunting—every turkey hunt that I've ever been on, and every turkey that I've ever harvested, they're always different.

What do you feel on a visceral level when you have that dead bird—any feelings of remorse?
NEELY: Respect. Respect for the bird. It's a truly majestic animal. You know, when I shoot that bird, a lot of times I won't get up right away. I'll just sit there for a minute or two. I don't know what runs through my mind. And then when I do walk up to that bird and I touch that bird, you know it just, it's just all. . . .

Respect is a pretty good word.
NEELY: Yeah, it's just respect, you know, respect. And I guess there is some regret too. But it's respect.

Tell me about killing your first turkey.
NEELY: Well, I have to approach that from two ways because the first bird I killed, I killed with a rifle and there was not a lot of thought to it. It was from a deer stand, with a high-powered rifle with a scope. I shot its head off. There was not a lot of

A classic eastern turkey taken in May 2011 in Pennsylvania. Neely was hunting with two excruciatingly painful crushed discs in his lower back. He postponed surgery until after turkey season. "When there's a will there's a way!" Clyde recalled that the bird came in from behind. "I had to wait for him to pass me before I could shoot him," he said.

thought to it. I killed a few like that. I saw a lot of turkeys. After watching the birds a while, I never shot another one with a rifle. I gained so much respect for the birds that I said, "I just don't want to do it this way, I don't want to just kill them."

When did you start hunting the birds properly?
NEELY: When I killed my first bird with a rifle, I was probably in my 30s and then it wasn't until I was in my 50s when I killed my first bird with a shotgun. The two experiences were—there's no comparison, I mean, utterly no comparison. I had developed respect for the bird. It's such a majestic and smart animal. After watching 'em a lot of years, I decided to start turkey hunting rather than just turkey shooting.

I guess that's where the old phrase "turkey shoot" comes from.
NEELY: I guess so. I was looking for something else to hunt in the spring. I had done much reading on turkey hunting and a lot of books on turkey biology. I purchased a lot of the old books on turkey hunting. Reading these classic books taught me how the masters had done it and how much respect they had for the birds. It just changed my whole outlook and attitude on the birds. And hell, I probably bought every DVD and CD—anything I could put my hands on about turkey hunting. If it was out there and I could find it, I bought it. I had what I called "gadget-itis." If there was something out there, I wanted to try it and I bought it.

When you did kill a turkey the way you wanted to do it—ethically, aesthetically—do you remember the bird, the particulars?

NEELY: I was so excited. There was a sense of pride, a sense of accomplishment. I was shaking.

When and where?

NEELY: It was April first and it was in east Texas. It was a jake. He was gobbling, gobbling, gobbling, coming in. And we had a little old cheap decoy out there, you know, just a little old cheap decoy sitting on the ground. Not a lot of camouflage or anything. But a dumb jake and, man, I was shaking like a leaf. While he was coming in, I mean, I thought I was gonna piss in my pants!

And here's a guy who has killed bears!

NEELY: Never, never been excited like that in my life. You know. The guide that was with me whispered to me that there's probably a big gobbler behind him. Shit, I couldn't wait. I mean, I just couldn't wait. BOOM! He said you probably should have waited because there's a big one behind him. I said "I don't care."

In all the years since, with all the wonderful experiences you've had, has that sense of excitement diminished?

NEELY: No, honestly, no. If I ever lose that excitement when I'm turkey hunting, I'll quit turkey hunting. The sense of accomplishment is still there. The excitement is still there. You get these birds that come in silent. You might catch a glimpse of them for a long, long, long way. You might just see 'em. But they're comin' in silent, never gobbling. I killed a bird like that in Louisiana on Giles Island. We knew there were birds there. I mean, that bird came from 300 or 400 yards. We'd catch a glimpse of him every once in a while. Never gobbled. That's when you're tense. That's when you're nervous. Then you just seen him stepping over a log or something. You catch parts of him moving. And that's when you're trying to stay dead-still. And, I mean, this may take place over 45 minutes. He's not in any hurry to get

One of many Rio Grande turkeys from Wheeler County in north Texas. On this April day in 2005, Neely said there were lots of vocal birds willing to come to the call.

to you—he's just trying to pinpoint where the call's coming from, you know what I'm saying? But they can't see you. They haven't picked you out yet, you know, and they're doing their best to pick you out. And as long as they don't get you picked out they're going to keep coming. So they'll walk a few steps and then stop. They'll be looking. And you're just a nervous wreck.

How long had you hunted turkeys before you killed your first bird that April?

NEELY: Actually, that was my first time, but I can tell you something else—ha! I went on a dry spell after that. Oh, crap, I probably went on 10 hunts after that before I ever killed another bird. [chuckling]

The rest of that whole season?

NEELY: No, I think I finally killed another bird at

the end of the season in another state. I remember thinking, *Well, maybe this ain't gonna be as hard as I thought it was gonna be.* And that's the way it always is. As many states and as many hunts as I made in some years, you get a year where you kill a bunch of birds in a bunch of states, you know, and you think, *If I have another year like this I'll have this thing almost wrapped up.* And then you get a year where you make it to 12 or 13 states and kill three birds. It's just so funny.

Why is that?

NEELY: Weather is a huge factor. I mean, you're planning these trips, and you're planning on driving or you're planning on flying or whatever else. You've got so many things to plan, you've got ac-

In the darkness?

NEELY: Yeah, in the darkness and we're facing this way on the pop-up blind, and when he gobbled, I mean we had to turn everything around in that pop-up blind. Got my gun out the window and he rounded the curve: BOOM! Just like that.

And it was a big bird?

NEELY: It was a *big* bird, a big gobbler. I mean it happened so fast it was just like this [snaps fingers], it was that fast.

Clyde, at any point did you have a turkey-hunting mentor?

NEELY: I had so many mentors, I can't name them all. You know, I hunted with friends and I hunted

> I learned so much along the way. It's unbelievable.
> I learned so much from so many people. And every bird you hunt,
> in my case, you learned something from every single bird.
> But to say I had one mentor? No, I had tons.

commodations to plan, flights to plan, your hotel. So many things to plan. And you can't plan the weather, you know, you just can't do it. There's so many things that can go wrong, you know what I'm saying?

Is weather always a problem?

NEELY: I killed my bird in Massachusetts in the hardest rainstorm that I have ever been in. And he was a giant bird. In fact, me and Henry, we walked in on a little old logging road right under the bird, you know, and didn't know it. It was raining so hard and we set up a little pop-up blind on the edge of a field and we started calling it, and he's gobbling.

with guides and you learn—I learned so much along the way. It's unbelievable. I learned so much from so many people. And every bird you hunt, in my case, you learned something from every single bird. But to say I had one mentor? No, I had tons. Lots and lots and lots of mentors. And a lot of the mentors were the birds I hunted. I hunted this one bird in North Carolina in the same field or off the edge of the same field for three years. Three years! Saw him every year, saw him multiple times, and never got that bird killed. Never got him killed.

Did you give him a name?

NEELY: Me and several others. [chuckling] Oh, I'm not gonna say it!

OVERLEAF: This North Carolina turkey was the first of a pair of impressive easterns Clyde Neely killed in the same area two days apart in April 2014. It scored 69.125, weighed 23.5 pounds, with spurs of 1.325 and 1.250 inches. The second bird had two beards, weighed 25 pounds, and had 1.325-inch spurs. Another bird eluded him for three years.

During that first season, when you went you killed a bird on your first hunt, but then went a long time without success, what mistakes do you remember?

NEELY: I think my biggest mistake was movement. The biggest mistake you can make in turkey hunting is movement. You know, most hunters can't sit still—they just *cannot* sit still. And the second thing that you have to learn is patience. I used to hunt a place, because I hunt spring and fall, I used to hunt a place in Texas and the guy said, "Man, I saw some birds over in this field." We went out there and it was about 3 o'clock in the afternoon. They'd come feed out in this field. Wasn't no feeder or nothing, you know. This was in the once a day. And not thinking we topped over that hill and those birds that were in there, *poof!* they were gone. Now it was about 4 o'clock in the afternoon. We had a pop-up blind in the vehicle with us, so we went ahead and grabbed that pop-up blind and sat it off in the brush close enough to where we thought if those birds came back the same place the next day, at any time, I might get a shot at them. I got in that blind at 5:30 the next morning. You know when I killed a bird? Five-thirty the next afternoon.

Are you kidding?

NEELY: I sat in that blind 12 hours. Never got out. Unzipped it to take a leak. And it got up to about

> The biggest mistake you can make in turkey hunting is movement. You know, most hunters can't sit still— they just *cannot* sit still. And the second thing that you have to learn is patience.

fall and hunting fall birds is way more difficult than spring.

How is that?

NEELY: Well, because their patterns are different. They'll come to a call but they come to a different call. There's no mating interest so you've got to hunt them. You've got to try and find out where they're feeding and where they're traveling and where they're roosting. It's more of an ambush-type hunt. But these birds were coming to this particular field and we had crept over this hill. And when we crept over that hill, there were four huge gobblers. A lot of times you'll get gobbler groups, you know, and that's an opportunity—if you're in a state where you can kill multiple gobblers—to get more than one bird. They'll feed sometimes in the morning and sometimes you don't know what time of day they're going to feed, you know what I'm saying? Maybe they'll feed 90° that day. I was down to my shorts; it was so damn hot. You have to have patience. You just you gotta. It's a mental thing, you know. Bring something to read if you feel like you're going to have a long sit. There's nothing wrong with bringing something to read and everything. I'll always bring me some water and I'll bring something to eat. I've sat there reading and, you know, you can hear or you have a sense something's there, something is coming. I like pop-up blinds: they allow you the movement that you wouldn't have if you were sitting in a chair, or you sitting in the open. That's the good thing about pop-up blinds, especially if you bring young hunters or an inexperienced hunter with you. It's the freedom it allows you. But sitting in that blind all day is just an example of having the patience.

Any other advice that you'd give a beginner based on your first season?

Another nice Texas Rio killed in April 2012 in Wheeler County—Neely's favorite place to hunt Rios. He values traditional turkey hunting methods with call and shotgun.

NEELY: Patience and movement, period.

Stay put and don't move?
NEELY: Yes, if you've identified where your birds are feeding or where they're roosting.

How do you identify where they are roosting?
NEELY: Scouting—you've gotta do the scouting before the season opens. You go out and hear them before they come off the roost, you know. Or at night, sometimes, right after dark they'll gobble a little bit. They'll be talking. That's how you do it. Or maybe somebody that's living there that's not a hunter, will tell you where birds have been roosting in trees there for years.

Have you kept track of how many wild turkeys you've killed, counting that April bird as your first one?
NEELY: I've killed probably 220 to 230 birds.

Over how many seasons?
NEELY: I mean, I'm not going back to the 1970s or anything. I don't know but probably over 12 to 13 years.

Do you recall the particular stage in your turkey hunting when you started thinking seriously

about killing a bird in all 49 states—thinking, *Yeah I can do this?*
NEELY: Probably around 2005, after I killed that bird in east Texas, I read an article in a magazine about this ranch in Durango, Mexico. And so I called 'em. I got to talking to this guy, the owner who was an attorney. And this ranch hadn't been open for turkey hunting but about a couple of years. So I was talking to the guy, a really nice gentleman, and I said "Well, do you have anybody else that's planning to go down there?" He said "Well, I've been talking to a guy from Littleton, Colorado." And I said, "Is he talking about going?" And he said, "Yeah." "Can I have his name and number?" And he said "Yeah, his name is Jerry Malloy." So I called him and I said, "I'm thinking about going but I'd like to go with somebody." And he started telling me about himself and we became great friends. Jerry was probably 10 years my senior. He was a race-car driver at one time—stock cars—and he got in an accident and he lost his leg. So he had an artificial leg. Then he lost part of his arm in a machine shop. So he had an artificial arm. He had started turkey hunting about seven years before. He would leave his house in Colorado when turkey season opened up, and stay gone for six or seven weeks, and hunt turkey somewhere in the United States in five, six, seven states. That's what he would do; he was already doing that. So Jerry and I went to Mexico together and we got to be pals and we hunted together. He killed two birds that trip and I killed two birds that trip. Every year from then on until he died, we hunted in one or two places together. We'd pick a couple of states we were going to hunt and we'd meet. In fact, I brought Jerry into the jungles of the Yucatán Peninsula, because he could hardly get around. I mean he really couldn't. Thinking about a trip, I'll tell you about a trip we made to Mississippi. Actually, Louisiana on Giles Island. We went to the jungles and the Yucatán. We went to Guatemala together and he killed two ocellated turkeys in Guatemala. But he wouldn't have gone if I wasn't going with him, you know, and that was a tough, tough hunt. The living conditions were

miserable. You rode in a little pickup truck, or in the back of a pickup, and rode for six miles on rutted road, which was the main road that the smugglers would take into Mexico. And then you drove up and you got out and there were two V-shaped deals made out of logs like this, and that was where you bathed. They'd bring you a bucket and then you walked up the hill and there were these little huts like you'd seen on the beach. The beds were made out of logs, you know, and they had an old mattress that looked like it came out of a charity hospital 40 years ago! And they had a mosquito net around the bed, and they had another log deal here that you'd put your stuff on. I mean it was

the day before and I had seen a bird come across that creek, come across that grading. But it was too far for me to shoot. Jerry had one of those little camp stools you fold up. I said: "You need to set up right here. Those birds are crossing right there." So I set him about 30 yards from where they were crossing. He sat on that little stool up— and it was only about this high [motions about a foot] off the ground—sure as hell, the bird came across and he went to shoot and the legs of the stool sunk in the sand and that son-of-a-bitch tumbled down that railroad grade backwards, shootin' BOOM! BOOM! in the air. I went scouting and I saw another bird. The next afternoon we

> The mosquito nets are so the scorpions don't fall on you when you're sleeping. And then the rug on the floor— so when you step down if you gotta take a piss, you don't step on a tarantula.

150 percent humidity and everything else. There was a little rug you'd throw on the floor. The mosquito nets are so the scorpions don't fall on you when you're sleeping. And then the rug on the floor—so when you step down if you gotta take a piss, you don't step on a tarantula. And you go in for five days. You gotta stay in for five days! It was pretty tough.

What about the Mississippi trip?
NEELY: Jerry struggled with that bum leg all the time. Jerry was with me on the trip I was telling you about when I had a bird creeping to me. Well, I had killed that bird—you could kill more than one bird—but Jerry hadn't had any success. They used to have railroads on Giles Island to haul the cypress out. I was sitting on an old railroad grade

went out and somehow Jerry and the guide locked the damn keys in the truck—the guide's truck. They couldn't get to the gun, so he couldn't go hunting. So Jerry is sitting on the bed of the truck and this gobbler walks by no more than 20 yards from him. Sittin' on the bed of a truck! So he didn't kill a bird, even though he had two opportunities.

So Jerry was your inspiration for your wild turkey adventures?
NEELY: I don't know how many states Jerry ended up with. He had 30-something states, I think, and then he developed brain cancer. The guy was so smart. He had a little pension. He developed a little machine to make the cups that golf balls fell in. He made them in his house, and he sold those cups to golf courses all over Japan, shipping them

FACING PAGE: April 2010—Yucatán, Peninsula, Mexico: Clyde killed this exotic ocellated wild turkey on the fifth and final day of a hot, humid, hard hunt in the jungle. Living conditions were primitive. "It was one of the toughest hunts I ever made," he said. OVERLEAF: Over the years Neely has methodically and meticulously recorded his birds.

"This bird was very special because, after seven years of dedication, it completed my U. S. Super Slam," Clyde said. "It is my last eastern bird. I killed this bird on the last setup right at 12 noon on the last day of my hunt, May 2, 2013."

to Japan. That's how he made his money to go hunting every year. Yes, he was my inspiration. And I dearly miss him to this day, you know. But he's the one that got me started on this U. S. Slam.

How many years did it take you to get there?
NEELY: I did it in seven years. I started April 1ˢᵗ, 2005, when I did east Texas—the first bird I registered—and I finished May 2ⁿᵈ, 2012: a little over seven years and a month.

Where did you tag your last one?
NEELY: West Virginia. When I killed that bird there was a guide way behind me. I was staying in a beautiful place on the West Virginia and Virginia line. They didn't do much hunting, you know, mostly trout fishing. Fabulous place. Golly, was it a fabulous place. Railroad depot, redone. Old general store across the street—that's where you

would eat. The country is rocky, rough, tough. Anyway, the guide was way behind me and we heard a bird and started calling to it. That bird answered and came and then I saw him. I shot and I stayed sitting. Finally he said, "Did you kill him?" I said, "Yeah," just low like that. "Where's he at?" I said, "He's right over there by those trees over the rise." That was the last one.

Sitting there, having pulled the trigger on your 49th bird, what were your emotions?
NEELY: I just said to myself, "I guess I did it." There were some points during that time when I got to about 40 birds when it seemed the quest went cold. I wasn't gaining on it at all, you know what I'm saying? And I said, "Shit, I'll never get this done." Sometimes I didn't know why I was trying to continue, other than I love to hunt. Then I'd make a little progress. And I got to where I had

about five birds to go, and then there was another period—no progress. I got to where there's that one bird left, you know, and I think I might have gone to a couple of places in West Virginia before. So I just sat there for a little while. The guide came walking up and said: "Are you sure you got him? Don't you wanna go get him?" I said, "Yeah, in a minute." I sat there for a couple of minutes and I got up and we walked and saw that I killed him stone dead.

Did you drive or fly mostly?
NEELY: I did both. When I would fly somewhere I tried to make it to at least two or three states.

scouting, you know, I'm going multiple places and everything else.

When you say access, you mean where it was tough to get permission?
NEELY: Tough to get permission and knowing where the birds are. A lot of times I hired a guide because the guide had access to the property and I'd actually do the calling and everything myself.

How many were bearded hens and how many jakes?
NEELY: Oh, they were all toms and one jake.

What drove you to get to 49?

> I like to travel and I like to hunt different places
> and meet different people—it was that more than anything.
> I had killed birds in 20-some states and then 35 and 36 states,
> and I said, "Well, why not try and get all 49?"

What's the maximum number of states you hunted in one season during your quest?
NEELY: Fourteen or so. In fact. I think one season I killed birds in 14 at least once. I made 17 hunts one spring and about 10 or 12 hunts that same fall.

How many of your 49 birds were taken during the spring and how many in the fall?
NEELY: The vast majority in the spring. Very few were in the fall.

How many did you take with a guide, and how many while hunting on your own?
NEELY: Probably about half and half.

Is there a particular reason why you chose to use a guide in certain places?
NEELY: Access. I am still working and don't have unlimited time off, so I didn't have time to do the

NEELY: I guess because I like to travel and I like to hunt different places and meet different people—it was that more than anything. I had killed birds in 20-some states and then 35 and 36 states, and I said, "Well, why not try and get all 49?"

Did you feel in any way competitive with other hunters or was it strictly a personal quest?
NEELY: It was personal. It was never about competition. The only competition I had was with myself, you know, how can I get this done?

You said there were times when you felt like quitting.
NEELY: Oh, yeah. When I got real discouraged.

What did you do to mentally stay with it? When you got to those last several birds, what did you do to push yourself?

OVERLEAF: This framed display of 49 U. S. Super Slam medals representing all the states hangs in Clyde's den.

NEELY: I love to hunt. I love to hear the birds. That was the determining factor. I figured I'm going to be huntin' somewhere so why not in one of theses states that I needed to get a bird? Bottom line is I knew there was states where I could go and where I had a lot more odds of success, you know, greater opportunities. And I had friends in some of those states where I hadn't killed a bird.

Talk about the importance of your friends.
NEELY: Oh, some of the best friends I have today are people that I've met turkey hunting. Turkey hunters in general are some of the closest-knit group you are ever going to meet. They're just good people. I've had so many good times with them. Not only in the field but after hunting and everything else. They're just a good group of people. And I still communicate with a lot of them.

away from my family. They support me.

When you were aiming to kill birds hundreds of miles away from your home, how did you figure out where to hunt?
NEELY: I made a lot of phone calls and did a lot, *a lot* of reading about where others had hunted in the past and with whom. I searched the Internet. I talked to National Wild Turkey Federation regional directors. I talked to a lot of guides and outfitters and narrowed it down to who and where I wanted to go to. But I spent *a lot* of time on the phone.

So homework. . . .
NEELY: A lot of homework. *A lot* of research—a lot, a lot of research. That's how I determined if I should go to a place. I tried to pinpoint areas by

> Some of them will come in silent.
> Some of them will sneak in. Some of them will come in direct.
> Every hunt is totally different, just so different, and that's
> because the birds themselves are different.

We have similar likes. A lot of the guys I hunted with were federal game wardens or law enforcement personnel. I mean, when you meet them in in the field, you would never imagine what they do in real life, you know? Almost like two different people. I guess we all have two different personalities. I had a real good time. I miss the ones that I don't see regularly.

Did the Super Slam put a strain on your family life?
NEELY: I've been very, very lucky. Both of my wives have been very supportive. Both of them said, "You can chase birds all you want as long as you don't chase women." [laughing] They knew what I was doing and they had no problem with my turkey hunting. Financially, I didn't take anything

looking at existing record books and harvest data from the states, where the most birds have been killed and everything else.

What was your easiest state?
NEELY: Well, Texas, certainly, because I'm here.

Most difficult?
NEELY: Vermont. I made eight trips to Vermont before I killed a bird. I could have killed a jake the first year but wanted a gobbler. Just couldn't get on a bird. I saw birds. And I have a friend of mine that I was hunting with that lived up there and he had access to all kinds of property. But I just *could not* get on a bird. [pauses] See 'em far. Just couldn't get 'em in. Finally killed a bird coming off the roost heading down a mountain at 5:30 in

"This was my fourth trip to Illinois to try and get a bird," Neely recalled. "It was April 16, 2010. He came in like he was on a string. He is my best typical, weighing 24 pounds., with spurs of 1.3750 and 1.250 inches, and a 11.4376-inch beard."

the morning in the biggest rainstorm you ever saw. That was my eighth individual trip specifically to Vermont.

That's determination.
NEELY: Eight trips!

Anything special about how you prepared for those trips?
NEELY: Making sure I've got all my equipment together, making make sure I've got all the travel details planned out. I tried to have everything packed and ready and in the vehicle the day before.

Do you remember your most difficult individual tom?
NEELY: I can tell you one I didn't kill—that one

in North Carolina. [chuckling] I guess that damn bird on Giles Island in Louisiana. I killed him but he never gobbled—he never gobbled. Yeah, every every three or four or five minutes I'd get a glimpse of him. This went on for an hour and a half until I finally got an open shot. That would probably be him. That would be him.

Has it been your experience that individual birds actually have personalities?
NEELY: Oh, yeah. Oh, yeah. Some of them will come in so vocal and gobble their heads off. I mean, you just hit the first call and [makes loud gobbling noise] they just really come in after you. Some of them will come in silent. Some of them will sneak in. Some of them will come in direct. Every hunt is totally different, just so different, and

that's because the birds themselves are different. Whether you're dealing with a dominant bird or a subdominant bird, you know what I'm saying? And then in the fall you really see a difference. When you get these groups of dominant gobblers after they've all bunched up, three or four dominant gobblers, that's when you see a difference. I've learned so much in the fall, seeing those birds traveling together. You see groups of three- or four-year-old birds and then you see groups of two-year-olds. It's just amazing. They are so different.

Where's the strangest place you've ever killed a wild turkey?

NEELY: I don't know. I don't know. [pauses] You know, they can pop up in the strangest places. I've had gobblers that I'm watching from a distance, to myself: "Come on. I'm not gonna kill you. You're too damn easy." [chuckling] And I could leave and come back the next day at another time and that bird would come right back. I never killed him. Just because of that.

Have you ever thought about what killing a turkey in all the states cost you?

NEELY: I don't want to talk about it. [laughing] I don't want anybody to know what I think they cost because they will think I'm totally out of my mind. Let me put it this way: I could buy another home, easily.

Would you recommend that other hunters try for a Super Slam?

NEELY: I don't know if I would make that recom-

> I could go to this one place and I could sit there every day and I could hit the call twice and that bird could come running in— and he was a mature gobbler. I said, "Come on." I said to myself: "Come on. I'm not gonna kill you. You're too damn easy."

sitting against a tree, and they disappear and the next thing I know they're gobbling right there behind me!

Did you ever purposefully pass up a bird could have easily killed?

NEELY: Oh, yeah.

When and why?

NEELY: I've hunted some gobblers that I had so much fun with. I had this one gobbler that I called "Easy." Because I could go to this one place and I could sit there every day and I could hit the call twice and that bird could come running it—and he was a mature gobbler. I said, "Come on." I said

mendation or not. I think the recommendation that I would make is to go out and enjoy turkey hunting. If you want to go out and hunt multiple states because you want to experience the pleasure of hunting in different states and the conditions in different states, and it leads you to pursue a Super Slam, then that's fine. But to go out and pursue this just to pursue a Super Slam, I don't think I'd recommend it to anybody. I just don't think I would.

What's the one secret you would share with somebody who does want to accomplish what you have?

NEELY: Do lots of research and don't get in any

FACING PAGE: This Wisconsin eastern was harvested in May 2008 on a State National Guard training area. "I was able to contact the retired commanding general and gain access," Clyde said. "He even gave me a personal tour of the area."

"My absolute favorite state and place to hunt Merriam's," Clyde said about this eastern South Dakota bird. He tagged it in Perkins County in March 2005.

hurry. Take your time. That's the best thing I can tell you.

Which states are your favorites?
NEELY: I'm going to say four because I like to cover all the subspecies. I'm going to say North Carolina, Florida, South Dakota and Texas.

And your No. 1 state—or is that not a fair question?
NEELY: I love to go to South Dakota because Merriam's are just so vocal and you can see 'em coming from two miles away. They really come to the call.

Does the countryside have something to do with it?
NEELY: They've got those rolling hills and Ponderosa pines. It's just a beautiful state. I like it a lot.

Your least favorite state?
NEELY: Some of the eastern states because of the

difficulty in getting access—Delaware, Rhode Island—simply because it's very hard to find places to hunt. That's the only reason. I enjoyed hunting them. It's just so hard to find a place to hunt. They're both wonderful states. And I love to eat lobster. [laughing]

These days is it most satisfying hunting a familiar piece of land or learning new ground?
NEELY: Today I like to go back and visit with my friends.

During the height of your quest, how many days did you devote to chasing turkeys?
NEELY: Seventy to 80 days, some years. I really did.

How much pre-season scouting?
NEELY: I did as much as I could from home on the phone, you know what I'm saying? I studied topographic maps and did as much research as much as I could from a distance, but when you go into a lot of different states there's only so much you can do until you get there.

Is there a key to effectively scouting a new area?
NEELY: The key is to physically get on the ground, if you have that option. If you've got a topo of the area, use it. Utilize all the tools you have.

What's on your checklist, what are you looking for?
NEELY: You're looking for food. You're looking for roosting trees. You're looking for good cover and you're looking for water—all the essentials that the turkeys are looking for.

Do you like to wait for the birds to come to you?
NEELY: I prefer to locate the birds and call them. I will run and gun if that's what I have to do, but I prefer to sit and call them myself. It's harder for them to pinpoint you. That's what I find. You know, it's all about avoiding movement, movement, *movement*. But sometimes you gotta run and gun if they're moving. Sometimes you can't find them

FACING PAGE: New Mexico Merriam's killed in April 2007 coming off the roost with four other gobblers.

New Hampshire eastern gobbler that Clyde killed after patterning for three days. Although the turkey scored 83.5, featured three beards totaling 23.5 inches, with a 1.25-inch spur and a 1.75-inch spur, it weighed only 17.5 pounds.

so you gotta run and gun until you find them.

What's your favorite gun?
NEELY: I have a Benelli Super Black Eagle with a pistol grip, three-and-a-half-inch, and I shoot No. 5 Hevi-Shot. The No. 5 shot performs really well in my gun, so I've stuck with it.

Do you use decoys?
NEELY: Sometimes the birds like a decoy, sometimes they don't. I have boxes of them. To say which is a favorite, I mean, there must be 50 brands. And every year one is "the best." [laughing] Oh yeah, oh yeah, oh yeah.

Do you have a particular choice of camouflage clothing?

NEELY: You need to have a good rain suit, for certain, and you need to have warm- and cold-weather clothing depending on where you're going. The camo brand, I don't think it matters. You need to have the pattern and color that blends in where you are hunting. I don't care if it's Mossy Oak or Realtree or any others—they all make good camo. But be ready for the conditions. I think waterproof leather boots are the best. And you need a good set of binoculars. Always, always. They don't have to be big but they need be quality.

Over the years how many different calls have you tried?
NEELY: Ten thousand. [laughing] I tend to like slate calls. Myself, I just I like the sound that comes out of them, you know. I've used diaphragm calls

and I've used box calls, but I like slate calls better.

When do you call aggressively and when do you back off?
NEELY: Depending on the bird's temperament and you just have to determine that for yourself. He's going to tell you how to call him. When you're not hunting, practice, practice, practice. Get you some tapes. Listen and try to mimic what you hear. That's the only way you're going to learn. But listening to the actual birds is better.

roost a bird. Then you go out before daylight and set up and get comfortable. Be still. Let him make his presence known. Let him make his morning call and then you can answer a bit and when he flies down you can start to call to him a little, and go from there

What about hunting at midday?
NEELY: Normally at midday, during breeding season, you're going to find the gobblers that have already bred the hens with them, and that's when they'll be more receptive to your calling. I like to

> If the bird is responding to your call and likes your call
> it makes no sense to change, you know what I'm saying?
> Just tone down your calling if the bird is coming to you, though.
> Don't stay loud and aggressive. Tone down, you know. Get lower.
> Stop when he's starting to get close.

In what circumstance do you stick with one call versus multiple calls?
NEELY: If the bird is responding to your call and likes your call it makes no sense to change, you know what I'm saying? Just tone down your calling if the bird is coming to you, though. Don't stay loud and aggressive. Tone down, you know. Get lower. Stop when he's starting to get close. You may not be able to see him but you can hear from his calling that he's getting pretty close.

How about a non-gobbling turkey—your Giles Island shadow bird?
NEELY: You just gotta call enough to keep them interested. That's it.

How about a drumming bird?
NEELY: Shut your mouth. Shut up. If you've got a drummin' bird, he's damn close!

How do you start your day in the woods?
NEELY: Preparation the night before, if you can

hunt at midday, personally.

In your experience, what are the ideal conditions for hunting?
NEELY: No wind and no rain. [chuckling] Wind is a killer. You don't want any wind and preferably no heavy rain. You don't want those at all.

Do you remember the largest gobbler you ever killed?
NEELY: Oh, he was about 28 pounds. Longest beard was about $14^{1}/_{4}$ inches.

What characteristics do you most admire in fellow hunters?
NEELY: Honor, dedication, respect for the animal, dignity.

Any single individual?
NEELY: A guy I think a lot of is Larry Profitt. He lives in Tennessee. He's killed so many Gould's. He's got 58 Grand Slams. He's a great caller and

just a good, dedicated, hard-hunting, old-fashioned turkey hunter. I've never actually met him but I know a lot about him and I think a lot of him. There's been lots of articles written about him and everything. He's a tremendous guy.

How has turkey hunting changed?
NEELY: A lot of the changes I don't like. It's become a competition to see who can get the most slams and who can get the most publicity for slams, and I don't think that's necessarily good. This is my strictly personal opinion. If the publicity does good things for the sport of turkey hunting, then I'm okay with it. But I wonder about the character of some of the people that it brings in to the sport. I wonder what their *personal* motivation is—is it recognition or is there something else driving it? My personal opinion only. It's the older turkey hunters I admire most, the older, devoted, *honorable* turkey hunters that are only going to hunt with a shotgun and only hunt in a certain way: "This is the tradition of turkey hunting. This is the way it should be done and that's the way we're going to do it." [claps hands lightly] Cut and dried. That's what I'm trying to say.

I do. And I'm sure nearly all serious turkey hunters share your sentiments. How about habitat—have you seen it change significantly in the places you've hunted?
NEELY: Yes, I have and in some cases yet for the better. So yes I think people are trying to manage habitat better for some species of game. But habitat can't be managed for all species of game. It just can't. It just doesn't work that way, you know. I've seen some successful efforts to manage habitat for wild species. I've seen some improvement in that. What I'm concerned about is that, yes, we're managing habitat, but are we leaving it open for hunting? I don't know. I mean, we've got so much government acreage that's closed up to hunting where it should be ours. It's all ours.

How about populations of wild turkeys where you've hunted: Are they sustainable and in pretty good shape?
NEELY: It's like any other game population. I think they're expanding in some areas and they're going down in others. What are the causes? I don't know; I'm not a biologist.

Where do you think the sport of turkey hunting is heading?
NEELY: I hope it's going to in a positive direction but I don't really know. I don't know where the sport of hunting is going. I hope it continues on forever. But I am very concerned about our children. They are not being brought up to hunt. There seems to be less and less interest, overall, in the sport of hunting. I wonder if one day it's not going to go away. And that's our own fault with all the gun control issues and everything else. Are we going to become like in a lot of European countries where you go to check out a gun to go hunting, and get to a point where an average man can't afford to hunt? I'm afraid that's where we're headed.

You have a wonderful sporting library here. Do you have a favorite book on turkey hunting or a writer whose words you find inspiring or helpful in some practical way?
NEELY: I have so many turkey-hunting books—and not only turkey hunting but big-game hunting—that to pinpoint one would be honestly really hard for me. I like a lot of the old literature. Some of these guys would hunt at night and kill over 2,000 turkeys in their lifetime. It's amazing. They would hunt day and night on these old southern plantations, you know, and it didn't matter whether they killed hens or gobblers. It can't sustain that anymore. But to go back and read about how it was done then you would go, "Golly." It's just amazing. Some are reproductions of the old, old books. I've got a bunch of biological books; I read and study that stuff, too. Sometimes it's hard to digest. But you learn so much. I'm going to go through all my book collection and find out what edition it was and who printed it and when, and try and sell it as a whole. Because my children aren't going to appreciate it, and I

This Arizona-hatched Gould's wild turkey example is currently ranked No. 2 non-typical in the world. Clyde Neely was was fortunate to win one of early Gould's tags auctioned at the National Wild Turkey Federation Convention. He harvested the bird in December 2007 near Fort Huachuca in Cochise County, site of the original stockings.

don't want to see it go to a used bookstore and sold piecemeal. I told my wife the other day, "I want to go through my book collection and make a list of and then see that it goes to somebody that will appreciate it." Simply for that reason. I'm 68 but my health is horrible and I would rather do that than see the books just disappear when something happens to me. And that's what so often happens.

Do you have a favorite recipe for wild turkey?
NEELY: I do have a favorite recipe and it's not eating the turkey as a whole. I have a friend that worked with me and he taught me about doing this with ducks. He'll take the turkey or duck or anything else and he'll slice it in little thin slices. Then he'll season it with lemon pepper salt and stick it in a Ziploc bag and fill that bag with Russian salad dressing and throw it in the refrigerator for two or three days. Then he'll take the meat and wrap it with bacon and cook it on the grill—not very long, you know, just like duck you don't want to overcook it—and serve it as an hors d'oeuvres. And it will knock your socks off. A lot of women will not eat wild game and I'll fix some of these for my friends' wives and I can't keep it on the plate: "Hmmm. What was that?"

Randy Stafford

HOME:
Franklinton, Louisiana

OCCUPATION:
Retired pharmacist

FIRST WILD TURKEY:
1966, Alabama

COMPLETED U.S. SUPER SLAM:
2010, Pennsylvania

OPENING PAGE: April 2010—Debbie Stafford with her Delaware turkey, the year husband Randy got his last two birds, Nos. 48 and 49. That year Randy Stafford suffered a detached retina in his right eye. The doctor said it was okay to hunt if he used a small-gauge shotgun and shot left-handed. He chose a 28-gauge Remington 1100 semi-automatic. In Delaware on April 24 Debbie killed the bird pictured at 7 a.m. By 11 a.m she had also taken a Maryland wild turkey. Two birds, two states, before noon—not bad! ABOVE: March 2009—San Carlos Indian Reservation, Apache Nation, Arizona. Randy Stafford recalled that he and wife Debbie were not having much success. He said that as they rode around, they came to a big pond in the woods. It was extremely windy; they could hear practically nothing but wind. Their guide walked off looking for sign. Debbie and Randy walked over to the dam. The wind was blowing straight down behind it. "I called several times as loud as I could on my box call," Randy said, "but heard nothing in reply." They started back for the truck. Debbie was lagging behind. Randy turned to see that she was on her knees motioning into the woods—two gobblers were coming down a drain not 20 yards away. "I leaned up against the rear of the truck," Randy said. "It was thick between me and the drain." The first bird stepped out. Arizona was a done deal.

I WAS IN "SPORTSMAN'S PARADISE" to talk with Randy Stafford about wild turkeys, but *Meleagris gallopavo* was not foremost on my mind as the plane touched down on the tarmac at Louis Armstrong New Orleans International Airport. *Crassostrea virginica* was. I checked into the charmingly aged Lafayette Hotel and made a beeline for Iberville Street, where I obediently slipped into the line below the green, pink and yellow neon sign: FELIX'S RESTAURANT OYSTERS.

"Bar okay?" asked the young woman at the door.

"More than okay," I replied, whereupon an exceptionally large black man and master shucker called M. J. smiled and began piling the watery, sweet, slightly briny gems of the Louisiana Gulf onto the bare counter in front of me faster than I could slurp them down.

"Another dry martini, please," I asked his skinny sidekick.

The last thing I remember that night was getting swept into the blaring off-key brass horns, drums and flashing blue lights of an impromptu parade up—or was it down?—Bourbon Street.

Randy Stafford was born in New Orleans in 1947. In 1954 his father, a medical doctor, moved the family north to rural Washington Parish, up toward the Mississippi border. His father didn't have much spare time. Randy and his older brother Pete grew up walking through the squirrel woods, following their grandfather.

"Granddad would lead us through the woods before daylight and sit us down by an old oak tree," Randy recalled. "He'd walk off in the dark and we was scared to death. That's the way we grew up, listening to the sounds of the woods."

Granddad chewed Beechnut tobacco and he made a loud spitting sound in the darkness. Randy thinks it was so his grandsons would know he was nearby.

Randy and Pete competed to see who could get his limit of squirrels first. But they were raised with a strict respect for game laws: "If you broke a game law you did it by accident—and you paid dearly for it." Once Pete killed his 12th and 13th dove with one shot. The limit was 12. Their father forbad him from hunting the rest of the season.

"We had 200 acres of woods to explore and we got so where we knew every foot of it," Stafford said. "That was really the beginning of our journey of learning woodsmanship."

The last day of spring I drove north through the pounding rain on the world's longest causeway over Lake Pontchartrain with the radio turned to Voodoo 104 FM. Regaining land, I passed a Baptist church and a Dollar General store. There was Beckie's Hair Salon on the left and Don's Barber Shop on the right. Red's Discount Fireworks. Another Baptist church. Another Dollar General. Ramsay's Crawdad & Bait. Suddenly the sunshine and the piney woods opened into magnificent green horse pastures edged in bright white fences stretching to infinity south of Washington Parish.

Why do you hunt?

RANDY STAFFORD: I grew up hunting. I grew up in a hunting family. It's always been exciting. It's not that challenging to sneak up on a squirrel. But deer and turkey are challenging, and that's where most of my time has been spent. The anticipation and trying to figure out what an animal is doing to be successful and just being in the woods. I mean it's where I'd rather spend my time.

DEBBIE STAFFORD: It's so peaceful, very peaceful. No phones—just God's wonderful bounty that he's given us to take care of.

What makes hunting wild turkeys so special?

STAFFORD: To me, for the turkey to stand out there and gobble, and tell you exactly where he is, and yet be so difficult to take, is just amazing. If you happen to be in a field or an open place where you can actually see 'em strut and gobble and do his thing—being there and watching all that is by far the most exciting thing to me. I've taken a lot of birds simply because Debbie made me stay there and wait.

Ahhh—the truth comes out.

DEBBIE: [laughing]

STAFFORD: If he's not a gobblin' and struttin' I lose interest pretty quick. That's my thing. I mean,

I want to be vocal with the birds. I want to challenge *him* to come to me.

And Debbie, what is it about turkey hunting that attracts you compared with other hunting?

DEBBIE: When you're deer hunting you sit in a tree stand and wait. With turkey you go to one spot and you do some locator calling. If you don't hear anything you go somewhere else. You locate a bird and play with it.

So you like the animation.

DEBBIE: Yes. You're active—it's not boring.

Randy, when did you kill your first turkey?

STAFFORD: I told you that my father was real strict on us. Well, there was one exception. My first cousin and I in the winter were going into a wood duck pond to hunt. I was going down a little narrow lane and there was a big log across and there was a big turkey squatting behind it. Just about the time I was going to step over he jumped up and took off and I guess it was just like a reflex—I didn't even remember shooting. But I was here scared to death to bring that bird home to my dad. Back then at that time in Washington Parish turkeys were unknown. That was the first wild turkey I'd ever *seen*. I'm going to guess and say it was around

1963—something right in that neighborhood. I was around 15 years old. I don't think I had my driver's license long. It was the first time and only time I ever heard him say it was okay. I don't know as he had ever seen a turkey. Turkeys were very, very scarce in Washington Parish. A little bit of history: There were probably less than a half-dozen older gentleman that turkey hunted in Washington Parish and they were extremely, extremely secretive because there weren't many birds.

Did you know any of them when you were a kid?
STAFFORD: I did know several of them. Dr. Smith was a dentist here in town—he was the one that actually got my brother into turkey hunting before I did and he went with Dr. Smith quite a few times to learn about turkeys and everything. I never did. Mr. Harvey Bryant was another one. I never did go with them or talked turkey hunting with them. Ray Duncan was another one. I pretty much knew all of them but I really wasn't acquainted with them at that time. I got to know them in their later years. But they were old-school turkey hunters. They would go sit in a spot and sit there all day. They might cluck one time and sit there and wait an hour, then cluck again. I mean, they were whole different breed of turkey hunter than what we have today. I actually wish I would have gone and got to know them a little bit more.

It would have been interesting.
STAFFORD: Yes, yes it would have been. But there were very few birds at that time and to hear one actually gobble was extremely rare, I think.

And Debbie, when did you tag your first turkey?
DEBBIE: Ninety-two or '93 in Mississippi.
STAFFORD: We were on that road in the camp up there by double-x. But I think you missed that one.
DEBBIE: Don't listen. [laughing]
STAFFORD: She actually knocked that turkey slap over and he just popped back up. That's where we did most of our hunting when we first got married. I was in a lease up in Mississippi, a hunting club, and that's where we turkey hunted.

DEBBIE: Was it on the power line—or was that in Louisiana?
STAFFORD: You killed a bird out on the power line but I know that wasn't your first turkey. That year we doubled. We doubled in just about every state we hunted.
DEBBIE: Yeah, we did that one year—doubled. We shot at the same time and we each got a bird. We did it in Florida, we did it in South Dakota, here in Louisiana.

When you were first getting serious about turkey hunting, Randy, did you have someone who taught you the ropes—a mentor?
STAFFORD: My brother was into it before I was, like I say, and we kind of pitter-pattered back and forth with turkey calls and all that stuff. But I have an uncle in Alabama that called up the first long-beard turkey that I killed while actually hunting turkeys. He was big into turkey hunting—still is. I learned a lot from him. But probably the one person that inspired me the most about turkey hunting is Preston Pittman. I didn't know him personally but I watched a lot of Preston's hunting videos. He was one of the first making videos. Preston was from Mississippi and was very big into game calling and had his own line of game calls, and everything. He's an extremely good turkey caller. He grew up hunting also and he knows how to think like a turkey. He made several videos but the one that really stands out is the one video where he went and got a Grand Slam—you know, the four different types of turkey—and he might have gotten a double in each one. But it talked about hunting and how to call and when to call in different situations. There are a lot of those instructional videos and audio out there now that will teach you how to call; I learned from several of them. I likely gagged to death trying to use a mouth call but we finally got it figured out. [laughing]

Debbie, I don't have to ask you who your mentor was. Be honest now: what kind of a teacher was he?
DEBBIE: He was an awesome teacher. He taught

me to shoot. I started shooting five out of 20 and Randy got me to 24 out of 25—sporting clays.

STAFFORD: We shot a lot of sporting clays. She got really good at it and after years went by other men shooters would say, "Hey, Miss Debbie beat you today." And I'd say, "Yeah, and she beat you too." [laughing] I introduced her to deer hunting and turkey hunting, some duck hunting. But most of what we've done is turkeys.

DEBBIE: He's a very good teacher, very patient. And it's so much fun. He can call 'em like right into your face.

STAFFORD: [playfully sarcastic] "But he doesn't do real well when he does that and I miss."

DEBBIE: Happens to everybody.

STAFFORD: Yes it does. I've missed quite a few.

What's the one piece of advice you would give to a beginner?

STAFFORD: Other than you know learning how to call and just practice, practice, practice, they need to start out really doing something in the woods other than turkey hunting. Squirrel hunting or deer hunting—squirrel hunting is probably the best because you're actually walking around in the woods, doing a lot more, doing stuff. They need to learn—and I say this over and over—*woodsmanship*. They need to be able to get out and think about what an animal is doing and why that animal is doing it. If they've got somebody they can go out turkey hunting with, fantastic. That's a lot of help. But you don't have to be an expert turkey caller. I'm not an expert. I don't think it really makes that much difference to a turkey if you're sounding perfect. Rhythm is very important. You just have to practice and don't get discouraged. You're going to learn. You don't have to worry about doing something right or wrong. That turkey's going to teach you!

Debbie, do you remember while you were learning

at what point something sort of clicked and you know you thought that you had gained some insight and thought, *okay, now I get this?*

DEBBIE: Oh, yes—sitting next to Randy in the woods and he's asleep. [laughing] I'll pick up a call and I start calling it. I don't say I'm very good at it. But I've called up my own turkey and woke him up with a boom.

A mouth call?

DEBBIE: Oh, no, slate. I like slate calls. I've done that several times. He'll be napping. It's so much fun.

And you woke him up with a boom—I think we have the title of the book. [laughing] Randy, do you recall the moment when you started thinking about killing a wild turkey in all 49 states?

STAFFORD: I had taken birds in eight or nine different states before I ever thought about it. Exactly when I thought about doing it was during a National Wild Turkey Federation Convention when they recognized a gentleman up on the stage for completing his 49 states. So I thought, *You know, I've already got several states—that would be a very interesting thing to do.*

When was that?

STAFFORD: Ninety-eight, '99, somewhere around there.

And Debbie, you went with Randy on many of these adventures.

DEBBIE: Oh, yes. It was just fantastic. Every state that we went to was different, whether you go on private land or public land—it was probably about 50-50—and every state has different rules. It was so exciting to do that.

Other than the actual hunting, did you enjoy the travel aspect?

DEBBIE: Oh, yes, very interesting and it doesn't

FACING PAGE: 2002—Kansas. Stafford shot this bird at a Boy Scout camp in southeast Kansas. It took him three days. He called in two good longbeards using a mouth call just after fly-down. He said he could have taken both. When the first one went down, the other just stood there. Randy called out aloud, "Get up, buddy, let's go!"

matter if I'm the only woman doing it—although I'm sure I'm not.

STAFFORD: Some of these pictures you see [sorting through shoe boxes of snapshots] she took out the window while we were riding down the road. She liked the scenery. She'd say, "Stop! stop! We need to take a picture here." Even if it was cold outside.

DEBBIE: That's because you wouldn't stop. We would stop only when I was driving.

And you had never been outside Louisiana. Turkey hunting was your way to see the America. Now you've seen the whole country.

> Well, the first turkey I actually called up for myself was here in Louisiana. Probably about three, four miles from here. And it was a jake. And I was as happy as a person could ever be, I promise you. It was such an exciting thing.

DEBBIE: It's wonderful, beautiful. Hawaii was so much fun, getting to go way over there—such an amazing place.

STAFFORD: I said drove to every state—all except Hawaii. [laughing]

That would have been quite the trek!

STAFFORD: That was a lot more interesting, you know, driving through all the states rather than flying because you actually got to go see a lot of the terrain, see the country, meet a lot of people in the different states and everything.

Have you kept track of how many wild turkeys you've killed over the years?

STAFFORD: I've never really thought about it. I'm going to say that probably in a neighborhood of 150 birds in my life. But spent most of my time in Mississippi, Texas, Wisconsin, Florida, South Dakota, Wyoming—there's probably a 100 birds in those select states right there.

And you, Debbie, now well on your way to your own Super Slam. How many states have you tagged?

DEBBIE: Goodness. Thirty-one.

Are you committed to getting there?

DEBBIE: Oh, yes. It' tremendous. He just has to keep up with me. [laughing]

How many years did it take you?

STAFFORD: Probably over 12 years once I started chasing it. From '98 to 2010 would probably pretty much cover it.

What was your first state?

STAFFORD: Well, the first turkey I actually called up for myself was here in Louisiana. Probably about three, four miles from here. And it was a jake. And I was as happy as a person could ever be, I promise you. It was such an exciting thing. It turned me on to turkey hunting, you know, actually have the bird respond and come to me finally.

And which state was first in the quest for your 49 birds?

STAFFORD: I don't remember which one, but I want to say South Dakota or Wisconsin, one of those states.

What was your last state?

STAFFORD: The last state was Pennsylvania.

Was that a tough one?

STAFFORD: Pennsylvania was tough. We hunted public land in Pennsylvania. There were maybe a half-dozen states that we actually had to go back

to a second time and probably two or three we had to go back to a third.

Pennsylvania was one of them. Ohio was one of them. I should have killed a bird first year I was in Ohio and missed him; it took me two more years to actually get one. Rhode Island was tough. I think we went to every single wildlife management area in Rhode Island. Of course, it's a small state. I think we saw one hen but never heard a turkey gobble. We ended up killing one. We finally found out that in Rhode Island if land is not marked posted then you could hunt on it.

That was finally the key to me getting a bird—you could go on private land that wasn't marked posted and take a bird. But, you know, Pennsylvania and Ohio were very tough. Of course it was public land. On those two states and it was mostly just difficult finding gobblin' birds. I'm not a person to go and sit in the woods and call.

Do you remember the feeling when you pulled the trigger and you walked up to that final bird?
STAFFORD: Oh, yeah. I mean it was a relief, I guess. That was the biggest thing. Completing a major goal that I set for myself, meeting the challenge and everything. I was just happy and excited. I pretty much had done what I wanted to do. And it's the same with deer hunting. I don't have any desire to ever take another deer. I don't have any desire to ever take another turkey. You know, I respect the animal and love hearing him gobble. My thing will be youth, ladies—you know, first-time hunters. I have a lease out here where I'll take young hunters and ladies and a few wounded warriors. Something like that does me a lot more good than actually taking a bird myself.

What was the maximum number of states you hunted in any one year?
STAFFORD: Oh, we hunted 11. I'm not going to say we hunted 11—we may have hunted more—but but we took turkeys in 11 different states one year. We actually took 13 turkeys that year. I killed 11 and she killed two.
DEBBIE: We went from right here in Louisiana all the way to Washington, Oregon, Idaho, California. We took about five or six states over there and then we came all the way back across the country and went to Maine. That was a big year.

Why did you decide to drive to all those places rather than fly?
STAFFORD: Well, just because I knew I had everything I needed in my vehicle. I knew I could do whatever I wanted to do when I got there. I went on several hunts, for example, in Colorado, deer hunting, where I was with a group and I got there and I found I was confined. I was limited to what I could do because I didn't have my own vehicle and my own equipment. That was probably a leading factor.

Of your 49 birds how many were taken during the spring and how many in the fall?
STAFFORD: That's an easy one—all in the spring. I hunt gobbling turkeys. The springtime is my time. I'm not a fall turkey hunter. I'm there because they gobble.

Did you take any of your birds with a hunting guide?
STAFFORD: I think I ended up with six or eight that I actually had someone else doing the calling. Now, I had other hunts where I was with an outfitter or something like that. They put me on birds and you just do your own thing.

How many were bearded hens or jakes?
STAFFORD: It's a good question. You know, I've seen quite a few bearded hens. Matter of fact, when I first started turkey hunting I took a bearded hen because I didn't realize there was any such a thing as a bearded hen. But we've seen quite a few bearded hens. I didn't take one on this quest or anything. They were all toms but one. There was one jake and it was in that year, I think, when we were hitting a lot of states. We were in another state and left birds because we had a hunt booked in New Jersey. So we got to New Jersey and the first morning got to working and calling up some

birds. We thought we were working mature birds and spent two or three hours to get them in; they ended up being three jakes. And I told her, "We should go ahead and take these two birds so we can get back." And now I wished I hadn't. That way they'd all be longbeard turkeys. But I wanted to get back to the birds in the other state. And I still may go back to New Jersey and get me a longbeard! [laughing]

How many different firearms or bows did you shoot?
STAFFORD: During the actual quest I only used a shotgun. I've taken birds with pistol and bow and shotgun. But it's difficult and expensive enough to get the birds that I didn't want to take the chance of missing an opportunity.

Looking back, what do you think drove you to to accomplish this?
STAFFORD: The challenge of doing it. Going to all these different places. People have to really comprehend how hard it is to go to a brand-new place you've never been before and get on a bird and harvest a bird. It's still mind boggling to me that we were as successful as we were. Because there were very few places that we didn't take a bird the first or second day.

The secret to your success?
STAFFORD: Research, planning—I don't know what all you can attribute it to but it still amazes me that we were so successful. You know, if I'm on a gobbling bird, I should take that bird within three days. Day 1 he's teaching me. Day 2 if I don't take him he's taught me something else. By Day 3 I should have that bird figured out and know what I gotta do to harvest that bird. That comes back to being a woodsman out there and thinking like a turkey, knowing why he's doing what he's doing.

Did you feel in any way competitive with other hunters?
STAFFORD: Totally, 100 percent personal. I didn't have any competition going. I didn't have any

timeframe that I was trying to complete it in. I just loved doing it and it was just a personal challenge to myself.

Were you at any point discouraged to where you felt like quitting?
STAFFORD: Never. Like I say, I love it. As long as he's gobblin' I'll play. I'm a happy camper. I don't have to take him but he's got to gobble! The biggest downtime for us was between turkey seasons. Those were depressing times. [laughing]

You want to get back out there.
STAFFORD: That's right. The biggest thing about this Super Slam is your planning and that's what that time between seasons is about. You've got to do your research. It's easy enough if you just find an outfitter and book a hunt and don't worry about it, you know. But if you're going on public land you've got to do your homework. You've got to do it ahead of time. And I think that's a lot of why we were successful in a short amount of time.

Some hunters who have accomplished the Super Slam—and I'm sure great many others obsessed with turkey hunting—the chase puts a serious strain on personal or family relationships. It sounds like the sport brought you two together.
STAFFORD: That's right. That's how you eliminate that problem—bring her with you! [laughing] Let her hunt. Everybody should do that. They should introduce their wives to hunting, bring them along. I think that's why we've been together as long as we have. It's being out there and enjoying this together.
DEBBIE: It was always really easy getting somebody to watch and make sure the kids were okay; we had grandparents to help. That was fine. And then with the hunting store we had friends that would come in and work. So it was never any problem. I enjoyed his company the whole time, even on those long road trips, but it was fun.

What's the longest you were ever away?
STAFFORD: We were probably gone for a month

and longer, really, because we were out there in the West Coast and then came back through here, stopped off to check on things and then back up into the Northeast.

So when you're aiming to to bag a wild turkey hundreds of miles away or even farther—a couple thousand miles—how did you decide where to focus your efforts?

STAFFORD: I tried to group states together where we could make a loop and hit five or six states at a time, so you cut down on your travel time. But there are a lot of sources that you can use to actually help you locate places to hunt in different states. We purchased a lot of hunts at N.W.T.F.

have presidents of local chapters, and most of the time when you tell some of them what you're trying to do they're very, very helpful. And in traveling around we talk to local people. You know, most turkey hunters are pretty stingy with their information. I remember in Michigan we just went into the local hunting store there to pick up our game licenses and got to talking to the owner and told him what we were doing. I could kind of feel like he wanted to tell us more but there were two other boys standing nearby but he was holding back. Finally when those boys left he said, "They's turkey hunters just like I am!" He told us exactly where to go in a local wildlife management area where he personally hunted and we took birds.

> I'll tell you places lot of people overlook: Corps of Engineers land around these lakes. We hunted several of those in Indiana and South Carolina, also Arkansas. There's very little public hunting pressure on these places. We found lots of birds.

conventions and sometimes that would determine where we might be going and, you know, we try to get more states right around that one. You can start with major wildlife management areas and contact the wildlife division there. Generally most of them have statistics on turkey harvest and they will gladly send this information to you. You go over it and pick out what state has the highest success rate, what state has the least amount of hunting pressure or something. I mean, you look at all of that and formulate a plan. You pick out a wildlife management area or a National Forest. I'll tell you places lots of people overlook: Corps of Engineers land around these lakes. We hunted several of those in Indiana and South Carolina, also Arkansas. There's very little public hunting pressure on these places. We found lots of birds. You can also contact the National Wild Turkey Federation in those states. I keep bringing up N.W.T.F.—I'm a huge fan. They have regional directors and they

Any other tips?

STAFFORD: Mail carriers. They're out there every day in a country. They see turkeys. They know where there are turkeys. We were in Tennessee and passed a mailman. He actually said, "Oh, man, this is where I hunt over here, but if y'all haven't killed one come on over by my house and hunt behind there." And we got one. West Virginia and Virginia were two states a little bit leery of because of the terrain. I'm not going up a mountain. Scott Wilson, the state chapter president, he invited us to come hunt in Virginia. He said, "Me and my wife usually take a bird here at our house but we have a couple other places and friends that will let us hunt there." Brian Perry from North Carolina, we spent three or four days with him in his lease getting birds there. I mean, we've run across some exceptional people, friendly people. We've made friends that will last a lifetime.

Once you've done your reconnaissence and you get to these places, how do you locate the birds?
STAFFORD: Two ways. If you got the access, the best way is to ride around and look at openings and whatnot and actually see the birds and know exactly what birds you've got there to hunt. Early in the morning or late in the evening and use locator calls before daylight, and late in the evening just before dark your owl call; crow calls during the day. But during daylight actually riding around checking openings and locating birds that way—that's just a key to trying to find your birds—and, as I say, we were just fortunate. We had a lot of help, I guess, that put us in good places to locate birds.

was a big turkey hunter. And I had a young boy with me. There was this turkey roost where there were so many turkeys in the live oaks that the turkey droppings, they were so thick they were stacked up a foot deep. It was so strong it was actually killing some of the trees. So I told this young boy to take my brother back there. I said: "Y'all get in there before daylight and sit down. Thirty minutes before daylight or so, you tell him to owl just to make sure y'all got at least one turkey there." [laughing] He must have had 50 turkeys gobblin' back at him. His eyes got about that big. He set there that morning and let longbeard after longbeard walk right by him because after they had flown down he had one bird way back over that he could see. He wanted that bird.

> The birds get pressure. And one of the biggest things there,
> I think, is you have a lot of beginning hunters, novice hunters
> that get out there not knowing a lot about what they're doing—
> they educate a lot of turkeys quickly.

Which was your easiest state to hunt?
STAFFORD: Texas.
DEBBIE: South Dakota.
STAFFORD: South Dakota, yes—both Texas and South Dakota. But Texas they got a lot of birds. I was in this lease for five years down there on the Kennedy Ranch and honestly turkeys were almost like dirt. They were everywhere. I sat on a fence row with live oak trees on both sides and road down both sides of the fence and actually owled at daylight, and it sound like a wave in a football stadium gobblin' just out of here over to the other side and back. A hundred birds gobblin'. I have to tell you this story. I brought my brother there. He

But after he let all those birds walk by that one went the other way! He came back without a turkey. [laughing] I probably enjoyed running with my brother just about more than anything. I've called up birds for him and I think one of his biggest prizes was when he called up a bird for me in South Dakota and it tickled him to death.

You shared your difficulties in Ohio and Pennsylvania. I don't know whether those were circumstantial difficulties or something else. But, in general, which would you say is the most difficult state to get a turkey?
STAFFORD: When you book an outfitter or guide

FACING PAGE: 2002—Wisconsin. Randy Stafford on a hunt at Bluff Country Outfitters with his friends Tom and Laurie Indrebo. Randy always bet Pat Reeves who would get the biggest bird. Randy said that Pat always lost—*Pat, are you reading this?* Friendly betting between sportsmen aside, this Badger State bird was huge: 28 pounds with 10½-inch beard and one-and-a-quarter-inch spurs. "I thought I was standing on him when I went to pick him up," Randy said.

you're pretty much guaranteed they're going to put you on turkeys. Public land hunting is going to be your hardest. The birds get pressure. And one of the biggest things there, I think, is you have a lot of beginning hunters, novice hunters that get out there not knowing a lot about what they're doing—they educate a lot of turkeys quickly. That makes the birds a lot more difficult. In Ohio and Pennsylvania, locating birds was the problem. Probably the one state that we worked the same bird more than any was Rhode Island. We hired a retired game warden as a guide and he took us to the same place, I think it was three years in a row. We did the same routine with the very same bird. He was in the same place. All three years. We set up and that bird just wasn't coming to you. The third year we hunted two days and worked this bird and when he flew down he hushed and it was over. And he told me he said: "I've got to go guide another person but I want to tell you this land is not posted. You can come in here tomorrow without me and hunt." I was in the woods an hour before daylight and I had two choices. He was either going to fly down in the woods where I was or into a field. We had done everything we could do to call it for three years. So I thought, I'm not going to make a sound. I set there and he started gobbling. I watched him fly out of the tree out into the field and he happened to land in the one spot I could see. He was probably 80 yards or so out there and I did one thing that really turned a light bulb on. I just scratched in the leaves like a hen. He looked right at me and he turned and came straight toward me and I took that bird. I never made a call to that bird. So they teach you something.

Debbie, do you remember your most challenging bird?
DEBBIE: Tennessee! [laughing] You can tell that story—it's hilarious.
STAFFORD: It was public land and we had hunted for a day or so when we were finally coming out one afternoon, and crossed a bridge and there were a couple of fields, and there were two strutting birds in the back corner. Over the weekend we had seen a young man and a boy and evidently these people had hunted there before. I had heard him shoot. I eased over there where he had set up and he had a decoy that was like 60 yards from the woods. I thought, *Man, there's no way—he's gonna cripple the bird or spook any bird he gits.* So we came back in there next day and set up where he had been. I think it was a Monday because we didn't see anybody else. And we got there and there were birds roosted on the other side of the river—the Cumberland River. They were on a little mountain right on the side and I said, "We got to get him to cross the river." So we sat there and got to calling. It was kind of foggy and he sailed out into the field. He was probably 100 yards away. I said to Debbie: "This bird been shot at. He knows we're here." We know there are hens here. I said: "I'm through calling. I'm just going to lay down. As long as he's coming and just let him keep coming." Every once in a while I'd say, "Is he still coming?" "Yeah," she said, "he's about 70 yards." "Okay, just let him keep coming." In a few minutes she said, "He dropped down a little bit and I lost him." He came back up and I said, "How far?" And she said, "He's about 50 yards but he's not coming this way anymore." I said, "That's close enough—go ahead and shoot." BOOM! I jumped up and he looked like a net spread over the ground. And so I took off running. I'm old and I don't run well anymore. [chuckling] Just as I get to him he gets on its feet and I jumped on him. Why I didn't twist his neck, I don't know. But I said, "You sit here and hold the bird, stand on him." So I go whatever, 20 yards, to get something to knock him on the head and I come back and he's just a floppin' away and I said, "Now don't you let him get away!" She was standing on his wing and I think she pulled practically every wing feather he had. He got loose and he takes off running. I said, "You've got a gun—shoot!" She shoots and misses. BOOM! she shoots again and misses again. And I knew she was out of shells. Finally, it was just lucky that I had enough angle and I caught up with him. I couldn't breathe! [laughing]

A shame you didn't have that on video.

STAFFORD: There was another bird that she took in South Dakota. I had two birds roosting and I put Debbie in front with me back behind her and I said, "Look, just let the first bird come and you shoot the second bird and I'll get the first bird." Well, I'm sitting there with my gun laying across my lap. And across the way on the side of the hill we can see them strutting and gobbling and working their way down to us. As soon as the first bird gets within range: BOOM! She misses him but he loops around and I take that bird. She's frustrated. She's mad. She says: "I quit. I don't want to hunt no more." So we get back to the truck and I said, "Let me try to call." So I called and some birds

said: "There's still no way he's coming across the road. We're going to have to go over there." And there was a hen started lost-call down below us: *yelp, yelp, yelp, yelp*—continuously almost. He wouldn't pay any attention to her. I hit the box call and he'd gobble. I said, "He's on our side of the road." And we barely sat down when that gobbler came at a full run with the hen behind him trying to catch up. And she took that bird.

So you thought it was going to cross the road?

DEBBIE: Yes, yes!

It's the old chicken-across-the-road joke.

STAFFORD: [laughing] That's one of the things

> I did one thing that really turned a light bulb on.
> I just scratched in the leaves like a hen. He looked right at me
> and he turned and came straight toward me and I took that bird.
> I never made a call to that bird. So they teach you something.

gobbled above us. She said, "Let's go, let's go." She was all over that quitting thing. [laughing] So we went up the side of the mountain and it was a couple of jakes we called up. We let 'em walk off and we kind of planned what we are going to do. We were standing on a pretty high mountain. It drops off to a highway. We hunted on the other side with big meadow and a big mountain and another ridge. So I said, "Let me call to see if we hear anything." So I hear the old box call and there was a pause. And she said, "I think I heard one." I said, "Where is he?" And she said, "Over on that mountain across from us." "Well," I said. "We can go around and drive over there and get up there to him. I know where he's at. Let me call again." So I called again and she said, "He's coming—he's closer." And I said, "Well, there's no way he's gonna come across the road." That turkey came down that mountain across that meadow where the ridge came out to the road and a cliff, a big cut. I

about South Dakota. Those turkeys will call and they will come.

How far away did you shoot that bird?

DEBBIE: Oh, maybe 10 yards.

STAFFORD: He was right there. He was just—oh, man—*coming on!*

DEBBIE: One reason why I started turkey hunting with Randy is that he can't hear very well. I can hear way off.

STAFFORD: She has extremely good ears. We sit side by side and she's got a stick about four or five feet long. [laughing]

Is that for you?

STAFFORD: Keeps me in check—if I want to leave she whops me. But she keeps that stick pointed in the direction of the turkey. I have hearing aids now so I can hear more but when they get in real close it's so loud, I mean, they could be

360—they could be anywhere around. But she keeps me looking in the right direction.

So you have a pretty powerful weapon. . . .
STAFFORD: Yes, she does. [laughing]
DEBBIE: Remember the one time we took Dave and Randall to Mississippi with us?
STAFFORD: And I got a bird to gobble and asked which direction and three of you pointed in a different direction! I said, "We're going where Davy says."

[laughing] She missed him.

All right, what's your side of the story?
DEBBIE: He was just too far and when I'm lookin' at a bird—whether he's 30 or 60 yards—my heart is pounding out of my chest. I mean, I can literally feel it in my head. My heart's just pounding. That might throw me off a little.
STAFFORD: But that's not the end of the story.
DEBBIE: Oh. . . .
STAFFORD: We left there because it was Saturday and hunting is closed on Sunday in Pennsylvania.

> Probably 95 percent of the birds taken across the country are going to be two-year olds. They haven't seen hunters and they haven't been educated. So they're going to be the easiest birds to take. That's simply a fact that they haven't been exposed to hunters.

Here's an interesting question for you both. What's the most challenging bird you know you never did kill? Maybe it's the one you had to chase down and tackle.
STAFFORD: Pennsylvania really sticks out. The same day I took my bird in Pennsylvania we had a guide and he had been trying to get her a bird. Then once I took my bird I went and tried to locate a bird same time they did. When I topped this little hill it looked like land was being cleared for a new subdivision but it was a logging site and there was a bird strutting at the bottom with a hen in a circle, around and around. I called them and I said if y'all haven't found anything there's a bird over here. They came over and walked down the woods and I watched him. He eased his head out to see where they were. And that old bird came down out of his strut and walked off with that hen. I said: "Look, the bird saw something he didn't like. Y'all give it 15 or 20 minutes and ease back down and call." They did and I heard BOOM! I thought, *All right—got it*. The guide comes out of the woods and throws his hat up.

The only nearby state that I knew we could hunt on Sunday was Rhode Island. That wasn't that far so we went on to Rhode Island and she got her bird there Sunday morning. We went on to Massachusetts and got a bird up to within 30 yards and she missed that bird. All right. We can make it back to Pennsylvania and we got enough time to hunt that bird until 12 o'clock. So we made it there and we eased down in the same place. I said, "Let's see if he's still here." So I gobbled and he started coming and we just kind of set down. We were probably 15 yards apart. I sat back up against the tree. I said, "He's coming." I waited 20 minutes or so and I eased up and could see her feet and her gun barrel. I clucked to see if I could get her attention to see if she heard anything. And when I did that gobbler let loose like he was right on top of her. It wasn't just a minute and BOOM. And we missed him again.
DEBBIE: There was this big rock and he was strutting back and forth behind that rock and, I mean, he didn't come very far and I don't know. . . .

Did you get the rock?
DEBBIE: I hit a tree [sighing].
STAFFORD: So she still has yet to take a bird in Pennsylvania.
DEBBIE: Yes, yes.

Are certain birds in your experience more predictable than others?
STAFFORD: Two-year-old birds are. Probably 95 percent of the birds taken across the country are going to be two-year-olds. They haven't seen hunters and they haven't been educated. So they're going to be the easiest birds to take. That's simply a fact that they haven't been exposed to hunters.

Where was the strangest place you ever killed a gobbler?
STAFFORD: A lady's backyard. That's got to be the weirdest place. It was in Oregon. And it's the only bird I ever took actually coming to roost. The birds were out in this big field all day long and they came across the road, through a lot, and flew into this backyard within 50 yards of her door. We watched this bird come across the field and come across the road. I don't take birds going to roost— that's the one and only one that I know I took.
DEBBIE: You took that one by the bulldozer.

Oh, that sounds like a better story!
DEBBIE: It was in New York—Hunter, New York.

In the Catskills.
DEBBIE: We were with a retired game warden— he was super nice. We were just driving around trying to locate birds and we heard one up a good-size little hill. And we got out and there was a bulldozer there so we just got behind the bulldozer.

What was it, a gravel pit?
STAFFORD: It was a state forest, a logging site, and we had made a big loop and had come back out. We could see the roofs of the houses down below. And we just stopped there and we were standing beside our Jeep which was right next to the bulldozer.

DEBBIE: Randy got around and got into a ditch next to a tree and he was turned one way and the bird was coming down the other way but he didn't see it. He didn't know. He couldn't hear. So I had to crawl around the bulldozer and get in the ditch and point him in the right direction.
STAFFORD: I felt this tap on my leg and she whispered, "He's over here, not over there."
DEBBIE: So he turned his gun around and is wasn't five minutes and he shot.

I like it: a bulldozer blind—was it a pop-up bulldozer?
DEBBIE: Oh, no, it was a real big one. [laughing]
STAFFORD: We left there—New York also closes at noon—and went down the road to another spot and stopped on this little blacktop country road. The old boy yelped and a bird gobbled. She and I got set up and I just laid down kind of behind her. He called that bird up and she shot the bird and I think it was like 15 minutes or less before 12 o'clock cut-off time. And being with a retired game warden we wasn't pushing that envelope!
DEBBIE: Alabama was a good one, too, with Nick. That bird came from way over and strutted. It took little baby steps and strutted over this huge field. It was my turn to hunt and I was by a fence. We had decoys out and he was coming to the girls. It took *forever* for him to come but it was a pretty show and Nick said, "Tell me when you want to shoot." I was just watching him the whole time, it was so pretty. Finally I said "okay" and he just clucked or something and then the turkey went down out of his strut and folded up. He stuck his head up and I shot.

Has either of you ever purposefully passed up a bird you could have easily killed?
STAFFORD: Only jakes. Never a longbeard.

Which turkeys or which displays of turkey behavior give you the most satisfaction?
STAFFORD: In South Dakota we've had some beautiful experiences. We had a bird that Debbie took that came from a long ways. He was up on a

ridge where we could see him. We watched that bird strut and there was a gravel road between us and him and we watched him with the hope that nobody would come down that gravel road. But he took his time. He strutted all the way down that ridge, crossed the road, got in a big old meadow running away from us. And just like she said he'd strut, take a few steps, and gobble. I mean it took *forever* for him to get to us. But to be able to watch a Merriam's turkey—which to me is the prettiest bird there is—come all the way up to her and she never saw the turkey!

DEBBIE: Never.

STAFFORD: She had a big pine tree between her and that turkey.

DEBBIE: The whole time.

her to just sit here and I will go down the ridge a little way to see if there's a break where they could come right through—it was solid snow. So I came back right there where she was sitting. But she's not there. Now I panic. Snow everywhere and I can see me calling search and rescue to come get her lost in the snow. So I start blowing my crow call. No answer. I finally get to the point where I start hollering.

No walkie talkie or phone?

STAFFORD: No.

DEBBIE: I was coming as fast as I could.

STAFFORD: And I'm fixin' to go to the truck to call for help. And she says, "What's you want?" [normal speaking voice] Just like that. She's standing

> I can't see her. I was tense, I promise you. I could just envision her lost in the National Forest and getting home and telling everybody: "Well, I lost Debbie in the Black Hills of South Dakota. We'll find her in the spring thaw." [laughing]

STAFFORD: And I'm watching him the whole way and he goes behind the pine tree and I'm thinking, *Man, if she doesn't shoot him*, I will! But she didn't see him until he stepped out.

What was the craziest turkey experience you've had?

DEBBIE: It's probably when he lost me in the woods in South Dakota. I knew exactly where I was the whole time but he didn't know where I was. I could hear him the whole time but I didn't have my crow call. That was how we could find each other if we got separated.

STAFFORD: We had some birds comin' to us. But there was a big snow bank over on a ridge between us and they just wouldn't come across. So I told

there looking at me. [laughing]

DEBBIE: Well, I'm dressed in camouflage and I'm going like this. [waving] I'm coming as fast as I could but he couldn't see me.

STAFFORD: Yep, she's in camouflage out in the woods. I can't see her. I was tense, I promise you. I could just envision her lost in the National Forest and getting home and telling everybody: "Well, I lost Debbie in the Black Hills of South Dakota. We'll find her in the spring thaw." [laughing]

DEBBIE: Oh, he was so mad at me.

STAFFORD: I was.

You'd think you would have been happy.

DEBBIE: I didn't forget my crow call after that.

FACING PAGE: 2004—Louisiana. Stafford called this home-state bird out of a creek bottom near a cemetery with his six hens and another longbeard. "He was a tough old boy," Randy said. Debbie got his buddy two days later.

Have you ever tallied up what those 49 birds actually cost you?
STAFFORD: Don't even want to think about it. [laughing] It's scary.
DEBBIE: Yes. Like I said, we travelled everywhere. I would be afraid to tally it up.

Was it was worth it?
DEBBIE: Oh, yes.
STAFFORD: Every penny of it.

From your experience, what are some of the more important considerations you would recommend to a hunter seeking his own Super Slam?

and Wisconsin probably No. 2.
DEBBIE: There are *huge* turkeys in Wisconsin.
STAFFORD: Texas just because it's easy. Florida because of the unique swamp—gators, bears, panthers.
DEBBIE: Yeah, we had to dodge the bears in Florida. There was a mama bear with two babies. If we were going down trails and she was coming toward us we just turned around and went the other way. We didn't want to get too close.

Any trouble with alligators?
DEBBIE: No, thank goodness.
STAFFORD: We saw plenty of them. But we were mostly on dry land, you know, the cypress bot-

> And honestly, that bird, she could've reached out the window and touched him. I'm talkin' about he was *right there*. He gobbled and I think she jumped about a foot.

STAFFORD: You're going to have to make sure you've got the time to do it and do the research, like I said. I feel sorry for somebody who thinks he's just going to pop out to a state blindly. If we had done that it would have taken forever. You got to do the planning and your research and talk to people.
DEBBIE: We stopped at a little gas station in the middle of nowhere in Virginia and I went in there and just was talking to the man behind the counter, and he says go up the road to the second house on the right past the school. The farmer was super, super nice and his wife just so sweet. He had a lot of land on both sides. It was this beautiful place.
STAFFORD: He was a retired sheriff, I think.
DEBBIE: He had had a stroke.
STAFFORD: I think he had actually been shot. But they were just super nice people.

What are your top five wild turkey states?
STAFFORD: South Dakota is going to be No. 1

toms and palmettos. It's a unique setting. Nebraska, Kansas are both good—they've got lots of birds.

You rank South Dakota at the top—what is it about South Dakota that is so appealing?
STAFFORD: The scenery is just fantastic. Being from down South, you know, it's hard to think about hunting turkeys in the snow. You hit a snowstorm with wind and overnight the snow can be a foot deep. But the birds up there are just fantastic. I mean they will gobble. The biggest problem in South Dakota is wind—the wind blows and you can't hear. But locating birds? You can go out there at 10 o'clock at night and blow an elk bugle or something like that and birds will gobble.
DEBBIE: I opened the door one night and it popped and one gobbled.
STAFFORD: We were under a roost. Like I say, they come so well.
DEBBIE: It's crazy.

STAFFORD: They will come whatever distance it takes if they can hear you. They will come. The birds respond so well. The first year I went to South Dakota it wasn't with Debbie—it was with my brother and four or five guys from down here. We went out the first morning with three of us—myself, my brother and Charles Ledner—and we got down in a long meadow and split up. I went one way and they went two different ways. I heard birds but I'm not sure they did. When we got back together I said, "I heard some birds—let's go fool with them." We went up and set my brother up as the shooter and Charles and I stayed back callin'. My brother's all tensed up there and I'm sitting there and all of a sudden I hear a strutting bird [makes sound] right there on a little dim trail going off. I ease around and shoot him, BOOM, and when I do my brother jumps up and says, "You can't even see that turkey." And I said: "I don't know what you talkin' about. My turkey's over here, dead!" [laughing]

DEBBIE: He came in quiet.

STAFFORD: I loved hunting with my brother.

Now that you've traveled all around the country and have your favorite states to hunt, which is your least favorite?

STAFFORD: The only bad experience I had with public hunting was in Michigan—but I'm not going to put down on Michigan because of it. I mean we had some fantastic hunts and met a lot of nice people. But we had an encounter with a very rude person. We had gotten into some birds and got in there early we were sitting there waiting to walk in—nobody else in there that I know of—and this guy pulled up right next to us. And I said, "We roosted a bird and we're about to go in." And he said: "Well, that's just tough luck—this is public hunting. Live with it." We went somewhere else. But that put a real big damper on our experience, you know, that kind of attitude and lack of ethics. If I'd have seen another vehicle parked there I never would have stopped, right? It's just common courtesy.

Now that you have achieved the Super Slam, do you find it most satisfying to hunt a familiar piece of land or explore a new place?

STAFFORD: More than likely we're going to be going back to the same states that I've harvested a bird and try to take her one. But locally it will be youth—calling up turkeys and getting young people involved in hunting and enjoying the outdoor experience. Or ladies or veterans. First-time hunters.

DEBBIE: I know what they're feeling. It's just so exciting for them, the first time in the woods, to hear a bird gobble. A couple of my girlfriends, they've gone with us, and I won't say anything. I'll hear the bird and I'll let them tell me where it is and everything. They get so excited. One forgot she was hunting and was sitting there watching the bird. The bird came right up next to the blind we were in. We had to tell her, "Shoot, shoot!"

STAFFORD: We were trying to help this lady take her bird and she's right next to the window over here. I'm sitting in the back corner and Debbie is right next to her. And honestly, that bird, she could've reached out the window and touched him. I'm talkin' about he was *right there*. He gobbled and I think she jumped about a foot.

DEBBIE: She was so excited!

STAFFORD: I said, "Just let him come around." And she let him come on around and she finally shot him. I don't think he was any more than, golly, 10 yards. That was extremely exciting for her. I mean, he was in her face.

How important is preseason scouting?

STAFFORD: If you're local it's very important. But if you're hunting away in other states you have to get intel online or information from talking to people and let them basically put you on birds where you're going. But locally you need to locate the birds by scouting. Go out in the evening for the last hour of daylight and owl. Learning the woods where you're going to hunt is hugely important. You need to know the terrain. There's so many different things can make a bird hang up—an old fence row. Birds are funny. I mean, they may not cross a logging road. They may not cut

Randy Stafford   **197**

across a ditch or a creek or something. You need to try to prevent having some kind of barrier between you and a bird that will prevent him from coming to you. But locating birds—you've got to locate your birds.

Do you have a process for effectively scouting a new area?
STAFFORD: Like I said, locate the birds at dawn and dusk. Get yourself a topographical map and if you have an opportunity to walk through the woods look for where they've been scratching in the grass or leaves. Look for dust bowls where the hens been dusting and look for strut marks in the sand or dirt where an old gobbler's been strutting around and dragging his wings. You find sign like that and you'll have a lot more success.

Do you prefer to sit and wait or run and gun?
STAFFORD: I prefer to sit and wait but the turkey is going to dictate what you do. If you're on a turkey at daybreak and set up and he's coming, just give him time. The big hangup with turkeys in the morning is having hens with him. If he has hens with him it's going to be difficult to get that bird to give up what he's got to come see what you are. But in that particular case, if he won't come to you make you some mental notes: Know what he did. Know where he went. Know why he didn't come to you. I'm going to say 90 percent of taking a turkey is being where that turkey wants to go anyway. If you're where he normally goes it's going to be a lot easier to get him to come to you. If you're trying to call him somewhere he doesn't like to go or doesn't usually go, it's going to be more difficult to get that bird to come to you.

Debbie?
DEBBIE: I prefer to sit and wait.
STAFFORD: She had been responsible for me taking a lot of birds by making me sit there once he hushes and comes in silent. I'll give him some time, but I have a point I get tired of sitting there waiting on him if he's not gobbling.
DEBBIE: Just wait, [whispering] just wait.

STAFFORD: And sure 'nuff he'll show up.

What is your basic strategy for a day's hunt?
STAFFORD: If I've got a bird roosted or located or if I'm pretty positive I've got a bird there, I'm going to try to get as close as I can to the bird before daylight. I'm going to say, oh, 100 yards. It depends on the terrain. You know, if it's wide open you can't get closer; if it's real thick then you can get a little closer. And when I start calling all I want to do is make sure he's there. I give him a real, real low yelp. If he gobbles I know he's there. That's all I want to do. And I don't like to sit there and call a lot. This is one of those things you learn in your learning process. I've called too much to a bird before he flies down. That old turkey will fly up into another tree where he can see. And if he didn't see that hen he's gonna leave. Several different times I messed up by calling too much and the bird, instead of flying down and coming in on the ground, you know, he'd fly over there in a tree— and I'm not going to shoot him off a limb. I wait till the bird gets on the ground. If I tree up and he gobbles, he knows I'm there. That's all I want. When he flies down then I'll start calling to that turkey and generally I'll just yelp. It depends on the turkey. He will dictate how much or how little I call. If he's fired up and he's coming I'll call very little. Mostly I'll call just to keep track of where he is and to make sure he hasn't given up on us. But if that turkey hangs up or has hens with him and they go off, I'm going to pay attention to where he went. I can try circling around to get ahead of him and call, but that doesn't usually work too well. Tomorrow when I come back and hunt him I'm going to be over there where he went, okay? I'm going to be in the direction he *wants* to go. And I'm going to do basically the same thing. By 10 o'-clock in the morning—something like that—generally all your hens will drift away from the gobbler. I like to find his strut zone. Generally a bird about that time of morning he'll find a particular place he'll go and he'll hang out there and gobble ever now and then. And the hens will come to him. That's his safe zone—that's where you can

take him. If you can get there before he does you can take that bird. That's pretty much how you're going to take most of your turkeys. If you're out there 10, 11, 12 o'clock and a bird responds to you when you call, more than likely his hens have left him. He's looking for a hen and he's a lot more receptive to coming to a hen. That's pretty much the huntin' day.

What shotgun do you like for wild turkeys?
STAFFORD: Any shotgun will do. There's been a lot of turkeys taken with No. 6 squirrel shot out of a two-and-three-quarter-inch shotgun shell. I shoot a 12 gauge—a Browning Gold Hunter. I shoot three-inch shells; I've shot three-and-a-half-inch a few times. I'm not interested in shooting a turkey 60 yards away. I want the bird in my face,

choke and which shell pattern best for you at 40 yards. Everybody needs to pattern their shotgun. Just about all the turkeys I took with a Nitro shell hand-loaded by a man in Missouri. If you tell him what shotgun you're shooting—he had done the work—he would tell you what constriction on your choke you needed and which shell he needed to send you. He would guarantee you so many pellets in a tiny circle at 40 yards if you just did what he said. He made some good shells—I never had a problem with them not doing what I wanted them to do. They were loaded with Hevi-Shot. He actually had a blend of 4s, 5s and 6s in that shell. I'll tell you, the thing coming now in shotgun shells is TSS. It's a tungsten shot. It's so much heavier. What it will do will just blow your mind. My son uses it for duck hunting. He reloads his

> Know where he went. Know why he didn't come to you.
> I'm going to say 90 percent of taking a turkey is being where that
> turkey wants to go anyway. If you're where he normally goes it's
> going to be a lot easier to get him to come to you.

preferably 25, 30, 35 yards. And you don't need a three-and-a-half-inch shell to take a bird at that distance. The Browning has probably got the least amount of recoil than any other automatic going. It's just a good automatic shotgun.

Barrel?
STAFFORD: Twenty-four-inch barrel—and the reason for that is when you go to swing on a close turkey, if you've got a tree sticking out, the short barrel is easier to maneuver. I started out turkey hunting with a Remington 1100 with a 30-inch barrel. [laughing]

Choke?
STAFFORD: You have to select your choke by shooting your gun. You're going to have to experiment with different chokes to find out which

own shells and just started using it. He said, "Dad, I've shot crippled ducks on the water at 70 yards—and I'm talking dead." So much penetration and you can use a smaller shot because it's so much more dense that you get more shot in your pattern. I think that's going to be the future of turkey-hunting shells. The bad thing about it is you give up some of the challenge of getting them in close. People are going to be shooting at distances they not normally ought to. But they're going to take birds.

What about off-the-shelf shells?
STAFFORD: If I had to shoot a commercial load already out there, Winchester makes Long Beard, and I like No. 5. I haven't shot that shell but I've called up birds for people who have. You know, generally when somebody shoots a bird the bird's

gonna flop—nerves and everything. But I've witnessed probably a half-dozen turkeys shot with that Longbeard shell. They don't flop. It amazed me. When they hit the ground they're there. It's a good shell.

Debbie, what about you—what's your shotgun?
DEBBIE: I started with the Remington 870 pump, 12-gauge, and then I took his old 1100 and had the barrel cut down with a new turkey choke. And now his Browning Gold now that he's not shooting.

What do you think of sighting devices?
STAFFORD: I've always used open sights that are on there and just put on some kind of fiber-optic sight that you can see. In most of the cases she has used the same thing. But after having a few

what was that? I said to him, "Shoot again." BOOM! They take a few steps they are still looking around. The gun was pointed up here. It was nowhere near the turkeys. So I said, "Let's just let them walk away—we'll come back next weekend." We practiced over the week.

Do you ever use decoys?
STAFFORD: Yes. Decoys are very valuable tool in turkey hunting. I don't use them all the time. There are situations when I'll just use a hen or situations when I'll use a hen and a jake. And there are situations when I'll use a hen and a full-fan decoy. Once in Nevada I had an old bird coming around a wood line and when that bird popped out and could see the decoy he ran the other way. Some birds if they see too many decoys, they get

> Once in Nevada I had an old bird coming around a wood line and when that bird popped out and could see the decoy he ran the other way. Some birds if they see too many decoys, they get spooky.

mishaps [chuckling] we basically put a red-dot type scope on there, so she can put the dot where she wants and we make sure she has it on the turkey. And she's done a whole lot better.
DEBBIE: It's good—it's really good.
STAFFORD: And that red-dot thing works really well for kids. I took my grandson on his first turkey hunt maybe four years ago. I had a couple of longbeards I was calling but they wouldn't come. Three jakes came up there 10 yards from us. The first turkey I shot was a jake so I let him shoot a jake his first turkey. So I'm sitting in the blind looking at him and he shoots—BOOM—and all three of the turkeys stick their heads up, wondering

spooky. But decoys are a valuable tool and their biggest value is it gets the eyes of the turkey focused on something other than looking for a hen they can't see. They're more likely to see you if they are looking for something than if they are already focused.

Do you have a favorite decoy?
STAFFORD: I've used most all of them. I've used a Feather Flex decoy and they are good and have been very productive. There are a lot of good decoys out there. The one that I'm using now is called Avian-X. They make a very good decoy. They've got a place where you can put a jake fan

FACING PAGE: 2009—Maryland. Randy could not get this spring gobbler to respond. The 12 noon deadline was fast approaching. Stafford swung into action with the "old low-turkey crawl." It wasn't pretty. He missed on the first shot. The bird jumped up and flew straight at him—he missed again. "I pulled the trigger when the bird was 10 yards over my head," Randy recalled. "Blew a hole about two inches through his right wing." The turkey hit the ground. The rundown was on.

in the back or a full fan from a fully mature bird—very, very realistic. I've seen all kinds of things: that skinny little thing that looks nothing like a turkey and looks more like a chicken. But they work. Again, they get the focus of the bird on something other than you.

Do you use decoys in all your hunts?
STAFFORD: No. I'd say probably half the time. If we're in a field or open area we're more likely to use them than if I were in the woods and your view is limited. He's going to be close enough you're going to see him anyway.

How about blinds?
STAFFORD: Not that much. Blinds I use if I have a youth or somebody that needs to get away with a lot of moving. In the rain I'm definitely going to be in a blind. But that's about the only time. Double Bull is what we used most of the time over the years.

How do you go about choosing your camouflage clothing?
STAFFORD: That depends on the time of year and your foliage. If you're hunting here in the spring I'm going to go with something that has a lot of green in the pattern. But if we go up North or to South Dakota and there's still snow on the ground, I'm not going to wear white, but I'm going to go with something brown, just regular old Mossy Oak or something like that. But your terrain and your foliage is going to dictate that.

Footwear?
STAFFORD: LaCrosse rubber boots are the ones I wear more than anything.
DEBBIE: Rocky snake boots, knee high. I've seen a big snake strike at him and he never saw it—a moccasin. All I could see is the mouth striking. We were walking down a dirt road and he walks right next to the snake. Ahhhh. . . . [Sighs in revulsion.]
STAFFORD: They don't bother you if you don't bother them.
DEBBIE: I just couldn't believe it. He almost

stepped on a rattlesnake.
STAFFORD: I had a rattlesnake in my face in Mississippi. We were just scouting. I was going up a pretty steep hill, you know. We were lucky. It was cold and he never moved. He was coiled up. My next step would have been right in his face. And since we were coming up he would have been thigh high. So it would have been bad.
DEBBIE: Yes.

Do you wear a turkey vest?
STAFFORD: Very seldom. Most of the time I just have a backpack on. She keeps a little fanny pack that she keeps some of her stuff in.

What essentials are you carrying?
STAFFORD: Most of the time I keep my mouth calls in my shirt pocket. Slate calls, box calls, gloves, face mask and binoculars. If you're in country you never have been you need a compass in there or a G.P.S.
DEBBIE: Thermacell.
STAFFORD: She's gonna have her Thermacell with her.
DEBBIE: Yes. I'll sit down and set it between us.
STAFFORD: Most of the time she puts it over on her side. [laughing] But they do work. And it's a whole lot easier to stay still not having to swat mosquitoes.
DEBBIE: But those ticks were really bad in Ohio—I never seen them that bad. He's always in front of me and there was like a brown wave coming out his legs. He stripped off those pants real fast—*oh!*
STAFFORD: She does pretty good with the tick repellent. We spray down our clothes at night, you know, and that pretty much keeps the ticks off.

How many different types of calls do you typically carry with you?
STAFFORD: I take a mouth, a box and a slate. I have all of them with me. In different states birds would not respond sometimes to a mouth call. But you hit a box and they'll hammer it. They might not respond to a box but you hit a slate and

they'll hammer it. So you need a variety of all those three calls.

Was there any rhyme or reason to their responding—or not?

STAFFORD: I don't really know why. But I've seen it happen in too many places. My go-to call is going to be the mouth call. That frees your hands. You're not having to put down a box and pick up your gun. You have a little more versatility with the mouth call than you do with just about any other call. And, you know, you can do just about any call: your cluck, your purr, your yelp, your cutting, your kee-kee, your cackling. I wouldn't rec-

Girl and I *never* picked up one of those calls and put it in my mouth that I couldn't get the same sound out of it as the last one I used. I don't know if it's the type of latex they use; they're just easy to blow. But it's all practice, over and over. And I still can't purr worth a flip. If I want to purr I'm going to use a box or a slate.

Debbie, do you call?

DEBBIE: Yes, with a slate. I like to play with it. I don't sound real good but they've come.

STAFFORD: I have hens walk past by me that sounded like somebody was trying to strangle them—the most terrible sound you have ever

> My go-to call is going to be the mouth call.
> That frees your hands. You're not having to put down a box
> and pick up your gun. You have a little more versatility with
> the mouth call than you do with just about any other call.

ommend somebody starting out using a gobble tube or a gobble call—mainly for the safety factor. Especially on public land, I just don't recommend shaking a gobble tube. You don't ever know who the other hunter is.

How did you learn to call?

STAFFORD: Like I said: practice, practice, practice. With the box call I pretty much learned from watching my uncle and working with him. With the mouth call it was pretty much trial and error—and it took me a while to get over the gag reflex with the mouth call. And I can't use any mouth call. I don't know what it is. I can't just go pick up any call. I started out using a Perfection call because that's the only one really that was around here. We had a local boy who repped them; he was a big turkey hunter. I hunted for a long time with Preston's Black Diamond. But I can't get the sound I want out of every call. The last few states we hunted I used a Tom Teaser Bad

heard come out of a turkey. So it's the rhythm that's more important.

In what circumstances do you stick with one call and when you use multiple calls?

STAFFORD: If it's raining I'm going to stick with my mouth call. [laughing] I'm going to stick with whatever that turkey's responding to. It doesn't matter which one. I'm going to use my call first and if they aren't responding I've got my other options.

Over the years what has been your single most productive turkey voice?

STAFFORD: Your yelp is going to be the basic call. But you're going to get more turkeys fired up and responding to cutting and cackling.

Of the 49 states do you remember how many birds you took in the morning and how many later in the day?

STAFFORD: I took two birds in the afternoon. That's it. Utah was about 4:30, 5 o'clock and that one bird in Oregon it was fixing to fly over.

Over the lady's laundry. . . .
STAFFORD: Yeah! Utah was another very enjoyable hunt. Locating a bird was hard but when we found one we got down there on that bird and I fooled with that bird from daylight to 11 o'clock. He would gobble and he would gobble but he would not come. I walked away from him still gobbling at 11 o'clock. I said, "This ain't happening." We came back over there at 3 o'clock and he had gone down a canyon. I said, "If he comes back up this canyon we gonna be here this afternoon." We got in there at probably about 4 o'clock and I

that was between me and him. And he stepped out past it and I mean there's nothing but air between me and him. But there's a stick, a limb coming off that cedar tree blocking his head and I'm sitting there and I thought, *Man, if he take one more step he's gone.* And I'm talking about he's from me to Debbie [across kitchen table]. That was probably the prettiest Meriam's turkey I've ever taken—that and a New Mexico bird.

You mentioned henned-up gobblers. What's your strategy?
STAFFORD: You've got two options. You can hope that later in the day the hens leave the gobbler and you can catch him by himself. If that works, fine. If that doesn't happen you're going to have to chal-

> You've got two options. You can hope that later in the day the hens leave the gobbler and you can catch him by himself. If that works, fine. If that doesn't happen you're going to have to challenge the hen. There's alway a boss hen.

said, "I'm going to see if he's still here." So I took a box call because I wanted to cover a long area. I cut with that box call and he gobbled way down in the canyon. So we just sat there. One reason we couldn't see him that morning is that he was back up in some cedar trees. Over 15 minutes or so I called and he was coming. I didn't hear anything from him for a little while so I yelped. We'll, I don't guess those cedar trees were 20 yards away and he was right above them. I was facing this way [gesturing direction] and he was back there. She's sitting right there to my side. I just slid down to another cedar tree and turned around and faced up the hill. That's the closest turkey I've ever killed. That turkey came through those cedar trees and I couldn't see him. Finally he got to where I could see his feet. And then he got to where I could see his body. When he got to where I could see his head he was right at the edge of the last cedar tree

lenge the hen. There's alway a boss hen. Pardon my French but you want to piss her off enough to make her want to come and whoop you—and hope he'll follow. That's the only two ways.

You also mentioned hung-up birds. In your experience what's the most common reason birds don't come?
STAFFORD: Most of the time it's because some obstacle they don't feel comfortable crossing. It can be a barbed-wire fence they could step under without any problem but won't. It could be an old net-wire fence that's down that's not a foot tall but they won't cross. It can be a stream. It can be a ditch. They should be able to see the hen they're hearing—if they don't see the hen they'll hang up. That's why if you're in an open spot the decoy is valuable. They should be able to see what they're hearing and hear what they're seeing.

What are your most memorable moments from the quest?

STAFFORD: There are many, many, many—including birds that Debbie took, where I could actually sit back and watch everything unfold.

DEBBIE: The doubles.

STAFFORD: The doubles, you know, when we got birds at the same time. I think we've had six Grand-Slam years together.

What's the oddest thing you've ever seen a wild turkey do?

STAFFORD: I didn't actually see the turkey do this but the weirdest thing is that I harvested a turkey in Mississippi, and when I was cleaning the bird I felt something in its craw. I thought it might have been some kind of growth or something. I wanted to make sure the meat wasn't messed up to eat or anything. So I cut it open. And that turkey had swallowed a hickory nut—I'm talking about a large hickory nut—and he had had it in his craw so long it was smooth as a steel ball bearing. It had just rolled around in there. I don't know how many years he had it but it was smooth and round. How he swallowed it or why he would have swallowed it, I don't know. I've taken turkeys with no spurs in Mississippi—they've got some weird turkeys in Mississippi. [chuckling] I've taken a lot of multi-bearded turkeys: double-bearded turkeys and triple-bearded turkeys. But I've never shot a turkey knowing he was a multi-bearded turkey before I pulled the trigger. The year we killed 13 turkeys in 11 states, I think four out of the first six had double beards.

What was your heaviest gobbler?

STAFFORD: Twenty-six pounds. Wisconsin. They got some big old birds. First one I shot when I picked him up I thought I was standing on his head. This old boy up there did him in a full strut—prettiest I've ever seen. I'd always heard that taxidermists had a hard time doing a bird in a full strut, just to get the feather to stand up. Unbelievably beautiful turkey mount.

Who is or was the best turkey hunter you've ever known?

STAFFORD: You mean besides myself? [chuckling] No, I'm not the best turkey hunter I've ever known. Preston Pittman I'm gonna have to put right there with the top people. Not only is he an extremely good turkey caller, but his woods knowledge and his ability to think like a turkey are without equal. He has a video where he's sitting next to a live oak in Texas and he's got a hen that's probably 10 yards away. And he gets up real slow—as close as from me to you—and actually act like a turkey. And that turkey just keeps on feeding. Now this is a wild turkey!

DEBBIE: He even looks like a turkey [chuckling].

STAFFORD: He does. But I'd have to say, locally, I would have to say Mr. Tim Hiak. He's a young man here. He is an extremely good caller. He yelps. Most people use a raspy call because it's easy to cover up mistakes. But he uses a mouth call in a very clear, clear voice. But I can almost say if that gentleman hears a turkey gobble, he gonna die. Now, I would never tell him that to his face.

He'll have to read it in this book.

STAFFORD: I had a friend, Bruce Hunt, who passed away from cancer several years back that was extremely good. I think the biggest plus for them is their knowledge of the woods and to be able to read the turkey and to know what he's got to do to make him come. It's the same thing with all the most successful hunters.

What changes have you seen in turkey hunting?

STAFFORD: Biggest change I think you're going to see is going to be loss of habitat. The National Wild Turkey Federation is responsible for us having turkeys in all 49 states and the efforts they put forth for wild turkeys and the hunting heritage is just awesome. But I think there's been a slight decline in turkey populations. I don't know why. Here in Louisiana our turkey population took a huge hit when Hurricane Katrina came through. We lost so much habitat. I mean we had hardwoods, pine trees, everything on the ground. And

May 14, 2014—Pennsylvania. *Bird No. 49!* Here is Randy Stafford with his guide Steve Moore on the left. Moore is a "super guide," Randy said. The team worked this stealthy eastern bird for two days. The first day the bird came in but the undergrowth was too thick for the hunters to see him—he walked away and disappeared across a road. The next morning he flew down and came looking for love. This time Stafford and Moore were on the right side of the road.

we're just now seeing the recovery of those turkeys. Our area should have been closed for turkeys—I want to say—for three years after Katrina. Period. But Wildlife and Fisheries were going to get a lot of flak from a lot of turkey hunters if they closed the season, so what they did is they kind of cut the limit back. But you saw what happened. We didn't get a hatch for that first year, for sure. Well, that means you didn't have any jakes the next year. Which means the year after that you didn't have any two-year-olds, which I told you is 90 percent of your turkey harvest. Good turkey hunters, they kill turkeys. So what they were doing is they killed all the two-year-olds, and then the few jakes that survived to make two-year-olds the next year they took them. So then there weren't nothing but old birds—three-and-a-half or four-and-a-half-year-old birds—they took them. So you lost gobblers to breed your hens. They should have backed off and allowed the flocks to restore themselves before they started hunting them again.

Are you seeing changes in turkey hunters?

STAFFORD: I think you've got a lot more hunters coming out. I don't think you've seen any real change in the attitude of the older turkey hunters who have been around. You've got a lot of new turkey hunters and what you're seeing basically is a lot more new people in the woods, which is educating turkeys. I did it. That's how you learn. That's how you learn how to turkey hunt—and what to do and what not to do. But the birds learn, too.

That's an interesting point. So you believe inexperienced hunters are actually shaping the behavior of the birds.

STAFFORD: Right. You get new things coming out in turkey hunting and the new things work well because turkeys haven't seen them before, like decoys when they first came out. Now you're getting to the point where more and more birds are decoys-shy, because they're seeing more of them and people are spooking them. Probably the biggest mistake I see beginners make—I'll say what I did: I bumped a lot of turkeys trying to get too close, not knowing where to stop, when to stop. I called too much, birds flying up instead of coming in on the ground. I spooked a lot of birds by getting up too early, thinking that they had gone somewhere else when they were actually still coming to you, coming in silent. All that educates birds. I think you're going to see more two-year-old birds become three-year-old birds because they're learning more from beginning hunters.

Finally, you've killed a turkey—how do you eat it?

DEBBIE: Wild turkey can get kind of tough if you overcook it. So the secret is cooking it done but not overly so.

STAFFORD: I like turkey deep fried because you know it kind of seals the meat quick and keeps it moist.

DEBBIE: Make little strips or nuggets and put

bacon around them. I also use Tony's Seasoning and batter it up.

STAFFORD: Seasoning is a southern thing, I think. That's one thing I noticed traveling across the country—people outside the South eat plain food. [laughing]

Debbie, you have 31 birds on your way to your own U. S. Super Slam. How are you going to get to 49—move to Hawaii?

DEBBIE: We decided we're going to go to the New England states and try to get those farthest away first and then come this way, since Pennsylvania has been a problem for me. Go to Maine. I have New Hampshire, don't I?

STAFFORD: You have New Hampshire.

DEBBIE: I already got a turkey in Rhode Island—that's the one I got on my own.

STAFFORD: Next year, if we get all the states we're hoping she'll get, Debbie will take a turkey in Maine, Vermont, Massachusetts, Connecticut, North Carolina, West Virginia and Arkansas. Those are my goals for next year. Arkansas is a kind of a tough place to find a place to hunt. And they've had a noticeable decline in their turkey population for some reason the last couple of years. But I've got a couple of good contacts up there. We get calls now and again from boys working on it, looking to come to Louisiana for a bird. I say, "What state you in? If you're in a state Miss Debbie needs and you got a turkey she can come kill, you way ahead of the game!" [laughing]

INDEX

Page numbers in **bold** indicate photograph

PHOTO CREDITS

Jonathan Barta
145, 146, 160–61, 164–65

Jeff Budz
vi, 13, 14, 18, 28, 31, 41, 57, 61, 62, 65

David J. Ellis
8, 10–11, 17, 21, 22–23, 26, 35, 38–39, 42, 50, 54, 58, 66–67

Timothy C. Flanigan
Front cover image of strutting gobbler, back cover, all images of live turkeys and feathers throughout book used as decorative graphics

Tony Hudak
70, 74, 75, 76, 79, 80–81, 82, 83, 84, 87, 88, 89, 91, 92, 93, 95, 96

Rob Keck
101, 102, 104, 108, 109, 118, 122, 132, 134, 141

Matt Lindler
Front cover image of hunters

Clyde F. Neely
149, 151, 152, 154–55, 157, 158, 162, 167, 168, 170, 171, 172, 175,

Thomas R. Pero
2–3, 4, 7, 24, 32–33, 45, 48–49, 69, 114–15, 126, 133

Randy Stafford
177, 178, 182, 189, 194, 201, 206

A Note From the Author

If you are—or anyone you know is—nearing completion of the quest for a United States Wild Turkey Super Slam, I would like to interview you for a new volume of *Turkey Men*. Please write or phone me at your convenience: tom@wildriverpress.com or 425-486-3638. Turkey hunters everywhere would like to hear your story.

Thomas R. Pero